Photo B. de Villentroy.

ALTAR OF OUR LADY OF LOURDES.

Igniting the 19th Century Embers of Lourdes

Archbishop Napoleon Joseph Perche' Consecrates the Archdiocese of New Orleans to Our Lady of Lourdes – December 8, 1873

By Mary Desforges Engler

ISBN NUMBER:

Paperbound: 1-59804-667-5
Hardcover: 1-59804-668-3

Distributed by:
CLAITOR'S PUBLISHING DIVISION
P.O. Box 261333, Baton Rouge, LA 70826-1333
800-274-1403 (In LA 225-344-0476)
Fax: 225-344-0480
Internet address:
e mail: claitors@claitors.com
World Wide Web: http://www.claitors.com

Dedication

Dedicated to the loves of my life - Nicholas, Matthew, Elizabeth and Kathryn - may Our Lady of Lourdes wrap her mantle of protection around each of you and remain with you throughout your lives.

Poetry by my mother, Joy Rittler Desforges, has been added throughout this book. So many of her poems seemed perfect as introductions or afterthoughts to certain portions of this book; they almost fit like a glove. They are included to enhance this work and to offer a meditative element to an otherwise historical account of a devotion that deserves the gentleness the poems add to the story.

A Difference

Lord, let me make a difference
To those I meet today.
Help me give good example
For following Your way.

Let my thought be kindly
And soft like angel wings
So I'll not be bogged down
With selfish, petty things.

Let my words have meaning,
Help me choose them carefully
So they will heal and never hurt
And praise Thee prayerfully.

Let me go about my work
With grateful dedication.
Remembering Thee at end of day
With healing meditation.

Armed with all these graces, Lord,
Point me to the way
That will make a decided difference
To those I meet today.

Table of Contents

Foreword

Sharing the same experience

At the grotto of Lourdes, France, each meeting with Our Lady changed the life of Bernadette Soubirous. Through that very deep experience, giving her life to Jesus, offering her life to God, day after day Bernadette became a true 'child of Mary'. Through Bernadette a lot of people still meet Our Lady and through the Blessed Virgin they meet the Saviour of the world, Jesus Christ.

When he came to Lourdes, France, Bishop Napoléon Joseph Perché had also a great experience. How do we know that? Only because as soon the Archbishop of New Orleans came back home, he spread the devotion to Our Lady of Lourdes in his diocese and Louisiana. By doing that he extended his own experience of Lourdes, his experience of the Gospel.

More than one century later the story of Mary E. Engler spreads in a way the experience of Bernadette, of Bishop Perché, of millions of Lourdes pilgrims. It is the story of a meeting with Our Lady of Lourdes. It is the story of a meeting which changes the life of someone, because this meeting opens to others through the witness and charity rooted in a simple prayer. It is a meeting which contains a treasure, but this treasure is only accessible when shared.

The story of Bernadette, of Bishop Perché, of Mary Engler happened on earth, but like the story of the Blessed Virgin, it was lived in the light of God. For that reason these three stories not only shed light on each other but also they help us as readers of this wonderful book to become more contemporaneous of all friends of God whose names are written in heaven.

After reading this book if we become ourselves true 'children of Mary', spreading through our own life the Good News of the love of God for all human beings, it means that through this book we also meet Our Lady of Lourdes.

Père Régis-Marie de La Teyssonnière

Chapelain de Notre-Dame de Lourdes

Lourdes July 16, 2012

Introduction

Some may ask why this book was worthy of being written. Others may say, "so what" if the Archdiocese of New Orleans was consecrated to Our Lady of Lourdes in 1873 – what is the meaning in that for us today? Still others may question why so much time might be spent poring over documents long forgotten from a time so distant from our own. We might hear from some Catholics that we have ongoing Marian apparitions that deserve our full attention now rather than on apparitions that have been concluded for years. The simple answer is I just couldn't resist finding out everything about the 19thcentury devotion to Our Lady of Lourdes. The fact is the embers of the Lourdes consecration, Arch-confraternity and message have been burning in our area since 1868 and with a small wind the ash can be blown from those embers and the burning fire re-ignited in the hearts and souls of the devoted today.

Although this book is about the historical devotion to Our Lady of Lourdes in South Louisiana, to understand my interest in this subject and entrance into the story that is Lourdes it is necessary to explain my association with the Shrine and the city.

Everyone who goes on pilgrimage has a "pilgrimage story" and so it is with me. In the summer of 2008, I was at an emotional low point in my life. My sister Nancy's concern for me brought an invitation from her to England to attend the 100th birthday party for her husband's, Geoff Hughes', mother. I didn't really want to go but we both knew getting away might help. I asked her if she would go to Medjugorje with me on a side trip. She declined; but she countered with an offer to go for one night to Lourdes, France.

My sister reminded me that Lourdes was an approved apparition. She also told me she took Bernadette as her Confirmation name and had always wanted to go there. The decision was made. We planned to meet in London, as we were taking different Trans Atlantic flights; and we would fly to Toulouse early the next morning, take the train to and from Lourdes, spend one night in Lourdes and fly back the next day in time for the big birthday party. Unfortunately, her overseas flight cancelled. I was in London, staying with her husband's family and couldn't decide whether or not to go on to Lourdes by myself as it was clear she would not make it to England in time to catch our scheduled early morning flight to France.

My son, Nick, urged me to go. With his encouragement, enveloped simultaneously in fear and courage I decided to go to Lourdes on my own. Sometimes bricks have to drop on my head to fully understand; in this case, it occurred to me that there was more going on than met the eye. In fact, the Lord had a plan for me on this journey that opened up a new life through His Mother, The Immaculate Conception, and Our Lady of Lourdes. It wouldn't take long for me to comprehend. With no preconceived notions about what to expect or what might be found in Lourdes, my pilgrimage began.

Most people who go to Lourdes do not go alone; most go in groups or if ill, with doctors, nurses, companions and supportive care. In Lourdes, we see people together with other people; mostly they are pushing them in wheelchairs, or pulling the voitures[1], or walking in uniforms, or scarves or other clothing that signifies that an individual is a part of a group – they are there on pilgrimage with someone else. Although my journey started as a single pilgrim, it wasn't carried out that way.

I was met by a stranger in the airport in London. Upon learning Lourdes was my destination, this kindhearted soul accompanied me on my pilgrimage. Fear and anxiousness

---

[1] Voiture is the blue cart which is used to transport the disabled pilgrims in Lourdes and is defined as a carriage, wagon or other wheeled vehicle. http://dictionary.reference.com/browse/voiture?s=t

were replaced by a sense of peace. My new companion, as it turns out, had been a volunteer serving the Sanctuaries at Lourdes for many years.

The feeling of being a mere traveler gave way instead to a distinct feeling of being invited, guided and drawn into the experience of Lourdes. We learned only days before leaving the US that Pope Benedict XVI was going to be in Lourdes that weekend. The Pope was not there during my 26-hour pilgrimage. However, the throng of pilgrims there to see him and to participate in the ongoing celebration of the 150th anniversary of the apparitions was everywhere. My companion was staying in Pau; so we parted but together attended Mass early the next day on September 13. By the time we reconnected, I had experienced the Friday night rosary procession, spent time in prayer virtually alone at the grotto in the wee hours of Saturday morning and bathed in the piscines all before Mass began. We attended mass in the underground Basilica; the number of people there was stunning – there were thousands!

In an instant, the meaning of the Universal Catholic Church was clearly apparent because I was present in the middle of it – right there in Lourdes. My new friend was familiar with the procedures for Communion, knew all the songs that were being sung and found a great vantage point from which to watch the beautiful Mass on the screens overhead. Recalling the experience now, listening to my companion sing sounded like the voice of an angel.

We spent the rest of the time praying at the grotto and walking by the river; having coffee in an outdoor café; strolling through the grand churches and exploring the town. I was drawn to the grotto and Our Lady for a final prayer and goodbye; and I was sad to leave after such a short visit. I knew, however, this visit would not be the last. I am not a person who has those sorts of feelings or certainties in her life; but this experience was different – I knew I would return. Also the clear belief came to me that Our Lady of Lourdes wanted me to do more for her Son through her. At that time, it wasn't apparent to me what, or how, or when but her gentle, inviting tug was unmistakable.

For a particular reason one evening in February of 2009, I was moved to investigate volunteering at Lourdes. Thinking back on it now, with a few years of prayer and reflection under my belt, I believe the Holy Spirit acted in me that evening, (as probably occurred before my first trip to Lourdes), to make the decision to volunteer as a Hospitalier in the service of the Sanctuaries at Lourdes. The decision was swift, certain and before I knew it; my paperwork was complete and I was journeying again – alone – to Lourdes. The plan was to meet with the rest of the unknown group in JFK and then on from there. The Lord and Our Lady had other plans. While checking in for the flight in New Orleans that early July, 2009, morning, a lady already at the counter, overheard my instructions to the attendant to check my bags through to Pau, France. On hearing this, she leaned over to ask, "Are you going to Lourdes with the North American Lourdes Volunteers?" To label this encounter a surprise would be an understatement!

When I said yes she happily told me that she and her husband were going too. Voila! Just like that, I was again being accompanied to Lourdes. As it turns out, we are still close friends; and we have journeyed to Lourdes two times since that original trip.

By means of my association with this group, I met Pere' Regis-Marie de la Teyssonniere. He is a priest assigned to the Sanctuaries at Lourdes and the Spiritual Director of the NALV. He writes a blog and on August 31, 2011, he blogged that the Archdiocese of New Orleans had been consecrated to Our Lady of Lourdes in 1873. This entry in his blog was the catalyst for this book.

Like earlier experiences, there was no question in my mind, I had to know more – I was moved to action. I wanted to understand why this consecration had taken place and what became of it. In that instant, I felt again like I was part of the Universal Catholic Church. I was not simply a traveler who had been to Lourdes; all of a sudden – a revelation - I had entered the story. My experiences had been that of others and theirs a part of mine; we were all in the story and experiencing Lourdes. That is to say, we were all experiencing our journeys, pilgrimages, conversions, our spiritual development, our lives, our prayers, our sorrows, the Gospels, Our Lord, the Sacrifice of the Mass – all by means of the invitation from Our Lady of Lourdes to come closer to her Son.

Upon researching the Lourdes story that unfolded in Louisiana in the 19th century, it was clear - the message of Lourdes was timeless and timely. Our Lady unceasingly invites us to come closer to her Son; she is beckoning us to enter the story that is Lourdes to experience the message of Lourdes. My mind flashed back to 2008 – for me, the dots were connected – just open the storybook and invite more pilgrims to enter. That is the "so what" that is the purpose of this book – Our Lady is continuously inviting us, the Catholic faithful of South Louisiana, to be a part of the Lourdes experience. This historical account of our forebears, their devotion and implementation of the consecration and arch confraternity are a legacy that each of us has inherited in our past and present. We are the present day pilgrims who have the same opportunity to share with our future generations the beautiful message of Lourdes and our own experiences in the story of Lourdes.

Pere' Regis-Marie told me that he frequently meets people around the world in areas where there may have been knowledge of or a devotion to Our Lady of Lourdes in the past. He said that sometimes when he spreads the message of Lourdes, it is like "blowing away the ashes from the still-burning embers beneath the surface". It is my ardent desire that upon reading this book, many will embrace the message of Lourdes; many will be moved to conversion; and that together we will blow away the ash and rekindle the still burning embers of Lourdes in the hearts, minds and souls of the faithful in our area, our state and our country.

Chronology/Timeline of the Archdiocese of New Orleans' Association with Immaculate Conception

January 7, 1844	Bernadette Soubirous was born.
May 10, 1846	The Sixth Provincial Council of Baltimore, the American bishops petitioned the Pope to make Mary, under the title of the Immaculate Conception, the patroness of the United States.[2]
June 16, 1846	Pope Pius IX elected Pope.
1847	The legal foundation of The College of the Immaculate Conception was laid in New Orleans by the Jesuits.[3]
July 19, 1850	New Orleans becomes Archdiocese; Blanc named Archbishop.
Summer/Fall 1853	Virulent yellow fever epidemic decimates New Orleans, especially the immigrant population.
December 8, 1854	Archbishop Antoine Blanc in Rome for Papal Proclamation of Dogma of the Immaculate Conception of Mary.
August 15, 1857	The first mass was offered at Immaculate Conception Church in New Orleans.
February 11, 1858	First apparition of Our Lady of Lourdes to Bernadette Soubirous in Lourdes, France.
July 16, 1858	Final apparition of The Immaculate Conception to Bernadette. Feast of Our Lady of Mt. Carmel.
January 26, 1861	Louisiana secedes from Union.

[2] (Wiseman October)

[3] (Immaculate Conception Parish 2012)

April 18, 1861	The Civil War begins in the United States.
January 18, 1862	Bishop Laurence wrote a mandamus[4] declaring the apparitions at Lourdes were officially recognized. Bishop Laurence recognized the miraculous healing of several pilgrims.
April 29, 1862	New Orleans captured, occupied by Federal forces.
August 29, 1862	Ministerial authorization is granted to build a chapel at Massabielle.
October 14, 1862	Construction of the Chapel of the Crypt.
April 9, 1865	Civil War ends.
July 8, 1866	Bernadette departs from Lourdes to enter the novitiate of Saint-Gildard's convent in Nevers.
July 19, 1866	Bernadette takes the habit and becomes Sister Marie-Bernard.
1867	Henri Lasserre agrees to write a history about Lourdes.
October 30, 1867	Bernadette's religious profession.
February 9, 1868	English-language newspaper, The Morning Star and Catholic Messenger, founded.
December 27, 1868	The Morning Star and Catholic Messenger published an article about a miraculous cure experienced by a Carmelite Friar, Father Hermann Cohen by using the water from Lourdes.
September, 1869	Lasserre published his book entitled Notre Dame du Lourdes.
October 17, 1869	The Morning Star and Catholic Messenger published a front page story submitted by a correspondent of the *London Univers* simply

[4] Mandamus is a bishop's letter.

	titled *Our Lady of Lourdes*. This article is the first local review of Lassserre's recent publication.
May 25, 1870	Archbishop Odin died and was buried in France; Perche' became Third Archbishop of New Orleans.
October 10, 1870	Perche' went to Rome to receive Pallium.
December 18, 1870	Perche' receives Pallium from Pope Pius IX at Vatican.
1871	Perche' made his first pilgrimage to Lourdes.
May 21, 1871	Perche' welcomed back to New Orleans.
November, 1872	Perche' engages George Soulier to construct an altar replica of Our Lady of Lourdes and the Grotto and St. Francis of Assisi at the Cathedral.
September 9, 1873	Two statues – one of Our Lady of Lourdes and the other of Bernadette were shipped to Perche' care of Am. Lutton on the steamer Missouri.
October 12, 1873	Perche' issued a Pastoral Letter announcing the inauguration of the monument erected in honor of Our Lady of Lourdes in the Metropolitan Church of New Orleans. At the same time he announced the intention to establish a confraternity to Our Lady of Lourdes and affiliate it to the Arch confraternity of Lourdes.
December 8, 1873	Perche' consecrated the Archdiocese of New Orleans to Our Lady of Lourdes.

January 25, 1874	Pope Pius IX gave the privilege of the affiliation to the confraternity to Our Lady of Lourdes to the Archdiocese of New Orleans in response to a letter from Perche' requesting same.
May, 1874	Diploma of Affiliation in the Arch confraternity of Our Lady of Lourdes was received in New Orleans.
July, 1874	First American pilgrimage to Lourdes; New Orleans sent a pilgrim.
April, 1875	Perche' traveled in Europe – England and France – to appeal for funds to assist his struggling Archdiocese.
June 10, 1876	Perche' visited Lourdes, France on his second pilgrimage.
July 1 - 3, 1876	Immaculate Conception Basilica was dedicated in Lourdes.
December, 1876	Perche' returned to New Orleans after his extended trip abroad.
April 20, 1877	Reconstruction in Louisiana officially ended; financial problems continued and grew.
September 8, 1877	Father Peyramale died.
February 7, 1878	Pope Pius IX died.
1878	Perche' spent two months in Grand Coteau during a yellow fever epidemic in New Orleans.
April 16, 1879	Bernadette died in Nevers.
1879 – 1880	Perche' may have made his final pilgrimage to Lourdes
December 27, 1883	Archbishop Perche' died; buried in St. Louis Cathedral.
December 8, 1933	Bernadette Soubirous is declared a saint - St. Bernadette.
2000	Pope John Paul II raised Pope Pius IX to blessed; his body was exhumed and found to be incorrupt.

Trusting Stone

When my star rose
sparked by divine fire
and came to rest in its carved-out space on earth,
a corner was born unlit.
It remains so today, deep and dark.
On occasions it catches light reflections
of passing, brilliant wisdoms.
Reaching from the depths, it strives
to imitate these lights,
to understand the darkness
and the sometimes dim, sometimes sparkling glow
of its connected body.
Always, it expects, anticipates
a lightning bolt of fire
to ultimately light the candle…
my corner of hope.

Excerpt from Rene' Laurentin's book, Bernadette Speaks from Chapter 15, Profession of Vows

"…Mere Josephine answered, "Monseigneur, she is good for nothing." This was said "with a smile," says Soeur Joseph Caldairou, and softly…

Bernadette had come forward.

"Is it true, Soeur Marie-Bernard, that you are good for nothing?" the bishop asked.

"It's true."

"Well then, my poor child, what are we going to do with you?"

"I told you in Lourdes when you wanted me to join the community; and you answered that it would make no difference…"

The bishop was not expecting this answer, and many of those present did not hear it, for the conversation was carried on softly. Bernadette was kneeling in front of the bishop to receive her book and her crucifix. At this point, the Superior General intervened, according to plan: "If you wish, Monseigneur, we could keep her here at the motherhouse, out of charity, and somehow use her in the infirmary, if only for cleaning up or preparing herbal teas. Since she's nearly always sick, it would suit her just fine."

According to Soeur Marie Bastide, the superior even added:

"SHE'S ONLY GOOD FOR BLOWING EMBERS INTO FLAME."

(Laurentin, pg. 369)

Lourdes Grotto

Strolling further along under some ilex trees one arrives at the highest point of the Vatican Gardens. At 71 metres above sea level it coincides with the spiritual heart of the park, the Lourdes Grotto. An exact replica of the one at Massabielle, it was donated by the French in 1902 to Pope Leo XIII (Vincenzo Gioacchino dei Conti Pecci, 1878- 1903). A statue of Our Lady is framed by a bright green mantle of American ivy (Parthenocissus tricuspidata Planch.) above the original altar of the grotto donated to Pope John XXIII (Angelo Giuseppe Roncalli, 1958-1963). It is a place where traditionally at the end of May each year the pope comes to pray and greet the faithful who have made their way up the hill in a torch-light procession.

The Pope Prays to Our Lady of Lourdes

Recently, I attended a Lourdes Experience. This experience is a presentation offered by Marlene Watkins, foundress of the North American Lourdes Volunteers, about Lourdes. One of the slides shows Pope Benedict XVI at the grotto in Lourdes. Mrs. Watkins stated that the Pope prays daily to Our Lady of Lourdes in his grotto garden and offers his prayers for all those who are praying to Our Lady of Lourdes.

[5] "…The pope then goes downstairs to take another walk, this time in the Vatican Gardens. He is usually joined by one or both of his secretaries and they pray the rosary before the replica of Our Lady of Lourdes…"[6]

Pope Benedict at Vatican Lourdes Grotto

[7]Pope Leo XIII was the first pope to pray "several hours daily in the Vatican gardens…"[8]

5 The Birds Will Still Sing: Pope Benedict XVI at Lourdes Grotto in the Vatican http://thebirdswillstillsing.blogspot.com/2010/06/pope-benedict-xvi-at-lourdes-grotto-in.html Screen clipping taken: 5/6/2012, 9:29 AM

6 Journalist chronicles a day in the life of Pope Benedict VATICAN CITY, February 20, 2012 (CNA/EWTN News)

7 Vatican Gardens http://www.vaticanstate.va/EN/Monuments/The_Vatican_Gardens/ Screen clipping taken: 5/6/2012, 9:39 AM

8 The Times Picayune. (1902) Present for Mgr. Guidi, Magnificent Travelling Case to the Apostolic Delegate. P. 2

CHAPTER 1

THE ARCHDIOCESE OF NEW ORLEANS CONSECRATED TO OUR LADY OF LOURDES,

THE IMMACULATE CONCEPTION AND PATRONESS OF THE UNITED STATES

Archdiocese of New Orleans – Consecrated to Our Lady of Lourdes

The Immaculate Conception

Catherine Laboure' Apparition

Catherine Laboure' is said to have experienced an apparition of the Virgin Mary in 1830 and as a result the miraculous medal was struck with the prayer "O Mary conceived without sin, pray for us who have recourse to thee."

Lourdes Website - Depiction of Apparition

Some say that apparition was the prelude to the Papal Bull declaring the dogma of the Immaculate Conception, while the apparitions of the Blessed Virgin to Bernadette Soubirous in 1858 became the confirmation. (Laurentin, p. 471)

The Archdiocese of New Orleans and Our Lady of Lourdes

As mentioned in the introduction, the blog posting by Pere' Regis-Marie was the catalyst for writing this book. Pere' Regis-Marie's blog can be found at this website: http://pereregismarie.blogspot.com/. It is written in French but easily translated by Google or Bing. I don't visit his website daily but on this occasion I dropped in and stumbled onto the following posting:

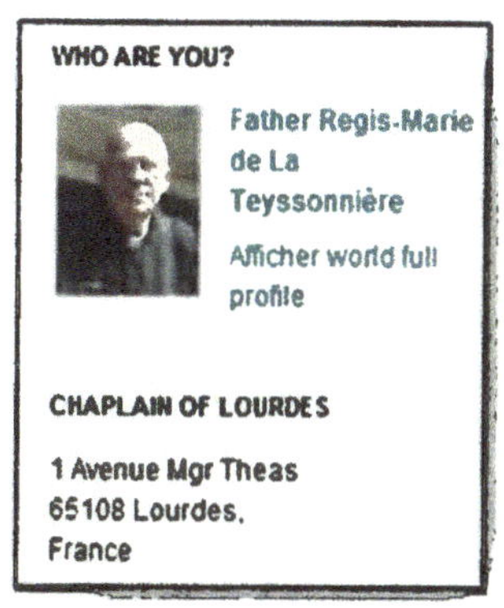

WHO ARE YOU?
Father Regis-Marie de La Teyssonnière
Afficher world full profile
CHAPLAIN OF LOURDES
1 Avenue Mgr Theas
65108 Lourdes.
France

Wednesday, August 31, 2011

New Orleans

On December 8, 1873, the Bishop of New Orleans spends (original French is "consacre") his diocese to Our Lady of Lourdes: "O Mary, conceived without sin, who have wished to confirm the dogmatic definition of the glorious privilege of your Immaculate Conception of the many miracles made at the Grotto of Lourdes, wanting to honor you and your special summon this title, now so dear to all Catholics, Our Lady of Lourdes, we have all dedicated ourselves to you, prostrate at the foot of this monument we have high in your honor as a small token of our trust and our love. On my behalf, on behalf of all the clergy and the faithful, I spent (original French is "consacre") the Diocese which has always been proud of you be committed "(Annals of Our Lady of Lourdes, 1874).

Posted by Father Regis-Marie de La Teyssonnière at 7:15

This posting moved my spirit. It was intriguing that our Archdiocese had been consecrated to Our Lady of Lourdes more than 100 years earlier. My devotion to Our Lady of Lourdes began in 2008 and in 2009 my service to the Sanctuary in Lourdes with the North American Lourdes Volunteers began. In the years that followed, we had returned to Lourdes and also worked with NALV to deliver virtual pilgrimages, known as a Lourdes Experience, locally. I became interested in the connections between Lourdes and my lay vocation as a novice in the Third Order of the Carmelites thereby inspiring more curiosity.

During these years, however, the fact that our Archdiocese was consecrated to Our Lady of Lourdes in 1873 had eluded not only me but just about everyone else I asked about the subject.

I wondered if – once consecrated – would the Archdiocese still be consecrated to Our Lady? The archdiocese was not only consecrated; but Archbishop Napoleon Joseph Perche' had built a monument to Our Lady of Lourdes as a side altar in St. Louis Cathedral – where is that altar, I wondered? Where are the statues? We weren't merely consecrated, but as an Archdiocese, we were enrolled in the Arch-Confraternity of Our Lady of Lourdes – what did that mean? Were we still enrolled? Who would revoke such an enrollment? How was this accomplished? Why didn't more people know about this? Where might answers be found?

For some time, I had felt compelled to spread the message of Lourdes – prayer, penance, - but how? I do not know many people; I have no influence among those I do know. How could Our Lady's message be spread far and wide throughout our area by someone like me? I stopped thinking about it except when the Virtual Pilgrimages of the NALV were approaching. This new information sparked my mind to once again think about Our Lady's message of Lourdes in our Archdiocese.

My mind searched for answers and my fingers began "Googling" the topic. As the days and weeks passed, I would come to learn much more about this subject. This book is my effort to report to those interested in the subject what my research has uncovered.

There was a grass roots effort by the faithful Catholics in our Archdiocese of the Reconstruction Era and beyond to consecrate our Parishes, the Archdiocese and the Province to Our Lady of Lourdes. (Catholic Church in Louisiana p.446) In response to great demand, Archbishop Perche' acted with haste, influence, authenticity and reverence to provide his faithful flock with a means to invoke the devotion they desired. Here is the story of our Archdiocese's consecration to Our Lady of Lourdes.

Immaculate Conception – Patroness of United States

Belief in the Immaculate Conception of the Blessed Virgin existed before the dogma was proclaimed. Catherine Laboure's 1830 apparition of Our Lady added confirmation to this belief in the hearts and minds of many faithful Catholics. Bishops in America were so convinced of this belief that "...In 1846, at the sixth provincial council of Baltimore, the American bishops petitioned the Pope to make Mary, under the title of the Immaculate Conception, the patroness of the United States." (Wiseman, 2003) This petition was granted.

Shortly afterward, the Jesuits embraced Our Lady under this title and carried this devotion to New Orleans. The Immaculate Conception church website in New Orleans reports that "... the Jesuits from Lyons, France, purchased this plot of land on which we are standing for $22,000. This is the second time the Jesuits took ownership of this same piece of property. They erected two buildings, which were to serve as a chapel, a residence and a college. The legal foundation of The College of the Immaculate Conception was built in 1847. The first mass was offered on August 15, 1857." (Church Website http://jesuitchurch.net/parish_history.htm 10/8/2011)

Although the first mass was offered AFTER the declaration of the dogma, the Jesuits of New Orleans had already accepted the belief that Mary was conceived in an Immaculate way as evidenced by the name of the church and college they erected in her honor years before.

Mid 19th Century New Orleans

In 1850, New Orleans had been elevated to a metropolitan diocese, or archdiocese, and Archbishop Blanc was installed in 1851. (Greene, p. x) In 1853 New Orleans was suffering under the weight of a Yellow Fever epidemic that was taking lives daily and leaving hundreds of orphans with nowhere to turn. "The epidemic of 1853 was by far the most terrifying: In a city of 154,000 people, nearly 8,000 died." (Times-Picayune, 1853) Many religious orders were founded during this time to care for and educate the children left orphans by the epidemic. (Greene, pgs. 160 – 161) In 1855 "...Henriette Delille founded the Catholic order of the Sisters of the Holy Family...Their mission included developing schools for the poor and orphaned in New Orleans." (Our Times, 1855) "The New Orleans Jewish Community was well established by the mid 19th century." Judah Touro, an unmarried wealthy philanthropist died leaving more than $500,000 to the City. (Our Times, 1854) That same year, Father Francis Xavier Seelos was transferred to Baltimore before coming later to New Orleans in 1866. According to John Kendall's book, *History of New Orleans*, General Lewis was elected mayor of New Orleans on April 10, 1854. Work on the New Orleans Opelousas and Great Northern Railroad was completed on November 6, 1854. The City of New Orleans was in debt of more than $11,000,000. (Kendall)

New Orleans Archbishop – In Rome for Ineffabilis Deus

As New Orleans was growing and suffering in the mid 1850's, across the Atlantic, Pope Pius IX was finalizing his papal bull declaring the dogma of the Immaculate Conception.

"...After consulting theologians, Pius IX, questioned the bishops of the universal church as to whether he should

Pope Pius IX Declaring Dogma of the Immaculate Conception

define the Immaculate Conception. 546 of the 603 bishops consulted responded affirmatively, four or five did not think it could be defined, twenty-four questioned whether the time was opportune, and ten preferred an indirect definition. Pius IX was assisted in composing his papal bull, Ineffabilis Deus, by a Jesuit theologian Perrone and by Dom Gueranger, Abbot of Solesmes. The document was not entirely completed when the Pope made the declaration on December 8, 1854. The essential definition was:

> "We declare, pronounce and define that the doctrine which holds that the Blessed Virgin Mary, at the first instant of her conception, by a singular privilege and grace of the Omnipotent God, in virtue of the merits of Jesus Christ, the Savior of mankind, was preserved immaculate from all stain of original sin, has been revealed by God, and therefore should firmly and constantly be believed by all the faithful.[34]" (Wiseman, 2002)

Image of Bernadette from Lasserre's Book – 1876 edition

Despite the many secular, charitable and religious issues facing New Orleans in 1854, Archbishop Anthony Blanc considered it of utmost importance to travel to Rome to witness and support Pope Pius the IX in this momentous declaration. (Pasquier, p. 133) The presence of the New Orleans Archbishop at the declaration provides a direct link from the time of the papal bull of this dogma declaring Our Lady's Immaculate Conception to the Shepherd of the Archdiocese of New Orleans. The Archdiocese of New Orleans was supportive of the Holy See and Our Lady in this dogma proclaimed in 1854. Did his leadership forecast the devotion of his flock less than 20 years hence?

For the theologians and the educated faithful, the final declaration of the dogma may have offered guidance, confirmation and clarity; but for the everyday Catholics struggling to find work; feed their families or remain faithful, it is unlikely this dogma was widely known.

As we come to learn, this was true of the small Pyrenees village of Lourdes also. The parish priest of Lourdes, Father Dominique Peyramale, was aware of the dogma declared by Pius IX in 1854, but had spent no time preaching to his faithful on the subject. According to Wonders of Lourdes, upon learning "Aquero's" (the word Bernadette used to describe who she saw) name from Bernadette after the 16th apparition, the priest "locked himself in his room…took up his pen to write to Bishop Laurence and warn him of what just happened." Father Peyramale further reflected on Bernadette's capacity to have prior knowledge of this lofty dogma. He thought "To be sure, Bernadette may have already heard the words "Immaculate Conception" at mass last December 8 but that was in French, not the dialect. Besides, a little peasant child had no propensity for theology." (Wonders, p. 71)

CHAPTER 2

THE STORY OF LOURDES

Local Newspapers Report and Stimulate Interest in the Apparitions and Cures in Lourdes

OUR LADY OF LOURDES APPEARS TO BERNADETTE SOUBIROUS – 1858

Among the earliest news reports in the United States, was the front-page article in The Morning Star and Catholic Messenger of New Orleans concerning the apparitions and cures at Lourdes from a correspondent with *London Univers* on October 17, 1869. This correspondent was attempting to accomplish two goals with this article; 1) he was first and foremost providing a review of the recent French publication of a book by Henri Lasserre entitled *Notre Dame du Lourdes* and 2) he was telling the story of Lourdes as he understood it from the contents of Lasserre's book. According to his assessment, this author provided a resounding endorsement of Lasserre, his work and the credibility of his findings. The unknown author puts it like this:

> "...This work is the production of M. Henri Lasserre, who had previously distinguished himself as a French Catholic author and it is precisely the very work, both as to matter and manner that is most needed at the present day. The great event that has so changed Lourdes is the apparition of the Immaculate Mother of God in the alcove of a rock near the hamlet, and the object of the learned and indefatigable writer, is to prove beyond the shadow of a doubt the reality of that apparition. The characteristic of religious error in this century is its denying or ignoring altogether the existence of the supernatural, and it is because the Catholic Church is the representative on earth of the supernatural, that so fierce a war is now-a-days waged against it. This being the case, we may reasonably expect that the supernatural should...vindicate itself by giving manifest proofs of its existence. Such a manifestation is said to have occurred at Lourdes..." (pg.1)

Shortly after this article about the French publication, the same newspaper followed with another article on February 13, 1870 after the subject book had been translated into English. This is how the newspaper article described the miraculous events of 1858 in Lourdes, France as reported by Henri Lasserre. The article commented on the new book written by noted French journalist Henri Lasserre and first published in 1869 to wide acclaim.

> "...The simple facts are these. On the 11th of February, 1858, an humble, ignorant, peasant child named Bernadette Soubirous, being sent by her parents, together with two companions, to fetch some dead wood by a mountain stream close to a grotto, known in the country by the name of "Grotto of Massabielle," suddenly saw in an inaccessible place an apparition, clothed in white and radiant beyond description...This apparition returned at stated times as it had promised on eighteen different occasions; it spoke to the child, commanding her to tell the clergy to have a chapel built on the spot; and at its word a miraculous spring burst forth under the hands of the child, in the presence of hundreds of spectators, from the dry hard rock of the grotto which miraculous source gave sight to the blind, feet to the lame and healing to the sick of all ages, conditions and maladies." (pg. 1)

Mgr Laurence, Bishop of Tarbes and Lourdes from 1844 – 1870 – Lourdes Website

The 1870 article goes on to state that the Bishop of Tarbes declared the apparitions to be authentic and quotes the articles as stating; "Article 1; We judge that the Immaculate Mary, Mother of God, did appear to Bernadette Soubirous on the 11th of February 1858 and the following days in the Grotto of Massabielle, in the town of Lourdes; that the apparition possesses all the characters of truth, and that the faithful have good reason for believing it to be certain. We humbly submit our judgment to that of the Sovereign Pontiff, who is charged with the government of the Universal Church. Art 2., We authorize in our diocese the "venite" of Our Lady of the Grotto of Lourdes; but we forbid any particular form of prayers, any hymn, or any book of devotion relating to this event to be published without our written approbation." (pg. 1)

This account was recorded by the local Catholic newspaper, The Morning Star and Catholic Messenger on February 13, 1870; twelve years after the apparitions occurred and eight years after the Bishop of Tarbes declared the apparitions valid. This article and possibly others no doubt had an impact on those who read them. We come to learn that the experiences in Lourdes would be spread throughout the world in a matter of a few short years causing the faithful to travel on pilgrimage there by the thousands.

Ave Maria

This holy air, it calms all fears,
comforts hearts, dries seas of tears,
helps overcome great sinful deeds,
begs intercession for all needs
from Mary as her presence nears.
This music plays, the dark sky clears.
Hope through Our Lady's light appears.
In knowledge that she always heeds
this holy air.
Our Lady's love lifts up and cheers.
Souls to her Son she gently steers.
When following her steps, she leads
to the Trinity as she pleads
each simple cause. The Spirit hears
this holy air.

The Apparitions and the Message of Lourdes

Before we explore deeper into the impact Lasserre's book had in spreading the story of Notre Dame du Lourdes, especially in New Orleans, let us first recall the apparitions to Bernadette and try to understand the message of Lourdes as it is understood today. The official Lourdes Website can be found at www.lourdes-france.org. The website summarizes the account of the 18 apparitions to Bernadette Soubirous as follows:

Illustration of Apparition - Lasserre 1876

"1st Apparition

Thursday 11th February 1858: the meeting

Accompanied by her sister and a friend, Bernadette went to Massabielle on the banks of the Gave to collect bones and dead wood. Removing her socks in order to cross the stream, she heard a noise like a gust of wind, she looked up towards the Grotto : "I SAW A LADY DRESSED IN WHITE, SHE WORE A WHITE DRESS, AN EQUALLY WHITE VEIL, A BLUE BELT AND A YELLOW ROSE ON EACH FOOT." Bernadette made the Sign of the Cross and said the Rosary with the lady. When the prayer ended the Lady suddenly vanished.

2nd Apparition

Sunday 14th February: Holy Water

Bernadette felt an inner force drawing her to the Grotto in spite of the fact that she was forbidden to go there by her parents. At her insistence, her mother allowed her; after the first decade of the Rosary, she saw the same lady appearing. She sprinkled holy water at her. The lady smiled and bent her head. When the Rosary ended she disappeared.

3rd Apparition

Thursday 18th February: the lady speaks

For the first time, the Lady spoke. Bernadette held out a pen and paper asking her to write her name. She replied; "It is not necessary" and she added: *"I do not promise to make you happy in this world but in the other. Would you be kind enough to come here for a fortnight?"*

4th Apparition

Friday 19th February: short and silent Apparition

Bernadette came to the Grotto with a lighted blessed candle. This is origin of carrying candles and lighting them in front of the Grotto.

5th Apparition

Saturday 20th February: In silence

The lady taught her a personal prayer. At the end of the vision Bernadette is overcome with a great sadness.

6th Apparition

Sunday 21st February: "Aquéro"

The Lady appeared to Bernadette very early in the morning. About one hundred people were present. Afterwards the Police Commissioner, Jacomet, questioned her. He wanted Bernadette to tell what she saw. Bernadette would only speak of "AQUÉRO" ("that thing" in local dialect)

7th Apparition

Tuesday 23rd February: The secret.

Surrounded by 150 persons, Bernadette arrived at the Grotto. The Apparition reveals to her a secret "only for her alone".

8th Apparition

Wednesday 24th February: Penance.

The message of the Lady: *"Penance! Penance! Penance! Pray to God for sinners. Kiss the ground as an act of penance for sinners!"*

Lourdes Website - Statue of Our Lady of Lourdes

9th Apparition

Thursday 25th February: The spring.

Three hundred people were present. Bernadette relates; "She told me to go, drink of the spring (....) I only found a little muddy water. At the fourth attempt I was able to drink. She also made me eat the bitter herbs that were found near the spring, and then the vision left and went away." In front of the crowd that was asking "Do you think that she is mad doing things like that?" she replied; "It is for sinners."

10th Apparition

Saturday 27th February: Silence

Eight hundred people were present. The Apparition was silent. Bernadette drank the water from the spring and carried out her usual acts of penance.

11th Apparition

Sunday 28th February: Penance

Over one thousand people were present at the ecstasy. Bernadette prayed, kissed the ground and moved on her knees as a sign of penance. She was then taken to the house of Judge Ribes who threatened to put her in prison.

12th Apparition

Monday 1st March: The First Miracle

Over one thousand five hundred people assembled and among them, for the first time, a priest. In the night, Catherine Latapie, a friend from Lourdes, went to the Grotto, she plunged her dislocated arm into the water of the Spring: her arm and her hand regained their movement.

13th Apparition

Tuesday 2nd March: Message to the priests.

The crowd becomes larger and larger. The Lady asked her: "Go, tell the priests to come here in procession and to build a chapel here." Bernadette spoke of this to Fr. Peyramale, the Parish Priest of Lourdes. He wanted to know only one thing: the Lady's name. He demanded another test; to see the wild rose bush flower at the Grotto in the middle of winter

14thApparition

Wednesday 3rd March: A smile

From 7 o'clock in the morning, in the presence of three thousand people, Bernadette arrives at the Grotto, but the vision did not appear! After school, she heard the inner invitation of the Lady. She went to the Grotto and asked her again for her name. The response was a smile. The Parish Priest told her again: "If the Lady really wishes that a chapel be built, then she must tell us her name and make the rose bush bloom at the Grotto."

15th Apparition

Thursday 4th March: The day all were waiting for!

The ever-greater crowd (about eight thousand people) waited for a miracle at the end of the fortnight. The vision was silent. Fr. Peyramale stuck to his position. For twenty days Bernadette did not go to the Grotto, she no longer felt the irresistible invitation.

16th Apparition

Thursday 25th March: The name they awaited for!

The vision finally revealed her name, but the wild rose bush, on which she stood during the Apparitions, did not bloom. Bernadette recounted; "She lifted up her eyes to heaven, joined her hands as though in prayer, that were held out and open towards the ground and said to me: Que soy era Immaculada Concepciou (I am the Immaculate Conception) ." The young visionary left and, running all the way, repeated continuously the words that she did not understand. These words troubled the brave Parish Priest. Bernadette was ignorant of the fact that this theological expression was assigned to the Blessed Virgin. Four years earlier, in 1854, Pope Pius IX declared this a truth of the Catholic Faith (a dogma)

17th Apparition

Wednesday 7th April: The miracle of the candle

During this Apparition, Bernadette had to keep her candle alight. The flame licked along her hand without burning it. A medical doctor, Dr. Douzous, immediately witnessed this fact.

The painting of the 16th Apparition - the miracle of the candle

Lourdes Website – Miracle of the Candle Lourdes Website

18th Apparition

Thursday16th July: The Final Apparition.

Bernadette receives the mysterious call to the Grotto, but her way was blocked and closed off by a barrier. She thus, arrived across from the Grotto to the other side of the Gave. "I felt that I was in front of the Grotto, at the same distance as before, I saw only the Blessed Virgin, and she was more beautiful than ever!" (Lourdes Website, 2012)

The 2012 Pastoral Theme of Lourdes is "With Bernadette praying the Rosary". It follows previous themes of "With Bernadette, let us make the Sign of the Cross" and "With Bernadette, Praying the Our Father." These themes are part of a three-year cycle "...consecrated to praying along with Bernadette..." (Lourdes Website, 2012) The 2012 theme provides insight and pastoral guidance for meditating on the apparitions. In the radiance of the Paschal Mystery, the first seven apparitions are contemplated and explained in the light of the Joyful Mysteries. During these apparitions Bernadette is being welcomed by the Blessed Virgin in silence and prayer. As the catechesis points out, "...As much as there is joy in Mary at having encountered "grace in the presence of God", so Bernadette displays joy in having encountered Mary..." The eighth through eleventh apparitions are referred to as the "penitential apparitions". During these apparitions Bernadette "...carries out three actions: she crawls on all fours and kisses the ground in the Grotto, she eats some grass and she smears her face with mud." Bernadette's actions were obedient acts of humility; during the ninth apparition the spring was revealed and then Mary told Bernadette to "Go to the spring and drink and wash..." When the Blessed Mother asks Bernadette to tell the priests to build a chapel and come in procession, these apparitions are referred to as the Glorious apparitions. As a result of these encounters, "...the grace received by Bernadette, is spread to all, everywhere and forever." The Mysteries of Light are brought to mind first because Bernadette brought with her to the grotto a candle to light her way from the 3rd apparition onward. During the 17th apparition, the candle flame touched Bernadette but did not burn her; the pastoral theme reminds us "...Christ, the light of the world did not come to condemn our humanity but to save it..." (Kemseke 2011)

Blind Faith

God never spoke to me in mortal voice.
I never had a vision of His Face,
though I would love to see Him had I choice.
Rather, I hear Him in a hidden place
there deep inside the corners of my soul
and trust that I obey, accept the grace.
I see Him when the sky has turned to gold
and when the stars shine in the velvet sky.
Too, when the signs of Spring again unfold.
But then, I doubt when things all go awry
and turn from Him much to my whining shame.
Forgetting Him, alone I sit and cry.
Through grace, new faith returns to my life's game
and hoping, once again, I call His Name.

THE MESSAGE OF LOURDES

Many accounts of the apparitions at Lourdes have been written including books, news articles, commentaries and others over the past 154 years; each has characterized the message of Lourdes in their own ways. We will explore various accounts which were directed to 19th century pilgrims, faithful and interested readers in New Orleans. Today, we find the message of Lourdes written simply on the official Lourdes website – Love, happiness in the other world, penance, meaning conversion, and prayer:

> "...At Lourdes, the fact that Mary had appeared in a dirty and obscure Grotto, in the place called Massabielle, the Old Rock, tells us that God comes to join us where we are,

in the midst of our poverty and failures. The Grotto is not only a place where something happened - a geographical place - it is also a place where God gives us a sign by revealing his heart and our heart. It is a place where God leaves us a message, a message that is nothing other than that of the Gospel. God comes to tell us that he loves us, - this is the heart of the Message of Lourdes, and he loves us as we are with all our successes but also with all our wounds, our weaknesses and our limitations." (Lourdes Website, 2012)

God's love is palpable at Lourdes. Many who journey to Lourdes on Pilgrimage feel called to be there; it is a feeling of being pulled into the heart of Mother Church. When we are there and see so many pilgrims, so many who are ill, disabled, wounded; and volunteers so dedicated to their care and assistance we are in the company of the true heart of God where all are welcome and loved and serving His loving purpose. It is just as important for us to understand the other messages that are of Lourdes and which consist of words Our Lady actually spoke to Bernadette:

"…The third statement of the Virgin was: *"I do not promise to make you happy in this world but in the other."* We know a world of violence, lies, sensuality, profit, and war. But we know also a world of charity, solidarity, and justice. These two worlds exist on our earth. When Jesus, in the Gospel, invites us to discover the Kingdom of Heaven, he invites us to discover in our world, as it is, "another world". Wherever love exists, God is present…

Bernadette was asked: 'Did the Lady say something to you?' She replied: "Yes, now and again she would say: *"Penance, penance, penance, pray for sinners"*. By penance we understand conversion. Conversion in the Church, as we learn from Christ, involves turning our heart towards God and towards others. "Pray for sinners". Praying brings us to the Spirit of God. Thus we understand that sin does not make us happy. We must understand that sin is something that is contrary to the love of God that is revealed to us through the Gospel." (Lourdes Website, 2012)

A discerning read of the official Lourdes website suggests that it is focusing on the known facts, the actual recorded statements, verifiable details, and benefits from a rich history of documents, studies and theological purity that give us reason to have confidence in the teachings about the messages of Lourdes recorded there.

What was written about Lourdes, Bernadette and the apparitions in the 19th century? Had the messages of Lourdes been evaluated in the light of their Gospel meanings or their theological implications at that time? How did the account of the Lourdes apparitions spread throughout the world and into the 19th century Archdiocese of New Orleans? Did these apparitions and the message of Lourdes bring meaning and purpose to 19th century believers as it has for so many today? If yes, why? Do the messages of Lourdes transcend time, place and people throughout our Universal Church?

My own experiences in Lourdes have told me that those who go there or have been there are linked through Mary to God's universal purpose for His people through the virtues of faith, hope and love. We see these virtues in practice in Lourdes through the spiritual and corporal works of mercy that are undertaken by ordinary people every day there. We will now investigate the Lourdes devotion as established in the Archdiocese of New Orleans more than 100 years ago.

Deep In South's Heart

Heaven seems far away in the lowlands.
Stars are not so reachable, not so bright,
so big as in Texas and other highlands.
Thunder, even, seems distant with its fright.
Folks must reach tall to touch angelic spheres.
'Neath sea level, one is tempted to yell
to assure Someone up there notes, well hears
and heeds poor supplicants' woes they must tell.
Thus, the host of church bells that peal and chime,
myriad choirs singing glory and praise,
rosaries, voice-filled processions each time
the faithful wish to sanctify their days.
Well-blessed would be land where such joyful noise
is raised to the Lord should He take sweet poise.

CHAPTER 3

STORIES OF MIRACLES REPORTED IN NEW ORLEANS

Early News of Miracles Reported in New Orleans

Fr. Hermann Cohen - T. Tierney, OCD

On December 27, 1868, The Morning Star and Catholic Messenger carried a story simply entitled *Father Hermann*. The article reported a story found in the *Monde* concerning a Carmelite friar who had undergone a miraculous cure by virtue of the use of Lourdes water upon his eyes. The account is recorded thusly:

> "For a year past my sight, fatigued by constant labor, became gradually weaker every day...The experienced oculist examined my eyes...he found them in an alarming state...a grayish tint on the bottom of the cribiform limina...he pronounced the existence of a malady which is known..by the name of glaucoma...Meanwhile, the idea was suggested to me to make a novena to Notre Dame de Lourdes, who had already miraculously cured several persons afflicted with blindness...The proposition pleased me much more than the prospect of a surgical operation...I began the novena on the 24th of October, the feast of St. Raphael, who himself had cured blindness in the case of Tobias. Every day I bathed my eyes with the salutary water taken from the miraculous grotto, and every day I prayed to the Immaculate Virgin, and many holy souls prayed with me...At last, on the last day, the feast of All Saints, being in the grotto itself and near the fountain, I no longer felt any symptoms..." (pg. 7)

The Carmelite Friar concluded his account of his miraculous cure by writing "I have obtained what I desired above, namely, the ability to continue to live the hermit life of our dear desert; in a word, I am radically cured, and my intimate conviction is that this cure is a miracle due to the intercession of the holy Virgin…" (pg. 7)

While Father Hermann Cohen experienced a cure for his glaucoma, it is also noteworthy that Father Hermann Cohen is documented as the first priest to lead a pilgrimage to Lourdes. Tadgh Tierney, OCD has uncovered and written about one of the most obscure but interesting facts discovered in this research. Hermann Cohen was an accomplished musician and pianist. He was Jewish and he was an atheist. He underwent a conversion and became a Carmelite friar. Tierney picks up the story of his life when he decided to found a "desert house". Tierney reports that:

> "…In the year 1856, amid his pioneering work in Lyons and Bagnères-de-Bigorres in the south of France, Hermann Cohen discovered a vast wooded solitude near the Pyrenees about twenty kilometers from Lourdes at a place called Tarasteix." (p. 2) To place the fortuitous location in context, Tierney reveals "...Hermann's choice of location for the desert could not be better…would have appealed to his spiritual father, St. John of the Cross… (from)Tarasteix…you can see the whole range of the Pyrenees… the shrine of Lourdes can be found. At the time when Hermann was surveying the area, a ten-year-old child near the hamlet of Bartrès was tending sheep in the hills overlooking Lourdes…Hermann could not have foreseen that two years later, not far away at the grotto…he would have the privilege of meeting Bernadette." (p. 2)

In the summer of 1858, Tierney recounts that Cohen and a friend of his, a journalist, Louis Veuillot, "were both disposed to believe in the apparitions. Both were afterwards to defend Lourdes - Veuillot in his frequent articles in L'Univers, and Hermann at the grotto itself by leading the first pilgrimage…Hermann Cohen was the first religious and priest to give public honor to God and Mary at Lourdes. He led hundreds of people in front of the grotto, although it was still enclosed behind barricades; and access was forbidden by the civil authorities. This happened on September 20, 1858, two months after the last apparition." (p. 4) One account reported from September 21, 1858 in the Commissary Dominic Jacomet stated that "there was a lot of agitation at the grotto caused by Fr. Hermann and Dr. Dozous who left the town together and went to the grotto, and there, surrounded by a curious crowd who had come with the Carmelite Fr. Hermann, they sang the Magnificat and another psalm so loudly that his voice could he heard on the way to Pau." (p. 4)

During this pilgrimage Father Cohen had an unusual experience. Tierney writes that Abbe' Rozies told the story like this: "Something unusual happened to Fr. Augustine (Hermann) when he bent down to drink from the spring at the grotto. As he did so, his breviary fell into the basin. A lady quickly tried to retrieve it, and the priest also looked to see if the pages had gotten wet. There was one particularly beautiful picture of Our Lady, which he expected to find soaked, but not only was the colored picture of Our Lady not spoiled, but a perfect copy of it was imprinted on the blank page of his breviary. Hermann remarked, "Holy Virgin, you have done me a great favor; instead of one picture of you, you have given me two." (p. 4)

While Father Hermann's cure appears to be the first reported in New Orleans, a book was being written by Henri Lasserre that would bring worldwide attention to the miraculous events that transpired at Lourdes within a few years hence.

Lasserre is Commissioned to Write the First Account of Lourdes Named the Lourdes Historian

Recalling the news articles from 1869 and 1870 about Lasserre's book, we learn from The Wonder of Lourdes that Lasserre was known to Father Peyramale, the Lourdes priest to whom Bernadette conveyed the messages from "Aquero"- the term of affection she used to describe the beautiful lady. On December 4, 1863, Father Peyramale received a letter from Henri Lasserre, a lawyer and Christian journalist known to have a "fiery pen…" A year earlier, in October, 1862, Lasserre had written to Peyramale asking for some of the Lourdes water in hopes that he might be cured from "a serious eye infection that no physician had succeeded in healing." (Wonders, p. 108) Father Peyramale sent the water and had "prayed a long time for Lasserre." The letter Father Peyramale held in his hand in 1863 was "an answer to his prayers". "Lasserre told of how, on October 10, 1862, after praying fervently, he had rubbed his eyes with a towel soaked in Lourdes water and found himself instantly cured." (Wonders, p. 109) This letter impressed the priest and "after a few hesitations" he asked "Lasserre to write the history of the apparitions of Lourdes." (Wonders, p. 109)

Henri Lasserre - Spirit of Notre Dame Website

Lasserre deliberated for several years but in August 1867 under the order of his confessor, Lasserre agreed to do

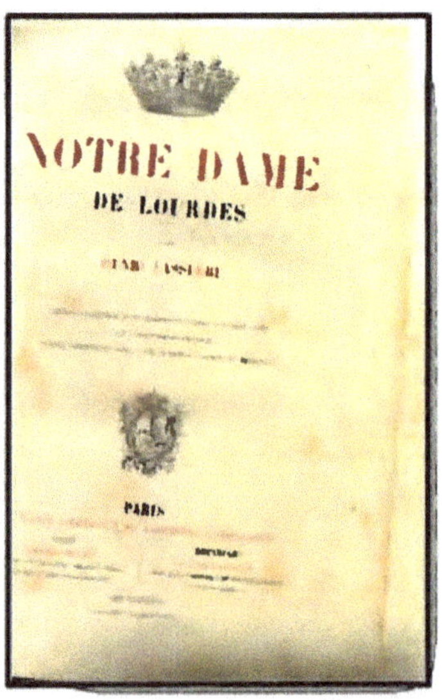

Title Page - Lasserre's Book 1876

as the priest had requested. (Wonders, p. 109) In 1869, he finished a single French volume and published a 504 page book entitled *Notre-Dame de Lourdes*. "The book became the nineteenth century's greatest publishing success." (Wonders, p. 110)

In February, 1870, the French population of New Orleans was already taking note of the book, and as the quoted news article reports, more importantly, becoming enthusiastic about the apparitions, miracles and cures as documented in the account by Lasserre; after all, he too had experienced a miraculous cure in 1862. The 1870 news account gives the New Orleans readers every reason to accept Lasserre's account as authentic; "M. Lasserre...has taken almost incredible trouble to verify every fact he relates. He has given the names and addresses of a host of witnesses both to the original facts and to the cures effected in consequence." (pg. 1) Not only did the author disclose the care and journalistic integrity with which he undertook this work, but the work also contains a letter in the preface of the book from Pope Pius IX dated September 4, 1869 in which the Pope extends his apostolic benediction and hope for success of the book.

Lasserre's book was criticized and his account called into question. This book, and other related works which Lasserre wrote and published later, earned Lasserre a "goldmine". (Wonders, p. 110) In the light of history, Lasserre's work is now considered to have "brushed aside historical accuracy." (Wonders, p. 111) "The history of the apparitions ...was portrayed as a struggle between good and evil, between little Bernadette's faith and an obtuse and meddling bureaucracy's contempt." (Wonders, p. 110) Notwithstanding the doubters and critics, the book underwent numerous republications and was translated into eighty-one languages. The result of this widespread publication of the account of the apparitions at Lourdes has been to make Lourdes one of the most popular pilgrimage sites, second only to Rome. (Wonders, p. 110)

Shortly after reading the newly published book by Lasserre, a man, identified as Pierre Joseph Hanquet, "...was filled with faith in the intercession of our Lady of Lourdes and implored his family to write...for some of the...water..." The account of his cure was reported in The Morning Star and Catholic Messenger on March 27, 1870. Entitled *Miracle at Liege*, the local paper picked up the story of a Belgian paper called *Journal de Liege*. The article reports:

Illustrated Lourdes Map - Lasserre 1876

> "...a touching account of a most remarkable event which took place on the 17th of November last. A man who had been confined to his bed for many years by paralysis, complicated by erysipelas and numerous abscesses...was restored to perfect health within two minutes after drinking and applying to his body some water from Notre Dame de Lourdes..."

The conclusion of Dr. C. Termonia was "...The wonderful cure of this patient can only be looked upon as the result of an intervention which is quite beyond all the laws of science." (pg. 6)

Local Stories Abound

The news accounts of miraculous cures and massive numbers of pilgrims to Lourdes continued to receive attention in New Orleans newspapers. Local readers were captivated by the stories of cures and miracles and the spring of water that was issued forth when Our Lady of Lourdes instructed Bernadette Soubirous to dig for the water in the Grotto of Massabielle.

On February 18, 1871, The Morning Star and Catholic Messenger carried a story entitled *Our Blessed Lady of Lourdes*. The article inserted a letter dated January 16, 1871 from a Sister at St. Paul's Convent, Selley Oak, Birmingham to the publication *Univers*. In this letter, the writer carefully details the illnesses of two sisters in the convent and the miraculous cures they experienced through the reverent use of Lourdes water in combination with a Novena which they began on the first day of May. (p. 2)

In a later edition of The Morning Star and Catholic Messenger dated November 3, 1872, a journalist writes an account of the pilgrimages to Lourdes. The author wrote:

> "...Many pilgrims are arriving from Brittany, and the Patrie estimates the number who have visited Lourdes during the year at 200,000...arrangements were made for thirty-eight extraordinary trains, besides twenty-one ordinary trains daily; each of which was to bring about 1,500 passengers, so great was the influx of pilgrims expected to keep the Feast of the Rosary at Lourdes...The crowd is described as incalculable, and the slopes of the mountains around are said to have been covered with people on their knees..." (pg. 8)

In December of 1872, The Times Picayune picked up an article from The St. Louis Democrat entitled *Notre Dame du Lourdes – The Miracles and The Pilgrimages to Lourdes*. It reads as follows:

> "...Lourdes could not be situated in a lovelier place...All is lighted by the sun of Southern France. What miracles this miracle has wrought...The miracle occurred on Shrove Thursday, February, 1858. Bernadette Soubirous, a girl fourteen years old, was gathering wood on the mountain. While near the Grotte de Massabielle she perceived in the grotto a woman of angelic beauty, wearing a long white dress with a blue belt.

Bernadette was terrified at first, but seeing la dame recite her beads she imitated her and fell on her knees and swooned."

The article continues with the well-known account of the apparitions, the spring of water and Bernadette's struggle to remain faithful to the duties and messages entrusted to her by Our Lady. What is, perhaps, most prophetic for that time period as well as our own is how the unknown author portrayed the relevancy of the apparitions at Lourdes. He put it this way:

"...Everybody cried a miracle has been wrought. Still, until Mr. Lasserre published his book, the miracle had merely a local reputation. The event of the last two years' current incident, the menacing future, have created in many minds a yearning for that support man finds only when he rests on heaven. The importance of religion as a social necessity is more keenly felt than ever. It is moreover, desirable for devout people to count themselves and to show the world how strong numerically they are. All causes combined have made this pilgrimage to Lourdes extremely important...25,000...came...the pilgrimage was imposing...There were eight bishops and two thousand priest, all of whom celebrated mass, and will carry back to their parishes stories likely to extend enthusiasm to Lourdes." (Times Picayune, 1872)

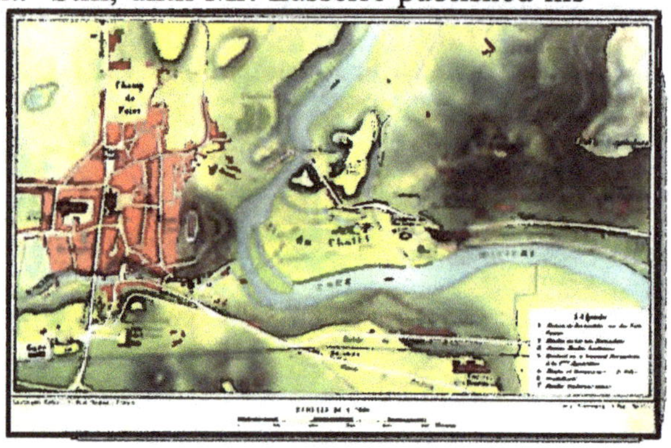

Illustrated Lourdes Map - Lasserre 1876

Upon reading this author's opinion concerning the importance "...for devout people to count themselves and to show the world how strong numerically they are..." one is likely to be reminded of the battle being waged today on behalf of religious freedoms in the United States and the leadership of the Catholic bishops in that struggle.

The Morning Star and Catholic Messenger carried another story about Lourdes in the Sunday, April, 6, 1873 edition. This article was entitled *Cures by the Water of Lourdes.* The article reads as follows:

"...A correspondent of the *Freeman's Journal* gives a translation of the attestation of the Mayor and several citizens of Chabris, concerning the miraculous cure wrought on a deaf mute, Aurelia Bruneau, by the use of the water of the Lourdes. Our readers will remember the famous letter of the New York *Herald's* correspondent, who witnessed a similar cure in the case of Constance L'Etst of Blois...We have been told by a personal friend of a lady in Boston, of a miraculous cure affected on her by the use of this water...The undersigned Mayor, and inhabitants of Chabris, certify that Miss Aurelia Bruneau, born at Chabris, April 24, 1853, was born deaf and dumb, and it is in their knowledge that this young girl – raised in the Asylum for the Deaf and Dumb at Deols and Orleans – never heard a sound until the 11th of October current...Fautereau, Mayor of Chabris...The above extracts, first published in Tours,...reproduced...Lourdes Annals...January, 1873. – Catholic Review" (pg. 8)

Yet another miraculous cure was reported by The Morning Star and Catholic Messenger on June 15, 1873. Entitled *Cures, Apparently Miraculous, at the Holy Grottos of Our Blessed Lady of Lourdes, May 1, 1873*, the account is:

"...from a private letter, sent...to St. Scholastica's Priory...there have been three cures that we know of for certain...The first was a girl of twenty four who had not walked without crutches since she was three years old...after having drunk some of the water, while she was praying in the Grotto she suddenly felt she was cured...and walked quite alone...The second was a child of six years who had not walked since she was born...The third we saw ourselves...a girl of twenty six...who had lost her voice...Everybody kept telling her to say "Mary" and to call on Our Lady...at first she could not...at last...she said quite aloud "Mary!..." (pg. 1)

Page 3 of the September 28, 1873 edition of The Morning Star and Catholic Messenger ran a story entitled *Another Miraculous Cure at Lourdes.* This article was taken from *The Semaine Catholique* and stated:

"...On the eve of the Assumption arrived at Lourdes the Baroness de la Rue...who has been suffering for twelve years with a terrible infirmity which obliged her to walk with crutches...The morning following her arrival she went to the grotto and, while praying before the shrine, was instantaneously and miraculously cured...A priest, Abbe de Musy, who has suffered for twenty years from exceeding weakness, has been also miraculously cured and upon the same day the Assumption of Our Lady..." (pg. 3)

On October 5, 1873 a story ran in the Sunday Morning edition of The Morning Star and Catholic Messenger which most certainly gave readers reason to feel increased devotion to Our Lady of Lourdes. The title line read – THE HOLY FATHER.

"...The Pope continues to enjoy most excellent health...the past week the Pope has received many deputations, and amongst others one from the Catholic schoolmistresses of Rome...He presented several of the ladies and their scholars with silver medals. An image of Our Lady of Lourdes, blessed by the Pope, has been placed in the Church of the Virgin. A *triduo*[9] was celebrated to its honor which commenced August 22d...This is the first statue of the Madonna under this invocation, which has been seen in Italy." (pg. 1)

[9] Triduo is a period of three days of prayer usually preceding a Roman Catholic feast. http://www.merriam-webster.com/dictionary/triduum

These early 1870's accounts of Lasserre's book, the attention it brought to the events in France and subsequent articles and attestations of miracles like the ones cited, documenting the vast numbers of pilgrims, surely had the effect to move the Catholic faithful of New Orleans toward a deeper understanding of and a fervent devotion to Our Lady of Lourdes under the French Shepherd of the Archdiocese, Napoleon Joseph Perche'. Papal acknowledgement of the invocation would also have served to confirm the authenticity of the apparitions.

Perhaps because these stories were found in newspapers, early accounts of the apparitions focused primarily on the water, miracles, cures and the struggle for religious freedom and goodness to triumph over the oppressive governments and the widespread evil which was taking root in the hearts of people throughout the world in the age of industrialization, reconstruction and scientific discoveries of the time. As the devotion evolved, Perche' would guide his archdiocese toward a deeper understanding of the apparitions and a genuine Marian devotion. Ultimately, Archbishop Perche' would lead the people of his archdiocese and province not only to Our Lady of Lourdes, but through Our Lady, he would lead thousands to Jesus.

The Water of the Lourdes Grotto

With reliable reported accounts of miraculous cures, it is no wonder that many were interested in obtaining some of the water from Lourdes.

In an article entitled *The Water from the Grottos of Lourdes* which ran in the Sunday edition of The Morning Star and Catholic Messenger on February 4, 1872 the paper ran a story they picked up from the New York Tablet concerning how to get the water.

"...we have made inquiries of the pastor of St. James' Church, Montreal, P.Q., and in reply received a letter...Montreal, Jan. 14, 1872...Mr. Editor – We have distributed all the water from Notre Dame de Lourdes which we had brought out from Lourdes; we will have none until spring. To get it, we address, directly, the Missionaries who serve the new church built at Lourdes in honor of Mary." (pg. 2)

In the Sunday, May 4, 1873 edition of The Morning Star and Catholic Messenger, the paper ran a story entitled *The Water of the Grotto of Lourdes* which was picked up from the Freeman's Journal. The story reported:

> "...By every mail we receive letters, and sometimes many in a day, asking us "where the Water of Lourdes can be obtained." Were it possible we would answer these letters. As it is not, we ask to refer to our previous publication...we greatly wish there was some depot, here in New York, for its reception and distribution, but there is none. By the permission, and even request of the "very Rev. A. Granger, C.S.C., Notre Dame, near South Bend, Indiana" Provincial of the Congregation of the Holy Cross, we stated sometime last February that he had a supply and was distributing it...he said:
>
> > "Since the publication of your article on the Water of Lourdes, we have been literally run down with letters, so as to require the service, not of one, but of three person – one to answer the letters, one to fix the vials, and the other to forward them to their proper places. But as I had already intimated in my former letter, our labors have not been in vain; most wonderful effects have been produced by the use of the precious water." (pg. 5)

Then, as now, the question of money came up. Anyone who has been to Lourdes, knows the water there is free. Everyone drinks of it plentifully, bathes in it and fills water bottles of all sizes to take home with them. Organizations like the one of which I am a member, obtain this water, bottle it and distribute it as an act of love and faith. The practical economics of costs associated with this worthy endeavor enters the picture today as it did in the 19th century.

The article attempts to shape expectations about the water from Lourdes thusly:

> "...Some of our correspondents add to their request for information as to how the Water of Lourdes may be obtained, an inquiry as to its "price?" In our estimation, the difficulty lies just here. Were it to enter into the category of things imported to be disposed of for a price like statuary, or wax-candles before they are blessed, we would not like to become the purchaser. But, on the other hand, our experience shows us that whoever undertakes to supply the demand will be subjected to an outlay, in various ways, of two to five thousand dollars a year – and increasing always...Those applying for the Water of Lourdes, according to their ability, may make a votive offering for the new Church of Our Lady at Notre Dame. The Religious receiving these...have no delicacy about receiving money in compensation for their expenses and labors. The pious Priests in charge of the Fountain of Lourdes notify applicants that the Water *cannot be sent by mail*...The phials...would, almost certainly, be broken...New York...agents...will refuse to receive glass containing fluids, unless packaged in wooden boxes...Father Granger had a dozen phials sent us, carefully packed in sawdust. When received, five of the twelve were broken." (pg. 5)

Today, we have plastic bottles which are lighter to ship. Also, there is air transportation and arguably more ease of shipment than in the 19th century. But, with the cost of fuel and air travel or overseas shipments increasing the Water of Lourdes remains a rare blessing among most of the Catholic faithful today as it was more than 150 years ago. This is one reason why attendance at local Lourdes Experiences continues to be such a gift to our faithful. Those who attend a Virtual Lourdes Experience as presented by the North American Lourdes Volunteers, are freely offered a small bottle of Lourdes water for each family in attendance. Most deposit a goodwill offering, knowing there are costs associated with bringing the water; but thankfully, the Volunteers do not require payment for same.

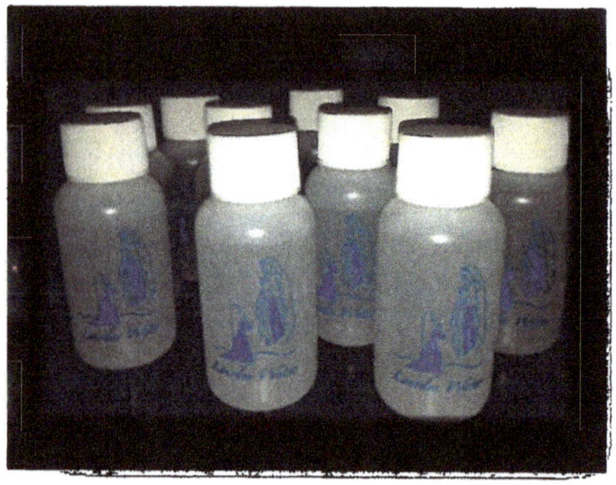

Small plastic bottles of Lourdes Water today

19th Century Devotion to Our Lady of Lourdes – New Orleans Faithful Adopt the Devotion

Reporting of the devotion to Our Lady of Lourdes in 19th century America was not limited to New Orleans Catholic newspapers. As we have seen, reports of Lourdes occurred in St. Louis and we can look to the website of the National Shrine to find that there was devotion to Our Lady of Lourdes in Maryland on a national level. A description of the National Shrine to Our of Lady of Lourdes in Emmitsburg, MD can be found on the website and states:

> "Several hundred yards back in the mountains, behind the site of Dubois' church, is the famous Grotto, the most ancient Mary-shrine in continuous existence in the original thirteen colonies, on which was begun in 1875 the first Lourdes Grotto in America." (National Shrine Website, 2012)

Although this outdoor grotto shrine may be the oldest outdoor shrine to Our Lady of Lourdes in America, the people of the Archdiocese of New Orleans were clamoring for an authentic devotion to Our Lady of Lourdes as early as 1872. (Messenger, 1872)

"..At the request of priests and members of the laity to promote devotion to Our Lady of Lourdes, publicly to have it established in the archdiocese...Archbishop Perche' arranged to have a grotto of Lourdes, a replica of the famous grotto in France, constructed in the chapel of the Blessed Virgin Mary at the St. Louis Cathedral." (Baudier, p. 446)

Louisiana: A Timeless Dream

In far eons, when earth was in a dream,
swirling mists flung by the great wand of God,
fell in diamond-dewdrop splendor to stream,
river, and lush green of a certain sod.
Holy, then, were the land and its creatures.
they thrived under moss-hung cypress and oaks
in bayous and eerie marshland features
and drew to themselves strong and kindly folks.
Earth recalls the dream again and again
and love's promise to a small, flowered part
of itself that defies tongue and pen
but is felt in soft places in the heart.
There can be heard softly tolling bells.
in the Louisiana dream, God dwells.

CHAPTER 4

ARCHBISHOP NAPOLEON JOSEPH PERCHE'

THE FRENCH ARCHBISHOP'S DEVOTION TO THE IMMACULATE CONCEPTION

Archbishop Napoleon Joseph Perche'

The focus of this research has always been Our Lady of Lourdes – the Consecration and the Arch Confraternity; however, as the story of this authentic Marian devotion has unfolded, it is clear that without Archbishop Napoleon Joseph Perche', none of it would have been possible. By means of his faith, stature, determination and zeal the archdiocese experienced the consecration with fervor.

At the advanced age of 65, Napoleon Joseph Perche' became the archbishop of the Archdiocese of New Orleans in 1870 after the death in France on May 25 of Archbishop Odin. (Baudier, p. 443)

Archbishop Napoleon Perche'
Find a Grave Website

Perche' was born in Angers, France on January 10, 1805. "At age 5, he was able to read and write and at age 13, he had begun his philosophy...He received Holy Orders on September 19, 1829." (Baudier, p. 443)

In 1837, he accompanied Bishop Flaget of Bardstown, after deciding to "devote himself to the missions of the United States." (Baudier, p. 443) He first began work in Kentucky, but while on a mission to get donations for his struggling efforts there, he was persuaded by Archbishop Blanc to come to New Orleans. He was found to be "a capable and eloquent orator" and was assigned as the "chaplain of the Ursuline convent". He spent much time traveling to all the parishes and was in high demand. (Baudier, p. 443)

Perche' founded the "first Catholic newspaper in Louisiana, "Le Propagateur Catholique"." (Baudier, p.443) Perche' was widely admired for his writings and "...his achievement in educating the general public as to the truth about Catholic tradition and discipline…" (Baudier, p. 443) He was known for writing "biting" articles in opposition to the Know-Nothings and was unpopular with many due to the fact that he exposed many errors. "…During the War Between the States he manifested an unswerving loyalty to the cause of the Confederacy…made him feared by the Federals…caused his imprisonment in his own house and the suppression of the Catholic newspaper." (Baudier, p. 443)

Perche' was "invested with the Pallium by the Holy Father on December 18, 1870"; a fact which he wrote to his flock in a letter from Rome. Another important declaration was reported by Perche'; in this letter. Pope Pius the IX while Perche' was in Rome announced that "…the Holy Father…had declared St. Joseph the patron of the Catholic Church…and decreed his feast, March 19…" (Baudier, p. 444)

Once having the Pallium, the question about wearing it was on Perche's mind during an audience with the Pope. From the Notre Dame Archives we find a letter from Perche' to Archbishop John Purcell of Cincinnati, Ohio dated November 17, 1871. It is summarized follows:

> "Having mislaid the faculty he had received when he was in Rome, Perche' now sends a copy to Purcell. The rescript (in Latin) from the Audience of Feb. 4, 1871 in answer to the petition of the Archbishop of New Orleans grants to him and to the other Archbishops of the United States the right to wear the pallium on the feast of the Immaculate Conception, the patronal of the country." (Archdiocese of New Orleans Collection, II-5-e)

From his earliest days as archbishop of New Orleans, Perche's thoughts were of honoring the Blessed Virgin under her title of The Immaculate Conception. He not only thought of this as to himself and his archdiocese, but he requested this approval for all archbishops since the United States had adopted the Immaculate Conception as the Patroness of the country.

Among the first efforts by Perche' was to erect a seminary to promote native clergy. The seminary was erected and dedicated while Perche' was attending the 1870 Ecumenical Council of the Vatican in Rome in late 1870; nevertheless, the dedication was carried out by designated representatives in his absence. It is worth mentioning that "...Among the noted priests who made their studies at Monseigneur Perche's seminary were...Father Joseph A. Coustarot of Lourdes, France..." (Baudier, p. 444)

Archbishop Perche' presided immediately after and during a time of great turmoil in the South in the years following the Civil War. He was known to be a "defender of the South" (Baudier, p. 446) and signed a petition taking a position against "exaggerations" by Phil Sheridan, who had been sent to New Orleans to assume command over the Department of the Gulf. Once Governor Nicholls was "installed as governor...the turmoil that had prevailed in the state...for a decade had come to an end." (Baudier, p. 446) Perche' seized the opportunity to seek peace and "...on May 1, 1877 he directed a letter to all pastors...asked all citizens to render thanks to God for His mercy in putting an end to the divisions...and urged all Catholics to join the religious and Christian views of the governor." (Baudier, p.446)

In the Tuesday edition of The Tri Weekly Capitolian in the latter part of 1881, an unknown author writes the following about Archbishop Perche':

> "This venerable prelate has been in our midst since last Sunday. At the advanced age of 77 years, spent in a life of inestimable usefulness to his fellow-men, he has come once again to confirm in their faith the one hundred and thirty Christians who will today, Tuesday, kneel at the altar of their God...His Grace, Archbishop Perche', has acquired a

name that will ever be prominent in the annals of the Diocese of Louisiana, which he has loved as a devoted son loves his mother. Those who will have been confirmed by him, will ever be proud to remember that it was by the hand of the noble Archbishop, whose pen was as brilliant as the sword of Napoleon, after whom he is named, and whose oratorical force has made him a tower of strength in propagating the faith taught by St. Peter, whose exemplary life he has emulated…we take inexpressible pride; in welcoming in him, the whilom journalist whose trenchant pen, has thrown dazzling luster upon the profession in our State." (Tri-Weekly Capitolian)

Archbishop Napoleon Joseph Perche' was a giant among Louisiana church Shepherds. He came to America and ultimately adopted the Archdiocese of New Orleans as his spiritual home and family. He faithfully carried out the duties of priest and archbishop during times of epidemic illness, war, reconstruction, financial difficulties and industrialization. He was ahead of his time in founding the first Catholic newspaper in the area and staunchly defended the faith through his written word. He was renowned by his peers. The Morning Star and Catholic Messenger issued on May 19, 1872 carried the following article praising Perche':

"From…*The San Francisco Guardian*, a new and able Catholic weekly…pays the following…tribute to Archbishop Perche', whom the Baltimore *Volkazeitung* very appropriately calls the "courageous Archbishop of New Orleans." That his great services as founder and editor of "the best Catholic paper in the United States,"…should be a source of pride to all his spiritual children…and that the Catholic Militant Union and the *Propagateur* will now…fight the good fight and triumph…over the enemies of our Holy Church…" (pg. 4)

In 1875, Archbishop Perche' found himself leading an Archdiocese which was in tremendous debt. In the April 25, 1875 issue of The Morning Star and Catholic Messenger, the paper reported that Perche' left "...yesterday...on his way to France..." The financial condition of the Archdiocese was "...very hard on our venerable Archbishop to be thus obliged by the debts of his Archdiocese to traverse the ocean in quest of pecuniary aid." It is significant to note the choice of words the author used to describe the relationship between France and Louisiana. He puts it this way:

> "...Catholic France, always open-handed in her generosity toward all works of zeal, considers herself, in some sort, the God mother of Louisiana, and, therefore, specially bound to see to her spiritual wants." (p. 4)

Upon leaving, Perche' issued a pastoral letter to his faithful in which he offered the following invitation:

> "...Whilst inviting you to continue to invoke with confidence Our Lady of Lourdes, so powerful and so merciful, to whom this Diocese is specially consecrated, and St. Joseph, the Patron of the Universal Church, we particularly recommend to you the devotion to the Sacred Heart of Jesus, under whose protection we have placed this Diocese and the whole Ecclesiastical Province...." (p. 4)

Whether Perche' knew he would be traveling abroad for almost 2 years in pursuit of donations for his diocese when he left in April of 1875 is unclear. However, the newspaper confirms his departure in April, 1875. Evidence about his return comes from a transcription by Harry Green of the Immigrant Ships Transcribers Guild that he returned to New York on the *SS France* on December 7, 1876. (Green) While he was abroad, he offered many sermons and speeches and seems to have been well received. One article from The Morning Star and Catholic

Messenger from Sunday, September 19, 1875, reports on Perche's remarks at the Congress of Catholics held in Poitiers, France during the month of August, 1875. The article was copied from Courrier de la Vienne and captures Perche's speech - parts of which are excerpted here:

> "...Mgr. Perche' rose in his turn...paid a new tribute...to the work of the Catholic Union. Of this work the venerable prelate had conceived the idea in the very audience accorded him by the Holy Father in 1871, an audience in which Pius IX had said to him: Until now there has been a *Union of Faith* among Catholics; it is necessary that henceforth there should be among them a *Union of Action.*
>
> ...Our age, which will be called in history the age of Pius IX, ought to be that of the triumph of the Church through the union of all Catholics. And when will this union be more easily affected than today, when it can be accomplished under a Pope uniting to the authority of the Supreme Pontiff a personal prestige such as no other name in history has possessed! "I united more than a hundred thousand persons in my diocese...to celebrate the Twenty-fifth Anniversary of the Pontificate of Pius IX, and Jews and Protestants came themselves to give testimony of their admiration.
>
> France! Let me...say to you in her regard a parting word. I have been separated from her for thirty-eight years, but I am none the less a Frenchman. I have in my diocese, which is as large as half of your country, 300,000 Catholics, and of this number 200,000 are of French origin and have preserved for the land of their ancestors all that affection with which their fathers were animated for French Louisiana. Well, over yonder while we do some good, it is for us a consolation to say to ourselves that we walk in the tracks of the mother country. Over yonder, as everywhere, they know that the destinies of France are

linked with those of the Church, that the latter suffers because the former is depressed, and that the triumph of the one will be the signal for the triumph of the other." (pg. 4)

Perche' told his enthusiastic listeners that twenty-five years earlier New Orleans had only four parishes and in 1875 had twenty nine. He told them that each of the churches had parochial schools, religious communities, chapels, charitable institutions and many societies. He wanted the potential donors to understand the "powerful organization" that was in place in his Archdiocese and he made a solid connection between France and New Orleans. The author who wrote the story reported:

> "To this powerful organization corresponds a devotion essentially Catholic in its manifestations and French in its origin. Mgr. Perche' obtained from the Holy Father permission to establish in his Diocese two pilgrimages, that of Lourdes and that of Paray-le-Monial, securing the same indulgences as those accorded to the pilgrimages in France. From thirty to thirty five thousand of the faithful followed each other during nine successive days in the churches designated by the Archbishop for these pilgrimages. His diocese is consecrated to Our Lady of Lourdes, his Province to the Sacred Heart." (p. 4)

Although the archdiocese was in bad financial debt under Perche's leadership, he seemed to take comfort in the strong spiritual leadership he had provided and the extensive organizations which he established despite the crushing economic times in which his administration took place. Perche' was publicly welcomed home to New Orleans by an official welcoming party called the Ancient Order of the Hibernians on December 29, 1876. (pg. 1)

According to the Encyclopedia Americana, Archbishop Perche' founded the Order of Our Lady of Lourdes on February 25, 1883. (p. 761) He also "...introduced into his diocese the

Carmelite Order of Nuns…A third academy of the Sisters of the Sacred Heart…and the Little Sisters of the Poor…" (Clark, pg. 366)

Photo of Holy Face Relic - Church in New Orleans

Perche' introduced the Confraternity of the Holy Face in conjunction with the Discalced Carmelites. "…the Confraternity of the Holy Face was established in the Sister's chapel and a replica of Veronica's Veil, received from the Carmelites in Tours, was placed in the choir; the devotion spread from there throughout the United States."[10] "…Archbishop Perché himself took the greatest interest in this devotion. The Carmelite chapel became a centre from which the devotion gradually spread throughout the United States. The names of Archbishop Perché and his coadjutor were the first inscribed on the register of the Confraternity that now numbers over 12,000 members, including several Archbishops and Bishops and a large number of priests and religious." (Currier, pg. 332) The veil pictured above is similar to the one that would have been in the choir.

Perche' Goes on Pilgrimage to Lourdes

It was on Perche's watch that the devotion to Our Lady of Lourdes made the first appearance in New Orleans and it was Perche' who appreciated the spiritual significance of the apparitions of the

Fleur De Lys and New Orleans

The iris flower so esteemed
is ancient symbol of hopes dreamed.
It graced the royal house of France
and in those time, on flags it gleamed.
It told of faith, and not by chance.
Charles V of France fixed fleur de lys
upon his arms, against blue shield
to number three to Trinity.
It's with us on our football field.
St. Louis, our Cathedral's name,
depicts the Saint on its Chancel
with fleur de lys of holy fame.
The iris lily of our state
is twin with it; is its soul mate.

[10] Nolan, C. (2000) A History of the Archdiocese of New Orleans. Archdiocese of New Orleans.

Immaculate Conception to Bernadette Soubirous in 1858. It is likely that his own pilgrimages to Lourdes played an important role in his devotion and decision to consecrate the archdiocese to Our Lady of Lourdes.

PERCHE'S FIRST LOURDES PILGRIMAGE

As already mentioned, Perche' received the Pallium[11] from Pope Pius IX in December 1870. Records from the archives at Notre Dame confirm that a letter was directed from C., S.W. of Rome, Italy to Perche' to an unknown location in France on April 1, 1871. (Archdiocese of New Orleans Collection, **VI-2-o)**

Another letter contained in these archives was mailed from Sister Mary of the Seven Dolors, M.S.C. of LeMans, France to Perche' on April 11, 1870 in Angers, France. From this, we know that Perche' traveled from Rome to Angers, France between December 1870 and April, 1871. (Archdiocese of New Orleans Collection, **VI-2-o)**

These two letters place Perche' in France in the Spring of 1871. Confirmation of Perche's first visit to Lourdes comes from the French book "Annales de Notre-dame de Lourdes" written in Lourdes by a chaplain of Lourdes and supplied to this researcher by a priest in Lourdes. According to this account, Archbishop Perche' visited Lourdes in 1871. This is an important discovery. Perche's implementation of the consecration and arch confraternity were so impressive and

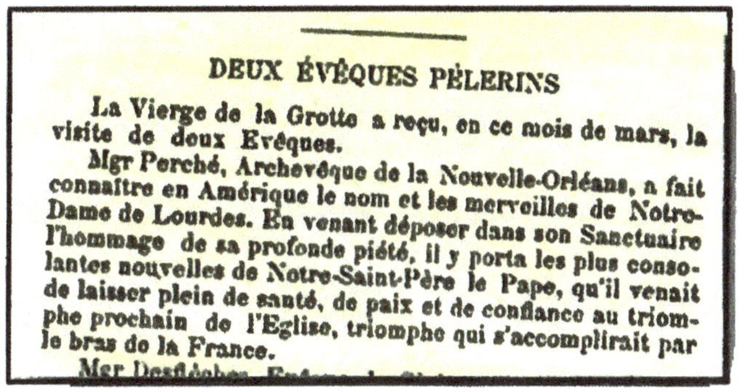

DEUX ÉVÊQUES PÈLERINS

La Vierge de la Grotte a reçu, en ce mois de mars, la visite de deux Evêques.

Mgr Perché, Archevêque de la Nouvelle-Orléans, a fait connaître en Amérique le nom et les merveilles de Notre-Dame de Lourdes. En venant déposer dans son Sanctuaire l'hommage de sa profonde piété, il y porta les plus consolantes nouvelles de Notre-Saint-Père le Pape, qu'il venait de laisser plein de santé, de paix et de confiance au triomphe prochain de l'Eglise, triomphe qui s'accomplirait par le bras de la France.

Courtesy of the Annals de Notre Dame du Lourdes

[11] Pallium is an *Ecclesiastical* vestment worn by the pope and conferred by him on archbishops and sometimes on bishops. Also called *pall*[1]. http://www.thefreedictionary.com/Pallium.

authentic that anyone considering his actions would have to imagine he had to have had his own Lourdes experience. This document confirms, indeed, Perche' was in Lourdes in 1871. His experience there must have been profound for him to return to New Orleans and ultimately consecrate his archdiocese to the Blessed Virgin under her title Our Lady of Lourdes.

PERCHE'S SECOND LOURDES PILGRIMAGE

The April, 1875 account of Perche's departure for Europe lists several priests who were in his company. The passenger list that documents his return in 1876 lists Father Joseph Coustarot as a passenger as well. It is likely that Father Joseph Coustarot was also present with Perche's departing party although his name was not mentioned. He was a native of the city of Lourdes, France and had been ordained only days before on April 10th and 17th by Archbishop Perche'. (Baurdier, pg. 4) Perhaps his recent ordination caused his presence to be overlooked.

There is a single document in the Notre Dame archives from Eugenie Brand of New Orleans to Archbishop Perche' in Lourdes, France under date of June 10, 1876. (Archdiocese of New Orleans Collection, **VI-2-o**) This letter confirms Archbishop Perche' was in Lourdes. It is probable Perche' was accompanied by newly ordained Lourdes native Father Joseph Coustarot, when he made a second pilgrimage to Lourdes in June, 1876. Perche' must have had a deep love for Our Lady of Lourdes and felt welcomed on his journeys there.

It is possible, if not likely, that Archbishop Perche' was in Lourdes at this time because the Immaculate Conception Basilica celebrations were taking place. These celebrations occurred on July 1 – 3, 1876. (Laurentin, p. 458) This writer has been unable as of the date of this writing to confirm whether Perche' was actually present; however, Laurentin described the ceremonies as follows:

"...The ceremonies of July 1 – 3, 1876, were elaborate and enthusiastic. A crowd without precedent was in attendance: thirty-five bishops, three thousand priests and nearly one hundred thousand pilgrims, from all over the world, assembled at the grotto. This was twice as many as had come to the "Banner Pilgrimage" (forty thousand people in 1872) and ten times the largest crowd drawn by the apparitions in 1858..." (Laurentin, pg. 460)

Whether Perche' was among the 35 bishops in attendance for these celebrations is not known but, given the timeframe of his confirmed presence there, it is indeed very likely.

POSSIBLY A THIRD PILGRIMAGE TO LOURDES

The Notre Dame archives contain a letter from Sister Theresa de Jesus, D.C. to Perche' dated August 1, 1879 addressed to him in France. The letter doesn't say where in France. He was from Angers and he may possibly have been there. (Archdiocese of New Orleans Collection, **VI-3-a**)

However, the same archives contain a letter from M. Delair of Lourdes, France dated December 28, 1879 to Perche' in Rome. In this letter she mentions that "She has not forgotten his promise to return to Lourdes before returning to his diocese." (Archdiocese of New Orleans Collection, **VI-3-a**)

Another letter comes from M. Delair of Lourdes; a summary of that letter follows:

1880 Dec. 19 Delair, Miss M.: Lourdes, France

to (Archbishop Napoleon Joseph Perché: New Orleans, Louisiana)

"She is still at Lourdes and asks him to pray for her as life is very hard. She has written three letters to Mother (Louise) Stephanie, (C.S.J.) without receiving any reply. She fears that the silence means bad news and she asks him to tell her want it is. She asks him to have the community (Sisters of St. Joseph) pray for her. She told him her entire situation at the time of his trip to Lourdes. She has taken a small apartment, but, not wishing to cause any commotion, she will have from the world only those who know her and her situation. Instead of recommending her to missionaries of the diocese (of New Orleans), she asks him to recommend her to other bishops and priests who will know her only through him. For the moment, she has no bread and still owes for half her meager furnishings. (P.S.) She told him that she would accept only frank and clear offers, seeking to unite her with others, be it for a work or for material business; provided that they hold no danger from the point of view of religion and that they are only temporary. That kind of frankness does not seem to exist anymore. (Signed also as:) Sister Theresa, C.S.J. Archdiocese of New Orleans Collection, **VI-3-b**

These documents support the conclusion that Archbishop Perche' was definitely in Lourdes, France on two occasions and almost certainly a third time.

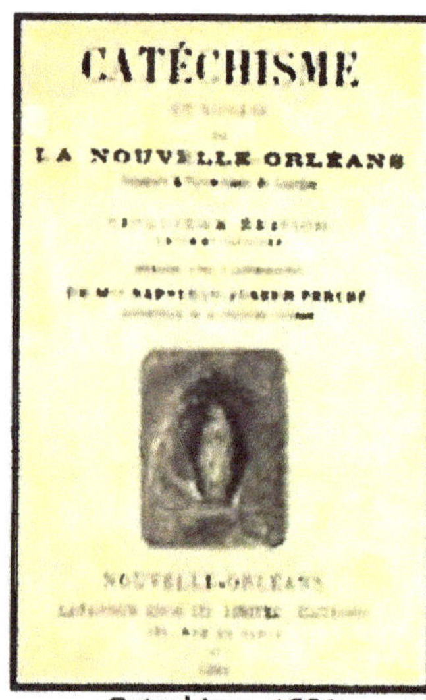

Catechism, 1891

Front cover of 1891 Catechism Book – Courtesy Archdiocese of New Orleans Website

One can only imagine the depth of Perche's devotion to Our Lady of Lourdes and the impact his pilgrimages there might have had on his own entrance into the story of the Lourdes experience or how these experiences may have influenced the implementation of the consecration of the Archdiocese to Our Lady. The archbishop's own experiences led him to invite his flock to participate in an authentic Lourdes experience; and he did so with the ultimate intention of pointing the faithful to Our Lady's Divine Son.

Perche's impact on the Archdiocese of New Orleans was most certainly influenced by his French nationality and surely by his devotion to Our Lady of Lourdes and the Sacred Heart of Jesus. This influence appears to have permeated the Catechism of the day. The cover of the 1891 Catechism book shows it was written in French and prominently displays Our Lady of Lourdes on its cover.

CHAPTER 5

THE ALTAR TO OUR LADY OF LOURDES ESTABLISHED AT ST. LOUIS CATHEDRAL

St. Louis Cathedral – Our Lady of Lourdes Altar

In early November, 1872, Perche' hired George Soulier to build two altars at the Cathedral of St. Louis in New Orleans. (Archdiocese of New Orleans Collection, VI-2-o) One altar was to be dedicated to St. Francis of Assisi and the other to Our Lady of Lourdes. Meanwhile, Perche' placed an order to a statuary builder in France for two statues, one of Our Lady of Lourdes and one of Bernadette. The cost of these statues was $956.25 and according to the invoice, from C. Wapler of Paris, France, (Archdiocese of New Orleans Collection VI-2-o) they were shipped on September 9, 1873 in care of Am. Lutton, on the steamer Missouri. (Archdiocese of New Orleans Collection, VI-2-o)

On February 1, 1874, The Morning Star and Catholic Messenger reported that they had received "...from Mr. P. F. Gogarty, 131 Camp Street...a copy of the photograph of the grotto of Lourdes in our Cathedral. The photograph was taken by Theo. Lillienthal, Esq., and is a good representation of this beautiful grotto, which was erected by His Grace...and dedicated by him...on the feast of the Immaculate Conception." On this same date, the paper reported that candles were being blessed in...front of this altar on February 2, 1874 on the Feast of the Purification of the Most Blessed Virgin." (pg. 4)

The Times-Picayune published an article on December 10, 1883 entitled *The Fountain of Lourdes – A beautiful Shrine Fitted Up in the Cathedral.* The article provides the confirmation of when the water feature was added to the altar and reads as follows:

> "Very Rev. G. A. Rouxel, Vicar General at St. Louis Cathedral, has had fitted up in the shrine which has long been dedicated to Our Lady of Lourdes, a striking and beautiful representation of the celebrated fountain at Lourdes, France, which has for some years

past been the borne of many important pilgrimages, and where many miraculous cures from disease and deformity are related to have been wrought.

The fountain in the Cathedral is beautifully arranged, a jet of pure water welling up in a little basin in the face of a rocky cliff down whose sides in numerous crevices the crystal fluid pours, finally losing itself among the rocks at the foot. On the summit of the cliff stands the chapel of Lourdes, and at its shrine is seen the Virgin to whom the place is sacred. The objects represented are full of interest from association and are tastefully and beautifully arranged. Our Lady of Lourdes has many devotees and admirers in this city and Father Rouxel has done much to minister to their sentiments of adoration and affection." (Times-Picayune, 1883)

Marigny/Mandeville Tombstone at St. Louis Cathedral in New Orleans

An account of the altar can be found in The Historical Sketch Book and Guide to New Orleans which was published in 1885. Here, we find "...The remains of the celebrated curate, Father Antoine, and many of his successors in office, lie buried under the floor of the vestry in the Cathedral, back of the altar of Notre Dame de Lourdes. Underneath the marble pavement of the Cathedral, in front of this altar and on the side opposite the grave of Don Almonaster, lie the remains of three cavaliers, of noble descent…" (Historical Sketch Book, p. 108)

The altar to Our Lady of Lourdes was reported among those sites to see when visiting New Orleans. In the book entitled New Orleans City Guide - *Outlines of the History of Louisiana* published in 1893 and authored by James S. Zacharie, he provided a descriptive account of the altar in the Churches section of the guide book. He states "The altar of our Lady of Lourdes, on the left, is in the form of a grotto representing the grotto of Lourdes, in France, with the figures of the Virgin and the peasant at the spring. Around the altar numerous and curious *exvotos*[12] (offerings) are hung by parties who have had some wish granted through the intercession of Our Lady of Lourdes. These offerings consist of tablets with dates inscribed, pictures, crosses, photographs and various kinds of articles. Before the altar is the family vault of the Marigny-Mandeville family, a distinguished noble family of France, long settled in Louisiana, and after whom several streets and villages are named." (New Orleans Guide, p. 71) A visit to St. Louis Cathedral in the French Quarter today reveals the tomb stone marker above and identifies the people buried there. This marker remains in front of an altar to the Blessed Virgin where the Altar to Our Lady of Lourdes would have once been located.

[12] Ex voto is an offering made in fulfillment of a vow, http://www.thefreedictionary.com/Ex+voto

THE ONLY REMAINING PHOTOGRAPH

Photo B. de Villentroy.

ALTAR OF OUR LADY OF LOURDES.

In and Around Old St. Louis Cathedral Page 83

In the 1908 book entitled In and Around the Old St. Louis Cathedral of New Orleans, written by Reverend Celestin M. Chambon, the altars dedicated to Our Lady of Lourdes and the Sacred Heart of Jesus in 1874 were described. It is within this book that we located the only remaining picture uncovered by this research. Chambon states "The side altar erected near the pulpit is dedicated to St. Francis of Assissium, whose picture is seen above, hung on the wall. The canopy of the altar supports a group representing the Apparition of Our Lord to the Blessed Marguerite Marie Alacoque which occurred in Paray le Monial (France)...often people designate this altar after the Sacred Heart. The other side altar is dedicated to the Virgin Mary under the title of Immaculate Conception. The rocks and panoramic view that cover the background of the chapel represent the famous shrine of Lourdes. There is seen a reproduction of one of the eighteen apparitions of the Virgin to a young girl named Bernadette Soubirous..." (pg. 81)

WHERE ARE THE ALTAR AND ITS STATUES TODAY?

"The altar of Our Lady of Lourdes, St. Joseph's altar, and the 1938 Mexican mahogany communion rail...have all been removed over the years." (Nolan, p.7)

A trip to the Cathedral today confirms that the wondrous 19th century creation of George Soulier has been removed. But, the statues seen in the foreground of the picture remain. In the forefront of the picture we see St. Anthony holding the Child Jesus and a statue of Our Lady of Poor Souls. Both of these statues are on display today in the St. Louis Cathedral, New Orleans, LA.

GENUINE LOURDES WATER FLOWS IN THE ALTAR

As mentioned earlier, the Altar was modified in 1883 to allow water to flow in it. At some point, real water from the Lourdes Grotto was added to the Altar. The Medical Standard, Volume 29, written in 1903 provides an early mention of Lourdes water in the Altar at the Cathedral. It states:

"...The lily of France mingles with the other decorations and modern France is represented by a replica of the grotto of Lourdes, down which trickles water brought by the faithful from this place of miracles..." (p. 314)

The 1904 publication called The Guide Book to the City of New Orleans published by The Picayune adds confirmation about the water which was flowing in the altar of Our Lady of Lourdes. In a chapter about St. Louis Cathedral the unknown author reports:

"...A reproduction of the famous grotto of Lourdes forms one of the side altars; the water which trickles perpetually over the rocks is supplied from the miraculous shrine at Lourdes..." (pg. 21)

In the periodical called Motor Age, Volume 29 from February 24, 1916, we obtain another account of Lourdes water flowing in the Altar.

"...In the church is a grotto dedicated to "our Lady of Lourdes" and over the rocks of the grotto water is continually flowing. This water is brought from Lourdes, France, especially for this purpose." (p. 10)

The assertion that the altar contained actual water from Lourdes was again made in a book published "...sometime in the early 1920's..." called A Condensed History of New Orleans – *America's Most Interesting City* by R. C. Duncan. Garrett County Press reprinted this book in 2010. In the chapter on the Cathedral, Duncan wrote:

"...A reproduction of the famous Grotto of Lourdes forms one of the side altars; the water which trickles perpetually over the bricks is imported from the miraculous shrine in France." (Duncan)

Still today we find evidence online of authentic Lourdes water flowing in the altar. Documented on the website www.storyvilledistrictnola.com the website reports that

"...A reproduction of the famous grotto of Lourdes forms one of the side altars; the water which trickles perpetually over the rocks is supplied from the miraculous shrine at Lourdes..." (http://www.storyvilledistrictnola.com/stlouis_cathedral.html)

With so many accounts of Lourdes water flowing in the grotto of the Altar to Our Lady of Lourdes for more than 20 years and the confirmation that the mechanism for a water fountain was added by Rouxel in 1883, there is no doubt that this Altar was particularly special indeed and above all for the time in which it was in use. Moving water from Lourdes to the United States today with all the modern transportation that is available is extremely expensive and difficult; one can only imagine the dedication which the Altar caregivers must have displayed to be sure Lourdes water was continuously flowing in the unique and sacred Altar.

INTERIOR CATHEDRAL, 1881.

In T. P. Thompson's book, St. Louis Cathedral of New Orleans, A Sketch, we find more fascinating particulars about a frescoe of Lourdes. Thompson wrote the book in 1918 to commemorate the bicentenary of the founding of the parent church of the Mississippi Valley. The book cover refers to it as a *"Restoration Souvenir 1718 – 1918"*.

The French artist employed to restore the church paintings and frescoes was Erasmus Humbrecht. (p. 24) Humbrecht restored the Cathedral with many retouched and original paintings. Among those is a frescoe on the ballastrade to the left of the entrance of the Cathedral. It is a depiction of the apparitions at the Grotto of Lourdes.

CREOLES AND QUADROONS ALIKE PRAY TO OUR LADY

We find another fascinating fact about the altar to our Lady of Lourdes in the New Orleans Guide from 1893. It is no surprise that devotion to Our Lady of Lourdes was universal. The Guide tells us "...The northern side entrance of the cathedral command it – a tall, dark, ecclesiastically severe archway...and Catholic quadroon women on their daily morning way to market habitually enter it with their baskets, to murmur a prayer in patois[13] before the shrine of *Notre Dame de Lourdes.*" (Guide, p. 295) The language Bernadette spoke was also referred to as a local patois. From this discovery we can conclude that Our Lady of Lourdes understands and speaks to those who listen in their unique language and in their hearts.

Leonard V. Huber provides another vignette about the Altar. In his 1980 book co-written with Roger Baudier, entitled Creole Collage, he says "...The older Creoles had an intense love for St. Louis Cathedral." (p. 55) In a chapter called "The Old Aunts" the story of Tante Camille is presented. "Every morning Camille made a visit to l'eglise Sainte Marie or she stopped at the Cathedral to pray a' l'autel de Notre Dame de Lourdes (the altar of Our Lady of Lourdes – a grotto-like altar in St. Louis Cathedral built in 1873 but later removed)." (p. 23)

[13] Patois is defined by Merriam-Webster online as a dialect other than the standard or literary dialect.

THE ALTAR AND SIGNS OF FAITH

In 1905, Carrie Moss Hawley wrote about an experience she had at the Cathedral in her article entitled *Faith as a Law of the Universe* in a publication called Mind, Volume 15. Hawley presented a viewpoint about faith that was enhanced by her experience at the Lourdes Altar in New Orleans.

"...A few years ago, I was sitting in the park one morning opposite the St. Louis Cathedral in New Orleans. I was not well, and, in addition to that, was very tired. Seeing the people going into and coming out of the cathedral, I concluded I would go in there for a while. I had been there before, as a sightseer, so it was not in a spirit of curiosity that I entered. My attention was soon drawn to the pale and maimed people kneeling before the shrine of Our Lady of Lourdes. A few crutches and canes near were silent witnesses of the efficacy of prayer at this altar. Of course I did not believe there was any marvelous power in the figure, or even that the saint herself had healed those who had been restored. Yet, I was deeply impressed. I *did* believe the weak had been made strong there in *some* way because I had been assured of numerous instances of marvelous cures by an authority not to be questioned. I analyzed it as some mysterious efficacy in prayer. Being somewhat discouraged over my own condition and ready to "try anything" to get into a better state, I concluded I, too, would pray to Our Lady of Lourdes, but without going up to the altar. I told myself that it was absurd for me to do this, because I did not really believe help would come from the one to whom I prayed. But why not try it. I reasoned again. Say to yourself I do believe in this; throw off all doubt for the moment. Just pray and keep saying, "I *do* believe, I *do* believe."

I did this for about fifteen or twenty minutes. Within half an hour after entering the cathedral I left it feeling better than I had felt in months, and perfectly rested. This condition remained not only through the day, but for several days. The incredulous will say, "You were undoubtedly all right when you went in there. The trouble was all in your mind." Even so, though I do not grant it, this does not touch the basic truth of my argument.

...To have faith we must come out of the atmosphere of doubt which envelops us. Faith kills fear, which paralyzes the energies. Faith never says "hold back," but always "press on." Faith and desire give us strength for anything. With these we can reach any goal. Jesus told the people that with faith they could do anything...Faith is the key...Why do we not make use of it – the faith that Jesus taught, which we now know is one of the subtle laws of the universe?"

(pgs. 386 – 387)

By all accounts, the Altar to Our Lady of Lourdes in St. Louis Cathedral was, indeed, very special. It was authentically constructed, eventually had Lourdes water flowing through it and people from all walks of life experienced Lourdes there in prayer, healing and conversion.

In the Deep South...

Sleigh bells do not ring out at Christmastime.
Oaks rustle, yet, sweet music through the air.
Bright birds of winter sing in the mild clime;
Gulf breezes waft gentleness everywhere.
The carols seem alien on a morn
when, through foggy mist, songs of the South ring,
camellias blush softly, sweet peas are born,
and the land basks in some magical spring.
Small seeds peek out in shy expectation
of the great advent whispered all around.
The sweet angel-sung annunciation
greets unmuffed ears awaiting the glad sound.
The South draws radiance from Mary's son
blessing the faithful, each and every one.

The Inauguration of a Monument

On Sunday, November 2, 1873, The Morning Star and Catholic Messenger carried Perche's Pastoral letter "announcing the inauguration of the monument erected in honor of our Lady of Lourdes, in the Metropolitan Church of New Orleans." (pg. 5)

Perche's letter is particularly moving and reverent. He writes:

"Our Catholic Population, always so remarkable by a most ardent devotion toward Mary, the Immaculate Virgin, the Mother of God, and the Queen of Angels and men, has been for a long time deeply moved at the recital of the wonderful miracles constantly performed at the Grotto of Lourdes, a place sanctified some sixteen years ago by the apparitions of the Blessed Virgin. On several occasions, pious members of the Clergy and Laity have manifested to us the wish that the devotion to our Lady of Lourdes should be established in our diocese in a public and solemn manner; and as this wish coincided with the inclination of our own heart and our filial love to that good and tender Mother, we have determined to erect in the chapel of the Blessed Virgin of our Metropolitan Church, a monument, which, in recalling as much as possible the Grotto of Lourdes, will transmit to those who will come after us an enduring memorial of our tender devotion towards her, who said of herself: *I am the Immaculate Conception.*" (pg. 5)

Illustration of Our Lady of Lourdes
Lasserre 1876

It is noteworthy that Perche' credits members of the Clergy and Laity with the desire for this devotion to Our Lady of Lourdes and that he was already thinking about "those who will come after us." The message of Lourdes was obviously moving the spirits of many in our country far from where the apparitions had occurred. Perche' was not to be satisfied with merely erected and dedicating an altar. His letter goes on to say:

> "The Feast of the Immaculate Conception which is celebrated on the 8th of December, being a feast of obligation for all the Catholics of the United States, and being moreover the patronal feast of the whole country, is naturally the most appropriate day for the inauguration of the monument of our Lady of Lourdes; it is the day we have selected for this ceremony; and by this solemn inauguration we intend placing in a special manner the city and diocese of New Orleans under the powerful and maternal protection of the Immaculate Mother of God."

While Perche' was responding to the popular demand for this devotion, his pastoral letter remains true to a core message of Our Lady of Lourdes – "Penance, Penance, Penance" and conversion - as he goes on to write:

> "Conformably to the words which she herself uttered in her apparitions at the Grotto, we shall beseech her to restrain the arm of her Divine Son, so justly raised against us; and to obtain for us that spirit of penance which alone can disarm the justice of the Lord; and in order that our prayers may be more favorably heard, we shall make to Him the sacrifice of our extravagance, follies, vanities, and sensual inclinations, and immoderate love of pleasure, and of all other evil habits which have drawn upon us the chastisements of heaven, and prepared for us, more than any other cause the ruin of our beloved country."

Though Perche' lived and wrote this letter 139 years ago, it could just as easily have been written about our city, the Archdiocese, our state, our country or the world today. In his letter, he tells the faithful what they shall ask of Our Lady of Lourdes through this devotion:

"We shall ask her to procure for the just the courage and firmness so necessary in these evil days to persevere unto the end, and to obtain for the sinner the grace of conversion, as well as for our wandering brethren the happiness to return to the only true Church, out of which there is no salvation.

As for us, we shall thank her from the bottom of our heart for the striking Catholic progress, which manifests itself more and more in our Diocese, and which we mainly attribute to her powerful intercession; we shall beg of her to keep it up, and develop it more and more; for it is our sweetest consolation in the midst of the trials and pains, which it has pleased Almighty God to send us. But at the same time we shall beg of her, to have pity on our dear Louisiana, now so severely tried, and to avert all those evils by which we see her so miserably oppressed, and against which all human efforts seem to be entirely powerless; we shall beg of her to restore to us our ancient prosperity, promising her at the same time, to make a better use of it, than we have in the past." (pg. 5)

Those reading this pastoral letter will undoubtedly be reminded of the current Family Prayer being said in churches at the end of Masses throughout the Archdiocese of New Orleans at the request of Archbishop Gregory Aymond in 2011 and 2012. The correlation between the needs of the late 19th century and those of the early 21st century are timeless in their appeal and devotion to Our Lady.

This inauguration of the monument was not inconsequential. On the contrary, Archbishop Perche' intended for it to be a solemn event that involved the entire Catholic assembly and carried with it the following expectations:

"We, therefore, after invoking the holy name of God, have ordained, and do ordain as follows:

1. The inauguration of the Monument erected in our Metropolitan Church in honor of our Lady of Lourdes will take place on Monday, the 8th of December, which is the Feast of the Immaculate Conception, in the afternoon, at an hour to be hereafter designated.
2. It is our desire that all the clergymen, who will be able, should attend this ceremony.
3. In all the Churches and Chapels of the Diocese, there will be on that day benediction of the Blessed Sacrament, followed by the singing of the *Te Deum.*
4. A Triduum of Prayers and public instructions will take place in our Metropolitan Church during the three days which will precede the inauguration.
5. We grant an indulgence of forty days to all the faithful who, visiting the Chapel of Our Lady of Lourdes will recite three Hail Marys to honor the mystery of the Immaculate Conception. They can gain this indulgence as many times each day as they visit the Chapel during the Triduum, the day of the Feast, and its octave. After the octave, they can gain it only once a day.
6. It is our intention to establish in our Metropolitan Church a Confraternity of Our Lady of Lourdes, which will be affiliated to the Arch-Confraternity of Lourdes; the person who may wish to become members of it may from this time give their names to Rev. Vicars of the Cathedral."

This letter was "given at New Orleans, on the Feast of the Maternity of the Blessed Virgin Mary, October 12, 1873." (pg. 5) The letter was published in its entirety in The Morning Star and Catholic Messenger on Sunday, November 2, 1873.

Archbishop Perche' was knowledgeable about current affairs in his time. Being a journalist at heart, he no doubt was keenly aware of an article that had been published in the May 11, 1873 edition of The Morning Star and Catholic Messenger entitled *Arch-Confraternity of Our Lady of Lourdes*. In this article readers learned that Father Pere' Sempe, Superior of the Missionaries of Notre Dame de Lourdes "...has just left Rome, where he has been staying...to settle various matters relating to the important work of which he holds the direction. His success at Rome has been complete. The Holy Father has been pleased to approve of the Arch-Confraternity of Our Lady of Lourdes recently founded, and has attached numerous indulgences to the new and splendid chapel lately erected near the Grotto of Miracles, where the Holy Virgin appeared to the young peasant of Lourdes..." (pg. 8)

On Sunday, November 30, 1873 anticipation for the consecration event was building. The Morning Star and Catholic Messenger published two stories on that date with more details about the upcoming event and a photo which had just become available for purchase.

> "*TRIDUUM AT THE CATHEDRAL.* – Preceding the inauguration of the statue of our Lady of Lourdes at the Cathedral, on the feast of the Immaculate Conception, a triduum of preparation will be celebrated in that church during the days of Friday, Saturday and Sunday, the 5th, 6th and 7th...The Archbishop will say Mass...he will preach...followed by benediction of the Blessed Sacrament...Vespers will be sung followed by the sermon and benediction. The exercises will be most imposing and interesting." (p.4)
>
> "...A very fine photographic view of the apparition of the Blessed Virgin in the grotto of Lourdes, with the grotto itself, has just been got out by Messrs. Murphy & Company, of Baltimore. The white figure of Our Lady is finely brought up against the dark background of the rocky Cave, while below, the little Bernadette is kneeling, scooping

out the earth with her fingers, under the direction of the celestial visitor, the miraculous fountain gushing forth as she does so. This commemorative picture may be had in three different sizes, the largest 9 by 12 inches. They are adapted for framing, and will make pretty ornaments in Catholic homes. P. F. Gogarty, Esq., 151 Camp Street, has a large number of them." (p. 4)

Notice was given to all in the Sunday, December 7, 1873 edition of The Morning Star and Catholic Messenger that on Monday, December, 8, 1873, the statue of Our Lady of Lourdes would be inaugurated at the Cathedral. The article makes clear that the event should be anticipated to be a solemn and reverent occasion.

"...His Grace, the Archbishop, will preach at the 8 o'clock Mass and afterward officiate pontifically at High Mass. On this occasion a new Mass composed by Mr. Curto for the occasion, will be executed by the choir under his personal direction...At 5 o'clock p.m., his Grace will start in procession from his residence to the Cathedral accompanied by all the clergy who will take a part in the ceremonies. Rev. Father Neitbardt will preach in English and his Grace in French. The Most Rev. Archbishop will then proceed solemnly, with all the clergy to the altar of Our Lady of Lourdes, when he will make the consecration of the diocese to Our Lady of Lourdes and perform the ceremonies usual in the benediction of a statue..." (pg. 4)

Thinking back on this Sunday before the consecration of the Archdiocese to Our Lady of Lourdes, it is important to realize now the inclusiveness with which this event was anticipated and implemented. This devotion was not meant for either French or English residents exclusively; this consecration was for all those in the Archdiocese of the time. New Orleans was well known for the melting pot that it was in the 19th century. Next to New York, New Orleans had some of the largest populations of Irish and German immigrants. It's French and Spanish roots ran deep in the culture of the time. (Greene, pgs. 157 – 161)

THE ACCOUNT OF THE CEREMONY

The Morning Star and Catholic Messenger dated Sunday, December, 14, 1873 carried the article entitled *The Ceremonies at the Cathedral.*

"Last Sunday will be ever memorable in Louisiana as the day of the consecration of this Diocese to Our Lady of Lourdes. That ceremony took place at the Cathedral in the presence of an immense congregation. We have never seen the grand old building more densely crowded, not a particle of vacant space, apparently being left. Large numbers of persons were unable to effect an entrance at all and occupied the street in a dense mass...Rev. Father Neithart...preached a short but forcible sermon in English...Most Rev. Archbishop ...in French...at the conclusion he knelt...read the following act of consecration:

> "O, Mary, conceived without sin, Thou has been willing to confirm the dogmatic definition of the glorious privilege of Thy Immaculate Conception by numerous prodigies accomplished at the Grotto of Lourdes; therefore, wishing to honor and invoke Thee in a special manner, under that title, henceforth so dear to every Catholic heart, of our Lady of Lourdes, we come, all of us, to consecrate ourselves to Thee, prostrate at the foot of this monument, which we have erected in Thy Honor as an imperfect token of our confidence and love.

> In my name, in the name of all the clergy and of all the faithful, I consecrate to Thee this diocese which was always so happy and so proud of being devoted to Thee.
>
> However unworthy we may be, renew for us, merciful Mother, those miracles which Thou hast worked for so many of our brethren, who no doubt, were more worthy of such favors. Look down upon us, O Mary! With one of those powerful and merciful looks which are an inexhaustible source of graces and blessings. Grant that all sinners may be converted, that the just may be strengthened in the belief and practice of our sacred truths, and obtain for all of us the precious gift of final perseverance.
>
> Avert from our dear country, so severely tried, the scourges of the justice of God, which was so often provoked by our iniquities, in order that, being grateful for the temporal and spiritual favors for which we will be indebted to Thy Motherly care and protection, we may serve Thee with a zeal and fervor every day renewed, until all together we be admitted to contemplate and praise Thee, with Thy Divine Son Jesus, in the splendors of glorious eternity. Amen," (pg. 4)

After the consecration, Perche' approached the side altar to Our Lady of Lourdes and conducted "the impressive ceremonies of blessing the statue"; the altar was described as "beautiful". The author goes on to describe the scene:

> "It is unnecessary for us to speak of the rare beauty of the statues of Our Lady and of the little girl Bernadette, or of the natural appearance given to the grottos by the skillful artist who constructed it…the beauty of the shrine, the loveliness of the statues, the harmony of

the music which echoed so grandly through the venerable pile, and even the magnificent ceremonial of the Church, were not the principal features of the occasion." (pg. 4)

In providing the eyewitness account of this ceremonial act of consecration on December 8, 1873, the unknown newspaper journalist places the words, the ceremony, the beauty of the scene and the vast numbers who attended behind the authentic reason why this consecration was so meaningful and moving. He describes it like this:

> "...They were all secondary to the profound devotion which we recognized as actuating the vast assemblage, and to the evidence before our eyes that Mary's image was enshrined in the hearts of our people and that the Church ceremonial was but an outward expression of a living worship which made a sanctuary in so many human hearts." (pg. 4)

Upon reading this account of the ceremony, I wondered, what exactly was it that was apparent to the eyewitness author that allowed him to see into so many human hearts that day? The author makes quite clear that the event was impressive, solemn, reverent, authentically Catholic and sacred in every way. But he distinguishes the external outward signs of the event from the "profound devotion" and the "living worship...made sanctuary in so many hearts." The parishioners, of the Catholic Church in New Orleans in 1873 who sought a relationship with Our Lady, were profoundly devoted to Our Lady of Lourdes, the Archdiocese was consecrated to Our Lady of Lourdes and the hearts of the citizenry were clearly on fire with this affection.

If one placed themselves in the vast crowd that day what would have been witnessed in human hearts? Why were so many hungry and thirsty for this devotion? What was the message from Lourdes that resounded most clearly for the people in the 19th century? Was that resounding message different then than it is today?

The Blessed Virgin appeared more than 154 years ago to a peasant girl in a remote place at a time when information was not instantaneously shared and transportation and travel were immensely difficult. Yet, this message was spread far and wide to great devotion in a few short years – why? What were people yearning for that the message of Lourdes quenched through "living worship…in their hearts"?

It is possible, if not likely, that then, as now, all people are searching for a means to connect with the Divine. The message of Lourdes was and remains one of prayer, penance and conversion – all people want the acceptance that Our Lady of Lourdes offers as our Divine Mother whose loving messages introduce us to her Son and the path we must follow to get there. After the terrible years of Civil War and the bitter period of Reconstruction that followed, perhaps the hearts of all were particularly open to the miraculous healing and inviting messages of Our Lady of Lourdes.

Commemorating the Ceremony

From the archives of the Archdiocese of New Orleans, the prayer card commemorating this consecration ceremony has been received. The prayer card reads, "In commemoration of the Solemn Dedication of the Arch-Diocese of New Orleans to "our Lady of Lourdes on the Feast of the Immaculate Conception, 8th December, 1873." The card was produced by J. A. McGee Publisher, 7 Barclay St., N.Y. This prayer card is truly a treasure that must have been a special memento of those who were in attendance that day. (Archdiocese of New Orleans Collection)

Commemorative prayer card courtesy of Archdiocese of New Orleans Collection

CHAPTER 6

POPE PIUS IX GRANTS ARCH CONFRATERNITY

Pope Pius IX Granted the Privilege of Affiliation to the Confraternity

By reason of a request from Archbishop Perche' to Pope Pius IX in Rome, Father John Simeoni, and Secretary of the Sacred Congregation of Propaganda: Rome, Italy responded on the back of Perche's request letter. Here the letter is summarized:

"Perche' asked the Holy Father that his Confraternity of Our Lady of Lourdes which he has erected in his cathedral be affiliated with the Confraternity in Lourdes itself. The superior of the missionaries at Lourdes told him that they can make such an affiliation only among the churches of France. Therefore he applied to the Holy Father for this affiliation. Also since many pastors of churches in his diocese also ask for affiliation both in his see city and in other cities he asks that they too obtain this affiliation. The faithful of the diocese have always had great devotion to Our Lady, especially in her title of the Immaculate Conception and have erected in his cathedral a magnificent statue of Our Lady of Lourdes. On the back of this letter written by Perché in his own hand is the letter of Simeoni in which he states that in the audience of January 25, 1874, Pope Pius IX gave the privilege of the affiliation to the confraternity not only in the cathedral but also in the parish churches of the diocese with the indulgences and privileges thereby attached." (Archdiocese of New Orleans Collection, VI-2-o)

Archbishop Perche's persistence was rewarded. The confraternity was established. The account of this affiliation was recorded in The Morning Star and Catholic Messenger on March 22, 1874. The account states:

"Our Most Rev. Archbishop has received from the Sovereign Pontiff the authorization of establishing, *canonically*, in his Cathedral, a confraternity of Our Lady of Lourdes and of affiliating it to the Arch confraternity established at Lourdes, thereby granting to the members an opportunity of gaining the same indulgences as are attached to the Arch confraternity. The ceremony will take place at the Cathedral on Friday, March 27th, Feast of the Compassion of the Blessed Virgin, at 6 o'clock p.m. After the sermon, to be preached by His Grace, the prelate will pronounce the canonical erection, and as soon as he shall have received from Lourdes the diploma of aggregation, he will inform the faithful, and then the members of the Confraternity will be entitled to gain the indulgence." (pg. 4)

"St. Louis Cathedral – Next Wednesday being the Feast of the Annunciation, the Most Rev. Archbishop will say his Mass at 7 o'clock at the altar of Our Lady of Lourdes...On Friday, Feast of the Compassion...His Grace will proceed to the solemn inauguration of the Confraternity of Our Lady of Lourdes, after which solemn Benediction of the Blessed Sacrament." (pg. 4)

Perche' took great care in establishing the devotion to Our Lady of Lourdes in the Archdiocese in an authentically Marian and Lourdes manner. He was meticulous in laying the groundwork for this devotion by having a proper altar constructed; ordering beautiful statues from France, making appropriate and timely announcements of his intentions in response to popular demand and in enacting this devotion with the core characteristics of the Lourdes pilgrimage and devotion experience – those being consecration to Our Lady, prayer, penance, procession, Holy Mass and Eucharistic Benediction and Adoration. He followed the act of consecration with the establishment of the Arch

Living Wine

The Spirit filled the golden cup,
Almost spilling over,
except for the consecrating hands
of the priest, gently settling it.
It licked up like white flames,
and rolled like a liquid cloud
before it settled into the cup,
leveling with the lip.
I rubbed my eyes...
had I seen the Spirit of Christ?
Does the priest see it everyday?
How can he handle such a wonder?
How can I?

confraternity subject to papal approval of Pope Pius IX whom Perche' so respected. (p.4) By all accounts, nothing of importance was left out of the establishment of this consecration and the confraternity.

PERCHE' SAYS MASS AT THE ALTAR TO OUR LADY OF LOURDES

The February 4, 1874 article in The Morning Star and Catholic Messenger demonstrates to us that Archbishop Perche' didn't establish this altar simply as a monument. He established this altar so that he might conduct the holy sacrifice of the Mass. Today, masses are conducted from within the grotto at Lourdes and Perche' did the same in 1874 at the altar he fashioned.

By Faith Alone

Whirling through space on a planet of blue,
small and unsure of where the ride ends,
seeing unreachable stars, blazing sun,
suffering and sorrow everyone's close friends,
having nowhere to turn, no place to run,
no one to care as urgent cry ascends.
God's creature, poor child, alone, blind and dumb?
Evidence of mountain, stream, blowing wheat,
perfection of the structure that is man.
Faith in the WORD in the soul's deepest place,
creature and Creator someday will meet.
And for the journey, there exists a grand plan...
at the end, Oh, Lord, to behold Thy Face!

"The Cathedral. Tomorrow, Monday, the Feast of the Purification of the Most Blessed Virgin, His Grace...will say Mass at 7 o'clock at the altar of our Lady of Lourdes..."

Research has confirmed that a future Bishop would be consecrated at this altar and many ex votos would be left at the altar in thanksgiving for healings that would occur.

Perche' and Our Lady of Lourdes Point the Archdiocese to Her Son – The Sacred Heart of Jesus

Heretofore, the pilgrimage spirit which had taken hold in the Archdiocese of New Orleans had as its focus Our Lady of Lourdes and the miraculous stories and devotions emanating from Lourdes, France. However, on March 25, 1874, the Feast of the Annunciation, Archbishop Perche' issued a Pastoral Letter, which was printed in its entirety on April 12, 1874 in The Morning Star and Catholic Messenger, and which took a decidedly Christ-centered point of view and focus. The Catholic faithful of New Orleans had been informed of the consecration of the diocese to Our Lady of Lourdes and the appeal made by His Grace for enrollment in the Arch confraternity. Perche' seized this enthusiasm and this opportunity to remind his congregation that Jesus Christ is the focus of our faith and salvation.

Illustration of Our Lady of Lourdes – Lourdes Website

At this juncture, we should stop to recall that March 25 has significance because it was on this date in 1858, during the 16th apparition that the Blessed Virgin announced her name to Bernadette by telling her I am the Immaculate Conception. It is likely Perche' selected this profound date to make the announcements about the dual consecrations and confraternities. Perche' respected not only the historical importance of the date he selected but undoubtedly, he had a deep appreciation of the spiritual significance as well.

With this pastoral letter, Perche' consecrated and enrolled the Archdiocese in the dual devotions to The Sacred Heart of Jesus and Our Lady of Lourdes. By linking the two together, Perche' demonstrated his piety (Baudier, p. 446) and taught by example the Church's long-standing teaching that Christ is the center of our beings and his Mother Mary is the perfect disciple, The Immaculate Conception, Queen Mother who lovingly draws the faithful to Her Divine Son. Here is excerpted a part of that letter:

> "...The Hierarchy of the United States, as remarkable for their zeal for the Church's growth, as for their Devotion to its Head, could not but feel that love for the Sacred Heart with which the heart of Christendom was yearning, and to which it was everywhere giving expression. Province after Province, Diocese after Diocese, in these States, has been laid at the feet of Jesus, to be united more closely to His Adorable Heart. And we, Dearly Beloved, eminently Catholic, sprang from Catholic parents, children of Catholic soil, in which Faith and Civilization have ever been a twin; we, through whose veins courses the best blood of France and of Ireland, of Italy, of Spain and of Germany; we, so diverse in origin, yet forming but one, grand, Glorious, Religious, Catholic Whole, now, do We intend to consecrate, in the most solemn manner possible, Our Diocese and Our Province to the Sacred Heart of Jesus.
>
> Therefore, seeing, Dearly Beloved, that the pilgrim spirit of the Middle Ages has been revived in our days, considering that the Sovereign Pontiff has granted Plenary Indulgences to the faithful who are visiting Paray-le-Monial, the centre of the Devotion to the Sacred Heart, and Lourdes, the choice Grottos of Mary Immaculate; and knowing that we are unable, almost every one of us, to visit those Miraculous Sanctuaries, We have asked and obtained from His Holiness, Pius IX, a favor, the

Image of Apparition of the Sacred Heart of Jesus - Website

bestowal of which proves his paternal interest in our regard. And not only for Our Diocese, but for all the Dioceses of the Province, We besought that favor, the acceptation of which depends on each of Our Venerable Brethren for his own Diocese. This privilege consists in the fact, that Pius IX has granted Plenary Indulgences in the same degree, and in the same manner, to the Novena of Pilgrimages, which We herein prescribe, and subject to the conditions, which We hereby append, as He has to the very Pilgrimage of Paray-le-Monial and of the Grotto of Lourdes.

...This Novena of Ours, Dearly Beloved, links us to that Pilgrim band – Our Brethren in the Faith, and portion of which will soon leave Our city for the Shrine of Mary Immaculate and the Tombs of the Apostles. Prostate at the feet of Christ's Vicar, they will tender Our undying love for His Holiness, and Our unswerving Devotion to the Successor of St. Peter. The precious boon of His Blessing He will bestow, not alone upon them – kneeling at His feet, but also upon Us and upon Our Province. To Us, Dearly Beloved, a more suitable preparation, for Our Grand Solemn Act of Consecration, is hardly conceivable."

The letter concludes by stating that the Consecration to the Sacred Heart of Jesus will take place in the Metropolitan Church on Sunday, 14th of June; the Sunday within the Octave of the Feast of the Sacred Heart of Jesus. Beginning with Sunday, April 19th and concluding on June 14th, the Novena of Pilgrimages was commenced and set to close on June 14 with the consecration of the Diocese. The pilgrimage churches and the order in which they were to be visited were prescribed by the letter. The schedule was to be as follows:

1. St. Mary's Chapel of the Archbishop, Sunday, 19th April.
2. Church of the Immaculate Conception, Jesuits, 26th April.

3. St. Mary's – German, 4th District, Redemptorists, Sunday 3rd May.
4. Church of the Nativity of B.V.M., Carrollton, Sunday, May 10th.
5. Church of the Holy Name of Mary, Algiers, Sunday, May 17th.
6. Church of Our Lady of the Sacred Heart, Sunday, May 24.
7. Church of Our Lady of Ready Help and St. Maurice, June 7th.
8. Cathedral Church, Sunday, June 14th, the day as aforesaid on which the Pilgrimage will be closed and the Act of Consecration made.

In the days after the Pastoral letter was issued, The Morning Star and Catholic Messenger of Sunday March 29, 1874, carried two stories which further linked the two devotions and consecrations. The first story entitled *The American Pilgrimage, Contributions Received,* details the names and contributions made for the purpose of sending "a representative on the American pilgrimage to Lourdes and Rome, in the person of Dr. Emile Doumeing. Six hundred dollars will be required for the purpose indicated." At publication, $254 had been collected. The story also mentions that Rev. C. Moynihan, pastor of St. Peter Church, Third District, also intended to join the American Pilgrimage set to leave New York on the 16th of May, 1874. This edition also carried an article entitled *Promises Made by Jesus Christ, to the Blessed Margaret Mary, Religious of the Visitation in Favor of those Devoted to His Sacred Heart.* They were enumerated as follows:

1. "...I will give them all the graces necessary in their state of life.
2. I will cause Peace to reign in their families.
3. I will console them in their sufferings.
4. I will be their assured refuge during life and above all in death.

5. I will show abundant benedictions on all their undertaking.
6. Sinners will find in my heart the source of an infinite ocean of mercy.
7. Tepid souls will become fervent.
8. Fervent souls will advance rapidly to a high perfection.
9. I will bless houses where the image of my Sacred Heart will be exposure and honored.
10. I will give Priest the talent of moving the most hardened hearts.
11. Those who propagate this devotion will have their names written in my Heart, from which they shall never be effaced…"

Under the sure-footed direction and leadership of Archbishop Perche', the Catholic faithful of New Orleans were being led to, consecrated to and enrolled in the Arch confraternities of the Sacred Heart of Jesus and Our Lady of Lourdes - both devotions carrying with them the pilgrim spirit that was swelling among Perche's flock.

Bishop G. A. Rouxel.

Times Picayune Sketch of Bishop Rouxel

DIPLOMA OF AFFILIATION

On May 17, 1874, The Morning Star and Catholic Messenger ran a story entitled *Confraternity of Our Lady of Lourdes.* In it, the author confirms that the Archdiocese has, indeed, been enrolled and the diploma of affiliation returned to Archbishop Perche'. By virtue of the diploma the author reported that "…By an indult[14] dated January 25, 1874, the Sovereign Pontiff authorizes

[14] Indult is a faculty granted by the pope to deviate from the common law of the Church http://www.thefreedictionary.com/indult

the Most Rev. Archbishop to affiliate with the Arch confraternity of Lourdes, the confraternity established in the Cathedral for this Archiepiscopal city, and one Confraternity for each parish in the country from which the pastor makes application...we are now authorized to state that all who desire to have their names registered can get certificates of membership by applying to the Rev. G. A. Rouxel, first curate of the Cathedral and Director of the Confraternity." (Messenger, 1874)

So began Rev. Gustave A. Rouxel's affiliation with Our Lady of Lourdes in the Archdiocese of New Orleans. Rev. Rouxel was later consecrated as an auxiliary bishop on April 9, 1899 at St. Louis Cathedral. Archbishop Chapelle conducted the "impressive service with pomp". (Times Picayune) Rev. Rouxel was consecrated an auxiliary bishop at the altar of Our Lady of Lourdes in the Cathedral. The account of the ceremony is extensive but here are the relevant connections to the altar and the role it played that day in this auspicious ceremony:

> "...The chapel of Our Lady of Lourdes was prepared for Bishop Rouxel and simultaneously with Archbishop Chapelle, who stood at the grand altar, the mass was offered...In the smaller chapel or shrine of Our Lady of Lourdes, where the bishop-elect was to officiate, the altar was prepared with two candlesticks, and all the vestments were in white..." (Times Picayune, 4/10/1899)

One can only imagine the devotion Rev. Rouxel must have had to Our Lady of Lourdes and perhaps even to little Bernadette for him to select that beautiful altar as the place for his consecration. According to the website www.neworleanschurches.com Bishop Rouxel died in the rectory at Annunciation church in 1908. (Website 2012) Although this church is closed today, there is still a grotto in the side yard at the church. Confirmation that a grotto to Our Lady of Lourdes was present in the side garden comes to us from the website www.storyvilledistrictnola.com which contains New Orleans history between 1897and 1917. It reads as follows:

> "...CHURCH OF THE ANNUNCIATION
>
> Two squares from Rampart street there stands on the corner of Marais and Mandeville Streets the little old French Church of the Annunciation, erected over fifty years ago for the French-speaking people of the Faubourg Marigny. It is in the old French style of architecture, as also the portion of the quaint presbytery, now the residence of Rt. Rev. Gustave A. Rouxel, auxiliary bishop of New Orleans. The beautiful old-fashioned garden, with its little shrine of Our Lady of Lourdes." (Storyville Website)

CHAPTER 7

DEVOTEES EMBARK ON PILGRIMAGES LOCALLY AND ABROAD

Close of the Novena Pilgrimages

On Sunday, June 14, 1874, the final procession of the novena pilgrimages took place with much solemnity and ceremony according to The Times Picayune article which reported the event.

> "...After an address in French by the Most Reverend Archbishop, and another in English by the Rev. Father McKiniry, S.J., His Grace the Archbishop read the act of consecration. The ceremonies in the Cathedral were watched with attention and followed with deep devotions by the immense congregation present. With the rocky grotto of Lourdes on the one hand, wherein stands a statue of Our Lady of Lourdes, of such enchanting beauty that we are almost inclined to think that the artist who formed it must have been inspired...the hearts of those present might easily drink in the aspirations appropriate to those distant shrines...the ceremonies...concluded...after which the clergy, with his Grace, repaired to Jackson Square. Here a large platform, festooned with the Papal colors and decorated with flags, had been erected. From this elevation, surrounded by the clergy, his Grace, Archbishop Perche', blessed the badges worn by the faithful, and the solemn Papal benediction, which was received kneeling by the assembled multitude, completed a day which will long be remembered by the Catholics of New Orleans." (Times Picayune, June 16, 1874)

First American Pilgrimage

When the Archdiocese of New Orleans became consecrated to Our Lady of Lourdes and later enrolled in the dual Arch Confraternities of the Sacred Heart of Jesus and Our Lady of

Lourdes, it was not a casual devotion. Catholic faithful knew that everyone could not make the pilgrimage to Lourdes, but to the extent possible, they supported the first American pilgrimage with donations and prayer. The pilgrim from New Orleans who was appointed to attend the event was Dr. Emile Doumeing. By the May 3, 1874 edition of The Morning Star and Catholic Messenger, the paper report that:

> "The following contributions have been received for the purpose of sending a representative on the American Pilgrimage to Lourdes and Rome in the person of Dr. Emile Doumeing. Six hundred dollars will be required...if the contributions exceed that amount, the surplus will be presented to our Holy Father, the Pope, by Dr. Doumeing...The list will remain open till...May 9th...The lady who so generously gave through Mr. Elder, thirty-nine dollars to the fund at the same time testified her devotion to the Holy Father by sending him $100 in gold." (p.4)

At the time of publication, $558 had been collected.

Still another local priest had plans to visit Lourdes. The April 12, 1874 Edition of The Morning Star and Catholic Messenger carried a story entitled *Departure of Father Massardier* and reported the following:

> "Last Wednesday evening the Rev. Father Massardier, curate of St. Theresa's Church, left here for New York...for his native place, St. Etienne...then he will join the American Pilgrimage to Lourdes and Rome." (p.4)

On May 17, 1874, The Morning Star and Catholic Messenger published Archbishop Perche's view of the upcoming American Pilgrimage:

> "As it is proper that we should be united, at least by our prayers, with the pilgrims who are going to the shrine of Our Lady of Lourdes and to Rome as the representatives of the

different dioceses of the United States, the Rev. Clergy will say at Mass the prayer Pro peregrinantibus,[15] till the end of June, the time when the pilgrimage will be completed." (p. 4)

The day arrived when the first pilgrimage to Lourdes would depart from New York and The Morning Star and Catholic Messenger reported the story in the news from Sunday, May 31, 1874 in an article titled *The Happy Pilgrimage. Solemn Ceremonies in the New York Cathedral. Departure of the Pilgrim.* which had been condensed from the Freeman's Journal. The article attempted to capture the enthusiasm and the solemnity of the occasion thusly:

"They are on the Ocean, on their favored way, of sacrifice and abnegation; and, so, of truest joy and contentment. They are on their way, *one hundred and eight souls* – the "First Pilgrimage from America." (1874)

This departure of 108 souls was no small undertaking according to the recorded account. This pilgrimage and those pilgrims were afforded every blessing possible. While some may think a word for word copy of this account is overkill, I have elected to insert almost all of the text as it appeared that day in May because I have never seen a record of such a magnificent disembarkation as the one written that day for this momentous and solemn Pilgrimage. Here is the *condensed* account from the *Freeman's Journal*:

"They reached New York in time; some of them not till late in the night of the 15th. On the morning of the 16th, the rain poured down in torrents. Most of them, notwithstanding, would not call carriages, but walked from the Metropolitan Hotel to the Cathedral. The good Catholic Societies, from the Church of the Holy Redeemer, and from St. Alphonsus, could not bring out their elegant flags and banners, as they had wished to do; but delegations of them, under the lead of Mr. Lerebe, to the number of nearly a hundred,

[15] Prayer Pro peregrinantibus is a prayer for sailors and travelers

were present as an escort. The Pilgrims, with Major Keiley, and other members of the Pilgrimage Committee, occupied the Gospel side of the nave of the Cathedral. The St. Michael's, the St. Aloysius, and the St Alphonsus Societies, of the guard of honor, occupied the Epistle side of the Cathedral nave.

The Very Rev. Father Quin F.G., who has shown a most tender and affectionate interest in the Pilgrimage, had left nothing unprepared for the commodious and edifying solemnity of the Mass inaugurating the Pilgrimage. All space possible without obstructing the solemnities, was given to the faithful, who thronged, on the rainy morning, to witness the ceremonies. Father Quin had in the Sanctuary a choir of the boys from the Cathedral Parish School, to chant the appropriate parts during the Mass. In the Organ loft there was a double Quartette who sang Ecclesiastical music during the Benediction of the Blessed Sacrament, after the Mass. Father Quin, with Fathers Kearny, McNamee, Farley, Secretary to the Archbishop, and other of the Cathedral clergy assisted. Bishop Dwenger, the spiritual Head of the Pilgrimage, in rochet[16], was seated on the Gospel side of the High Altar.

The beautiful Banner for Our Lady of Lourdes had been displayed, for a moment, at the door of the Hotel, but the rain compelled its being folded and sheathed, till it reached the Cathedral. It was, then, brought from the Sacristy, and placed beside a pillar at the Sanctuary railing.

His Grace, Dr. McCloskey, Archbishop of New York, entered the Sanctuary, and after being clothed in his Pontificals, proceeded to bless the Banner, according to the Roman Ritual. Mr. Patrick Farrely, its honored Bearer to the Basilica of Lourdes, supported it,

[16] Rochet is a vestment of linen or lawn, resembling a surplice, worn especially by bishops and abbots. http://dictionary.reference.com/browse/rochet?s=t

assisted, on the right by Major Kelley, Chairman of the Resident Pilgrimage Committee, and on left, by Judge Paul E. Theard, of New Orleans, Chairman of the Committee accompanying the Pilgrimage. After being blessed, it was set in the stanchion prepared for it, at the head of the body of Pilgrims.

His Grace the Archbishop said the Mass for the Pilgrimage. All the Pilgrims communed, except those of the Priesthood who had already, at an early hour, said Mass.

At the end of the Mass, the Most Rev. Archbishop, with a suppressed, but evidently deep emotion, delivered a most eloquent address to the Pilgrims.

The Benediction

At the conclusion of his impressive address, the Archbishop proceeded with the Blessing of Pilgrims setting forth to visit Sacred Shrines, according to the Roman Ritual; and then, with mitre[17] and crozier[18], gave his Episcopal Blessing. After this the Blessed Sacrament was brought forth for Adoration, and his Grace gave the Benediction of the Most Holy. The scene in the Cathedral will never be forgotten by those who took part in it. After the public ceremonies, the display of faith, on the part of the simple Catholic people was affecting. The Banner had hung, on the evening preceding, in St. Alphonsus' Church, during the evening devotions of the Month of Mary. It was intended that it should have hung in St. Patrick's during the morning of the sixteenth. But the eager crowd was so pressing to touch with crucifixes, and beads, and scapulars, the beautiful Banner so soon to be deposited in the Basilica of Lourdes, that – though it seemed cruel, it had to be folded, and removed to the Sacristy, to keep it from defacement or soiling.

[17] Mitre is the liturgical headdress of a bishop or abbot, in most western churches consisting of a tall pointed cleft cap with two bands hanging down at the back. http://dictionary.reference.com/browse/mitre?s=t

[18] Crozier is a staff surmounted by a crook or cross, carried by bishops as a symbol of pastoral office. http://dictionary.reference.com/browse/crozier?s=t

Shortly after two o'clock, the Pilgrims, except those whose health rendered it imprudent, were gathered at the Metropolitan Hotel. It was still raining. The prepared programme of escorting Societies, with the elegant Pontifical Flag from Holy Redeemer Church, St. Michael's Banner, a Catholic music Band, etc. – had been abandoned; but it was time to start for the steamer. Umbrellas were up all along Broadway. But it was a singular fact, that, at the moment Major Kelley gave the signal to open the private door of the Hotel, to march to the Steamer, the rain suddenly ceased. Not a drop more of cold water – abundant till then – fell on the Pilgrimage!

Arrived at the wharf of the French Steamer Company, on it, and all around, there were as many thousands as could find footing – most of them Catholics, came to show their interest and devotion.

Promptly, at four o'clock, the Steamer *Pereire* began to cast off her fastenings to the wharf. Those who were to go down the Bay, in accompany Steamers, sprang for their several vessels...

Apostolical Benediction on the Pilgrimage

A little after midnight of May 15-16th, Major Keiley dispatched a telegram to the Holy Father, in Latin, of which the following is the translation: "The Rt. Rev. Jos. Dwenger, with many of the clergy, and laity, in number over one hundred, setting forth on their holy Pilgrimage, implore Thy Apostolic Benediction." This was received in Rome by one that Major Keiley's forethought had put on the alert to expect it. Before eleven o'clock on the 16thth, the following reply came to the Major: "The Holy Father imparts His most loving Benediction to Bishop Dwenger, and the Pilgrims accompanying him." (1874)

LETTER FROM "OUR" PILGRIM

The pilgrim "E.D." mailed a letter under date of June 10, 1874 to the editor of The Morning Star which published it in the paper on July 5, 1874 with his account of their "...arrival at Lourdes and devotions at the shrine of Our Lady..." (p. 4) The letter is lengthy but of great importance. The New Orleanians who contributed money and prayers to be with the delegated pilgrims going to Lourdes were most certainly anxious to hear about the experience and the author provides good details in his account of their experience. Most of the letter is included as follows:

"...the American pilgrims set out (from Paris) on the first of June for Lourdes...by express train of the "Chemin de fer d'Orleans."...only first class cars can be secured...they are luxuriantly gotten up, and for one desirous of travelling a short distance they are very convenient. But to him who leaves Paris for Lourdes...and has...to spend a whole night in them after having spent a full day, it is barbarous in the extreme. The French are far behind the American in the art of travelling. No Pullman sleeping cars...no accommodations whatsoever...you may well imagine how fatigued the pilgrims must have been...our Bishop-Director...remarked to us that a pilgrimage is a penance, we had to exercise great patience...besides...the importance of the destination made us overlook many little difficulties which were more than compensated by the great consolations in store for us." (p. 4)

A significant portion of the letter is devoted to settling into hotels and getting situated before their first trip to the grotto. The letter then picks up with:

"...we were soon to be found wending our way to the hallowed grotto where our Blessed Mother appeared eighteen times to Bernadette...On the same evening of our arrival, the pilgrims went in procession to the holy shrine from the church...with the banner of the Immaculate Conception which was made in New York and destined to be left in the chapel of the our Lady of Lourdes as a perpetual memorial of the first American pilgrimage and with the American flag...On our arrival at the church, which is built upon the rock, in which is contained the grotto, solemn Vespers were sung, followed by benediction of the Blessed Sacrament...we proceeded in procession to the grotto, where we knelt before a statue of the Blessed Virgin and sang a hymn to her and offered up our prayers...

The next morning we went to Mass and received Holy Communion...from Bishop Dwenger. Scarcely had the Mass for our pilgrims been said when there came pouring in a numerous pilgrimage from...Toulouse, composed of the pupils of the Jesuits' College and a great number of pious Catholic families. They were preceded by the college brass band. Theirs was a more imposing ceremony than ours...Great was...the regret of the American pilgrims that a previous contract with a French vessel to take us from Marseilles...did not permit us to spend more than two days at Lourdes...

...we hurried to the house of Bernadette where her sister, Marie Soubirous, still resides...She received us with great kindness and showed us the bedroom of Bernadette and the oratory before which she knelt every day.

We could not help prostrating ourselves before this same oratory and offering up our prayers in thanksgiving to our Blessed Mother who had bestowed so many favors to the poor peasant girl...our curiosity was considerably awakened and many were the questions which we put to Bernadette's sister...we learned...that her father had died three years ago and her mother eight years...she had two brothers, one a religious and the other in the army…then went to the hotel…returned to the beautiful church of our Lady of Lourdes…and then paid a last visit to the grotto, whence with difficulty we had to snatch ourselves. We had the privilege of entering within the sanctuary protected by the iron railing, and therefore had the satisfaction of embracing the very spot over which our Lady of Lourdes appeared. Must I say that none of our friends in New Orleans were forgotten. One by one the many requests made were offered and I can say that, as far as that is concerned, I have done my duty. I have also had Masses offered for the intentions of all those who were united with us in prayer and in spirit during the entire pilgrimage…we left on the 4th…E.D." (pg. 4)

The Lord's Saving Words

This is My Body, the Lord said.
This is My Blood, do be fed
with the earth's bread and wine.
Remember Me, I am the vine.
Do this, you will never be dead.
By these signs the Church has been led
through two millennia – wine and bread.
First Christians said, when they would dine –
This is My Body.
On the cross, His scourged Body bled.
From the sight, the devils fled
and do today when the divine
Sacrifice repeats at each shrine.
Each Church on earth, these words are said:
This is My Body.

Emile Domingue certainly provided a thorough account of his pilgrimage on behalf of all those who made his trip possible as well as those praying for the pilgrimage. His description would have allowed all those following this important pilgrimage to vicariously enter the Lourdes story. By all measure, he appears to have been an excellent designee for this Lourdes Experience.

ARCH CONFRATERNITY CANONICALLY APPROVED AT ST. MARY'S CARROLLTON

The December 13, 1874 edition of The Morning Star and Catholic Messenger carried a story entitled *Our Lady of Lourdes – Pilgrimage of St. Henry's Congregation to Her Shrine in Carrollton.* The story reported that on the Feast of the Immaculate Conception that was celebrated the previous Tuesday the first pilgrimage to the shrine to Our Lady of Lourdes occurred from St. Henry's to St. Mary's Church. This celebration was the first anniversary of the consecration of the Archdiocese to Our Lady of Lourdes and the article reported the important fact that the Confraternity of Our Lady of Lourdes was "now canonically established in St. Mary's Church, Carrollton. The latter invested with the Scapular of the Immaculate Conception." The correspondent recorded the event like this:

> "...the Sixth District witnessed a religious celebration...although simple in form and unostentatious, was none the less sublime, if we consider the purely religious motives which inspired it and the truly Catholic manner in which it was carried out...the 8th of December had been fixed...by Catholics of St. Henry's congregation to perform the first pilgrimage to the shrine of Our Lady of Lourdes in St. Mary's Church Carrollton...fully 1,000 strong...proceeded from the...church to make the intended pilgrimage. Slowly and solemnly the assemblage of pious worshippers moved through the streets of our beautiful suburb, carrying also the adorable sign of Redemption...there was no interruption in praying or singing of religious hymns...it was truly a *praying procession, pilgrimage*...After an hour and a half's march the pilgrims arrived...were greeted...by the congregation of St. Mary...both congregations proceeded to the church, where the services were inaugurated by an appropriate address, delivered in German by the Rev J.

B. Bogaerts, pastor at St. Henry's Church. The address concluded, prayer was offered up to Our Lady of Lourdes in behalf of the Church and the Holy Father. It was an affecting sight which caused many a tear to flow, to see this vast assemblage, which by numerous accession, had now become fully 1,500 strong, prostrated before the throne of Mary, united in one common prayer for the deliverance of the Church and the Holy Father. For it must be remembered that the first object of the pilgrimage was to obtain through the intercession of Mary Immaculate the speedy triumph of the Church over her enemies…At the conclusion of the devotion numerous pilgrims came forward to make the offering of the candles usual on such occasions and a still greater number had their named enrolled in the Confraternity of Our Lady of Lourdes…" (pg. 4)

The St. Mary's Church Carrollton referred to in this article was called St. Mary's Nativity. (Baudier, p. 559) There were two churches in Carrollton until 1898 – St. Mary's and Mater Dolorosa. St. Mary's served the French speaking people and Mater Dolorosa the Germans. Father Vallee died in 1892. The website for Mater Dolorosa Catholic Church and School provides a short history of the church as follows:

"Organized in 1847 and known as the Church of St. Mary of the Nativity, the church's congregation was predominantly French and German. The first church was on Cambaronne Street in what was then the town of Carrollton. However, divisions occurred within the church and, in 1871, the German congregants moved across the street and formed a church they called Mater Dolorosa (also, known as the German Mater Dolorosa Church). By the end of the century, however, the rifts had been repaired and the two congregations came together under the name of Mater Dolorosa." (2012)

Archbishop Chapelle had sent Rev. John Francis Prim, the prior chancellor of the Archdiocese, to Carrollton "...with instruction to combine the two congregations..." in July, 1898. (Baudier, p. 559)

A visit to this church reveals two stunning alcoves dedicated to the Sacred Heart of Jesus and to Our Lady of Lourdes.

The presence of these two altars with statues of the Sacred Heart and Our Lady of Lourdes suggest the dual Arch confraternities were transferred to Mater Dolorosa when the two churches were combined. There is no confirmation whether the current alcoves and altars are the same or different from those which may have been in place in the early 20th century; but the fact that both are present there provides strong evidence that the early congregations embraced the Arch confraternities and perhaps preserved them for future generations to rediscover.

The statues of the Sacred Heart and Our Lady of Lourdes appear to be newer and more ornate than the statue of Bernadette. Bernadette's statue is authentic in its depiction of her but the statue is plain with evidence of wear. This statue appears to be one in which a candle could be placed in her left hand. She is not holding rosary beads, which makes this depiction somewhat unique when compared with many others which all seem to show her holding or praying her rosary. Her eyes are fixed above as if in a state of rapture. The base of this statue does not match that of Our Lady nor the Sacred Heart.

A careful comparison between this statue and that of the one shown in the black and white photo of the altar at St. Louis Cathedral suggests this could be the same statue; however this research has been unable to confirm this suspicion

CHAPTER 8

LOURDES GROTTOS, REPLICAS, STAINED GLASS AND STATUES

COMMEMORATE THE CONSECRATION TO OUR LADY OF LOURDES

Lourdes Grottos, Altars, Monuments, Replicas and Statues

When one explores the numerous ways which Our Lady of Lourdes, the Grotto of Massabielle and Bernadette have been memorialized, venerated, or honored for more than a century, the realization that the people who constructed these memorials have provided different interpretations of the Apparition scenes is apparent. Not all of the "so-called" grottos are in fact, grottos.

The online Merriam-Webster dictionary defines a grotto as a "cave" or an "artificial recess or structure made to resemble a natural cave."

The same source defines an altar as "a usually raised structure or place on which sacrifices are offered or incense is burned in worship —often used figuratively to describe a thing given great or undue precedence...a table on which the Eucharistic elements are consecrated or which serves as a center of worship or ritual."

Monument has several possible definitions; among them the online dictionary offers this definition: "a lasting evidence, reminder, or example of someone or something notable or great...a distinguished person...a memorial stone or a building erected in remembrance of a person or event..."

A replica is defined as "an exact reproduction (as of a painting) executed by the original artist..."

Finally, this dictionary defines a statue as "a three-dimensional representation usually of a person, animal, or mythical being that is produced by sculpturing, modeling, or casting."

Each of these interpretations of the Apparition events may stimulate us to remember and venerate the experience but we should be careful to designate the representation accurately.

With these definitions in mind, this researcher now shares the many places we have explored in the pursuit of information for this work. The 1873 altar in St. Louis Cathedral had been erected as an indoor monument, as it was referred to by Archbishop Perche', that was a very good replica of the Grotto of Masabielle.

The National Shrine at Emmitsburg, MD reports the first outdoor Lourdes Grotto in America was erected there in 1875. The National Shrine is quite beautiful and authentic. I had the pleasure of making a pilgrimage to that Shrine in 2009 with my granddaughter. It is accurately described as a grotto and authentically places Bernadette, Our Lady of Lourdes and the grotto to depict an accurate representation of the original. Like the Grotto in Lourdes an altar is situated between the Blessed Virgin and Bernadette – within the grotto where the Holy Eucharist is celebrated.

My granddaughter Elizabeth and I at Our Lady of Lourdes National Shrine in Emmitsburg, MD in 2009

ST. MARTIN DE TOURS CATHOLIC CHURCH – ST. MARTINVILLE, LOUISIANA

This research has uncovered an interesting assertion in a book entitled Moon Handbooks New Orleans: Including Cajun Country and the River Road… by Andrew Collins. The first printing of this book was in 2004 with the second edition in March, 2007. He reported:

"St. Martin de Tours Catholic Church (Bridge and Main Sts., St. Martinville), which dates to 1765 and is one of the oldest churches in the Gulf South. It contains a replica of the Grotto of Lourdes, which was added in 1870." (Collins, pgs. 2-3)

This account conflicts with another account on the website Online Highways Home. According to that version the grotto was built 13 years later. Here is their account:

> "St. Martin is one of the oldest churches in the state, it was established in 1765. The present edifice, built in 1836, has an 1883 replica of the Grotto of Lourdes…" (Online Highways Home, 2012)

More accounts of this wondrous grotto can be accessed through the Louisiana Collection at the State Library. Their research department has provided these additional accounts to provide further historical references to this sculpture.

St. Martin de Tours – The Mother Church is Restored

Sunday Advocate Magazine July 29, 1973

". . . One of the remarkable features of the church is the magnificent Chapel of the Grotto of Lourdes. It was designed and built by Paul Martinez, a St. Martinville octoroon, in the 1870s. Using mud and clay from the bayou, Martinez produced the replica of the site of the appearance of Our Lady of Lourdes, with a picture post card as his model."

St. Martin de Tours reflects area's French heritage *The Advocate* February 18, 2002

". . . One of the most striking parts of the church is the grotto to the left of the main altar. It is a replica of the Grotto of Lourdes in France and was made in the late 1870s by Paul Martinez, who had only seen a picture of the French grotto.

A lady from St. Martinville had gone to Lourdes and brought a postcard back with her," [Inez] Gauthier [who is descended from early French settlers] said. "Paul Martinez looked at the card and said, 'I can do that.' With mud and moss he constructed it."

Small marble signs placed on the grotto are expressions of gratitude for favors granted. . ."

If Mr. Collins' account is accurate, this indoor grotto to Our Lady of Lourdes would be the earliest one located by this researcher in the country; however, the 1973 and 2002 accounts suggest the grotto may have been built in the late 1870's.

ST. MICHAEL THE ARCHANGEL – CONVENT, LOUISIANA

In 1876 St. Michael the Archangel Church in Convent, LA erected an indoor grotto behind the main altar of the historic church. Their website reveals the details as follows:

> "...The Grotto behind the main altar is made of bagasse clinkers. It was dedicated in 1876 and is the first of its kind in the United States. St. Michael the Archangel is the first Marist foundation in the United States..." (St. Michael, 2012)

This representation is among the most authentic I have had the privilege to visit and has a rich history associated to it. Stones Beside The River – A History of the Church on the East Bank of St. James Parish – 1809 – 2009 by Frank M. Uter

contains a thorough account of the origin of this grotto. From his account, we learn Florian Dicharry designed and constructed this Lourdes Grotto in 1876. Uter asserts that "It is considered among the first, if not the first, Lourdes Grotto to be constructed in America, built eighteen years after the first apparition…" (p. 61)

Uter has provided his readers with details about this grotto of immense interest. He tells us the following"

"…its rock structure is made from charred clinkers of sugar cane bagasse, a byproduct of

sugar cane processing. Clinkers were hard rock remnants…made of varied sizes and shapes…put together by Christophe Colomb, a skilled artist and stone mason from Convent…the come over the altar recessed within the Grotto is made of a large sugar kettle…the base and side of the altar are decorated with hundreds of small clam shells from the Mississippi River…many ex voto slabs…indicate gratitude to God and the Blessed Virgin for her intercession for favors granted. One of the largest is dated July 25, 1876 and was donated by the Vasseur Weber family for his being safely found after being lost four days in the swamps.

Father George Meiluta, S.M…recorded that on Easter Sunday, April 17, 1876, "St. Michael Church was filled to capacity…Father J. Bigot, S.M…blessed the large Immaculate Conception statue (the same one there to this day) which was carried through the church on the shoulder of eight men and then hoisted to its present niche. Facing the statue is a nearly life size kneeling statue of St. Bernadette." (p.62)

In this designer's view of Bernadette, she is kneeling, hands clasped together and looking up at Our Lady in ecstasy. There is no candle in her hand but her rosary beads are held tightly in prayer. Bernadette began bringing a candle to the grotto on her third journey there. (Website, 2012)

In yet another account of this grotto, Lillian C. Bourgeois provides more details in her book Cabanocey – This History, Customs and Folklore of St. James Parish which was first printed in 1957. She credits the Marist Fathers with the undertaking of the construction of "the Chapel of Lourdes at St. Michel." (p. 44)

She provides the following interesting details about the story of this grotto:

"...The work for this, one of the first grottos of Lourdes in America, was placed in the skilled hands of Christophe Colomb, artist and artisan. Mr. Colomb, believed to be a descendant of Christopher Columbus, was surely part French...and it was he who left the singularly interesting and beautiful grotto of Lourdes at St. Michel." (p. 44)

About the ex votos attached to the grotto by the Weber family Bourgeois states:

"Mr. Webre and two companions went on a hunt at Nita Plantation. They became lost and for several days wandered aimlessly and hopelessly through the woods and swamps back of Nita...Mr. Webre alternately prayed, hoped and called. He promised our Lady of Lourdes public recognition if they were rescued. At the end of the fourth day, they were found...Mr. Webre's little marble "ex voto" is perched in a conspicuous place...It reads: "Ex-voto – le 25 Juliet 1876. Reconnaissance a N.D de Lourdes." (p. 45)

IMMACULATE CONCEPTION CHURCH, LAKE CHARLES, LOUISIANA

The first pastor of Immaculate Conception Church was appointed by Archbishop Napoleon Joseph Perche' in 1870 when he sent Father Badoil to serve there. When Badoil was transferred in 1874, he was followed by Father Cuny and then by Father Kelly. (Greene, pg. 132)

The Old Convent.
1883.

First Convent owned by the Marianites in Lake Charles, LA
Courtesy of Frazier Memorial Library McNeese State University

Elaine Bodin wrote a history of St. Charles Academy which states that Father Michael Kelly asked the Marianite order to staff the academy in July of 1881. There had been a hurricane on August 22, 1879 which destroyed the church property. Father Kelly completed the Church of the Immaculate Conception on October 2, 1881. He then moved the chapel and adapted it for use as a schoolhouse. The first day of school for the girls was September 11, 1882. But, he was concerned about the boys as well; so, he opened a school for them in March, 1883. The first commencement exercise of St. Charles Academy was held on July 17, 1883. Following these priorities, Father Kelly completed a new convent for the Sisters by December, 1884 and formally blessed it on February 7, 1885. There is no mention in Bodin's history specifically about this grotto replica, but these photo are included in her history.

Section of Garden Showing Grotto.

Courtesy Frazier Memorial Library – McNeese State University

In the foreground of this picture in front of the first Marianite Convent in Lake Charles, LA we find a replica of one of the Lourdes apparitions in the center of a courtyard dominating the entryway to this beautiful building. The photo is from the Maude Reid scrapbook and suggests this photo was taken in 1883. She does go on to write:

"On the Feast of the Immaculate Conception, December 8, 1885, the Societies of the Children of Mary and of the Holy Angels were organized. During the following month of May 1886, the first local public observance was held in honor of the Blessed Virgin. The Sodalists walked in procession from the convent to the church carrying Our Lady's Banner. After a sermon on the dignity and virtues of Mary, the Banner was blessed and aspirants to both Sodalities were received. Then the statue of the Blessed Virgin was crowned." (Bodin)

ST. JOSEPH CHURCH AND CEMETERY, THIBODAUX, LOUISIANA

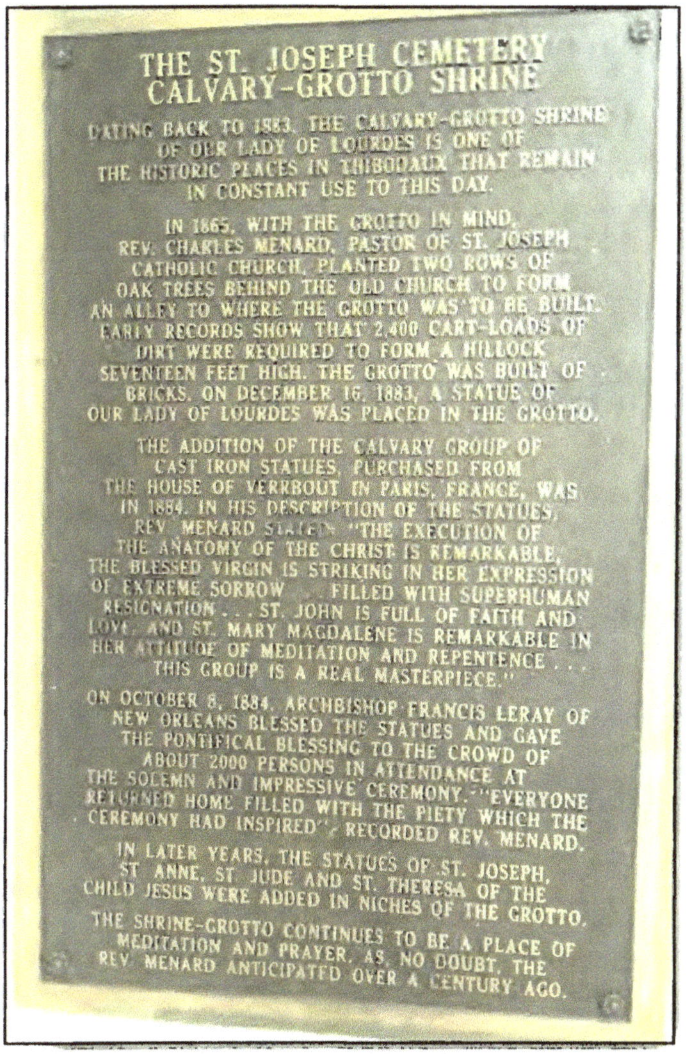

In Thibodaux a cemetery grotto replica was erected by Rev. Charles Menard after planning to do so for a long time. The bronze plaque inside the niche with the statue of Our Lady of Lourdes provides the story of this grotto. Rev. Menard was a canon at St. Louis Cathedral according to the history provided on a plaque on the front of St. Joseph's Church in 1874. He would have been acquainted with Archbishop Napoleon Joseph Perche'. The plaque at the grotto says that Menard had planned since 1865 to build this grotto. This fact would make Rev. Menard among the first in the United States to have knowledge of Our Lady of Lourdes and would make the plans laid down for this grotto likely to be the first in the country.

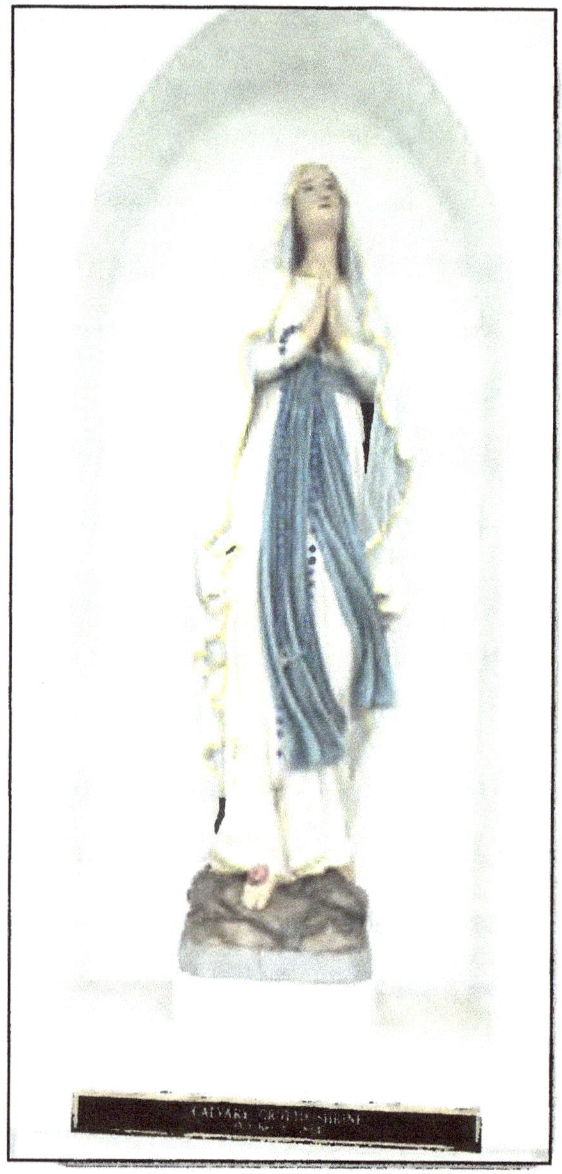

The plaque reads Calvary Grotto Shrine October 8, 1884

ST. VINCENT DE PAUL CHURCH AND THE SISTERS OF THE IMMACULATE CONCEPTION, NEW ORLEANS, LOUISIANA

Today, the St. Vincent de Paul Church on Dauphine Street has been renamed Blessed Seelos. The church website states that "St. Vincent de Paul Church is a federally registered Historical Building. Within the city of New Orleans it ranks as the 5th oldest Catholic Church, after Saints Peter and Paul (antebellum), St Patrick's, Our Lady of Guadalupe (the mortuary Chapel of the old city) and the St Louis Cathedral." (Website, 2012)

In 1879, Father Adolphe Chappuis was the pastor of the church of the church. His plans for opening a school succeeded and in that year he turned the administration of the school over to the Sisters of the Immaculate Conception. (Baudier, p. 455)

It is unknown when, but at some point on the grounds adjacent to the convent, a shrine to Our Lady of Lourdes was erected. Because it is on the grounds of the convent, it is reasonable to imagine this shrine was associated with the convent and the school perhaps, more so than the church itself and might, therefore date back to its founding.

This shrine was constructed of stone, and has a niche where the statue of Our Lady of Lourdes is slightly elevated above a kneeling statue of Bernadette.

The image of Bernadette is marred by a missing left arm more or less from the elbow to the hand. On inspection, one can imagine this arm was likely extended and like others probably was meant to hold a candle. This image does have rosary beads draped in front of her clothing and held in her right hand.

OUR LADY OF LOURDES CHURCH, NEW ORLEANS, LOUISIANA

Our Lady of Lourdes Church was dedicated in 1908 in a triduum of services which began on February 9, 2008 and would conclude on the fiftieth anniversary of the first apparition on February 11, 1908. More about this church and how it commemorated the apparitions appears later; for now, we focus on the beautiful grotto of Our Lady of Lourdes which was dedicated in July, 1908 according to an article in The Times Picayune dated July 19, 1908.

During the semi centennial celebration in February, 1908, Lawrence Fabacher, "...an ardent Catholic..." donated a "life-size statue of Our Lady of Lourdes, a duplicate of the image in the wonder grotto..." This statue was surely admired by all who looked upon it because it was not only purchased while Fabacher was in Paris but "...He took the statue with him on a pilgrimage to the famous shrine, had it blessed there, and secured permission for it to rest for a time upon the stone which figured in the miracle. Thus consecrated, he prized the precious relic highly and brought it with him to his palatial home here...The gift is much greater than its intrinsic value, and was one of the glorious features of the religious festival..." (Times Picayune, 2/10/1908)

Courtesy of Times Picayune - Photo of Grotto at Our Lady of Lourdes Church in 1908

OUR LADY OF LOURDES GROTTO.

Unfortunately, this church is now closed. However, the article contains a good description of this grotto and a black and white photo. Under the title of *Famous Lourdes Grotto – Reproduced Here at the Church on Napoleon Avenue – Through the Generosity of Friend of Father Kavanaugh and His Congregation*, the article describes the grotto:

"In the pretty little Church of Our Lady of Lourdes a handsome grotto has just been completed...This grotto is the gift of Mr. W. J. Waguespack. The statue of the Blessed Virgin which occupies a niche in the grotto was donated...by Mr. Lawrence Fabacher. It was brought by that gentleman from Lourdes on one of his recent visits to that famous spot. The statue apart from its beauty, is valued for the fact that it has touched the very spot where the apparition of the blessed Virgin first Appeared to Bernadette Soubirous...The entire grotto is a thing of wondrous beauty, the towering tocks forming an impressive picture...A tiny rivulet of water falling down the side of the mountain adds a touch of realism..." (Picayune, 1908)

Photo of Grotto at Our Lady of Lourdes courtesy of John and Kathleen DeMajo – www.neworleanschurches.com

From the website www.neworleanschurches.com we obtain a photograph taken and used with permission by John and Kathleen DeMajo of the grotto a Our Lady of Lourdes Church before hurricane Katrina. The photo shown at the inset captures the grotto, the altar and Bernadette kneeling before Our Lady.

ST. SCHOLASTICA ACADEMY - COVINGTON, LOUISIANA

The school website provides a history of this school founded by the Benedictine Sisters in 1902 and opened on September 5, 1903. The website goes on to state:

"When the bell rang in 1910, it was for the dedication of the Grotto of Our Lady of Lourdes, which is where the May Crowning is held for our students..." (Website, 2012)

ACADEMY OF THE SACRED HEART, NEW ORLEANS, LOUISIANA

Within the next decade, a Lourdes grotto was constructed at the Academy of the Sacred Heart on St. Charles Avenue in New Orleans. Sally Kittredge Reeves documented the story behind this lovely grotto in her book, *Legacy of a Century*, published in 1987. The story was reported as follows:

"…Here, Mother Chatard was known to have staged an extra crowning for chronic offenders who "really tried" to keep the practice during Mary's month of May but went nevertheless unrecognized. The stone grotto was erected in 1920. Statue given by Samuel Segari family in memory of their daughter Beulah, who would have graduated in 1919." (Kittredge, pg. 120)

In the summer of 2011, the Academy website reported that the grotto was originally erected on the "…back square of the Rosary campus…In the summer of 2011, the grotto was moved to a new location beside the chapel in the side yard of the main campus." (Website, 2011) A visit to the campus reveals that the original grotto was deconstructed very carefully and that the same materials were used to re-erect the grotto on the new campus location.

OUR LADY OF LOURDES SHRINE, LACOMBE, LOUISIANA

Along a solitary country road in Lacombe, located north of Lake Pontchartrain, Father Francis Balay, OSB, erected a shrine to Our Lady of Lourdes in a small chapel in 1923 as the sign clearly says. Although one can see the chapel from the road, a bridge over a small stream must be crossed to reach it. Inside the chapel a small replica of the apparition is situated to the right of the altar.

Once inside this simple chapel the side altar to Our Lady of Lourdes is evident. Bernadette is looking up at Our Lady and a basin with running water forms a base for the altar.

This shrine is a peaceful place. The shrine is a simple but reverent depiction in honor or remembrance of the miraculous apparitions at Lourdes in 1858. This chapel is a place of welcome. On Sundays the Rosary is prayed at 2:00pm. On one of the days spent visiting this chapel, this pilgrim saw parishioners of Sacred Heart Church in Lacombe undertaking extensive cleanup work to eliminate the brush and clear the way to this chapel.

SACRED HEART CHURCH, MORGAN CITY, LOUISIANA

Between 1922 and 1924 Father Andrew Souby constructed a Lourdes grotto for his parishioners at Sacred Heart. This grotto is unique in that it is built as a part of a structure called a Baptistery. This structure is well preserved and still beautiful today. Father Souby is actually buried there. Julie Delaune wrote a history book about Sacred Heart parish. As a result of an interview with Ms. Delaune, we have learned that Father Souby was a native of New Orleans and was ordained with approval of Archbishop Janssens in Genoa, Italy on May 19, 1894. (The Bayou Catholic, pg. 20) Before returning to the United States, he was given permission to make two side trips to Rome and Lourdes. He was not inclined to believe in the apparitions and miracles in Lourdes but he was evidently curious and open to the truth. While he was there, Father Souby witnessed "...several miracles at the Shrine of Massabielle..." (The Bayou Catholic, pg. 20) From that point on, Father Souby had a great devotion to Our Lady of Lourdes. He was the pastor at Sacred Heart from 1898 until his death in 1938. Father Souby also contributed to the founding of Morgan City's Catholic Daughters of the America, Court Massabielle #1134; so named for the grotto in Lourdes.

The Bayou Catholic article of August 21, 1985 provides details about the Baptistery and the grotto replica.

"...One unique feature of Sacred Heart parish is its baptistery. It is rare to find the baptistery apart from the main church. The building served four purposes for Souby – a baptistery, a memorial to his family…the grotto is a shrine to the miracles he witnessed at Lourdes and finally, his final resting place…

The plans were drawn by Souby. The building is in the shape of an octagon with three extensions…His specification called for a water tight wine cellar. His actual intent was for his own grave. He purchased the marble slab covering and had it engraved with all pertinent information with one exception – the date of his death…

The interior…holds 10 statues…St. Agnes, St. Lucy, St. Catherine, St Margaret Mary, St. Teresa, St. Elizabeth, St. Ann, St. Aloysius, St. Thomas Aquinas and St. Vincent de Paul. These statues were blessed by Bishop Laval…January 1, 1926." (The Bayou Catholic, pg. 34)

Like Bernadette, Father Souby was a chronic sufferer of tuberculosis. During the early 1920's he was reassigned to a dryer climate in New Mexico but returned to Morgan City. (The Bayou Catholic, pg. 29) Father Souby continued his priestly work at Sacred Heart in Morgan City, LA until his death on October 14, 1938. He was laid to rest in the tomb he prepared.

OUR LADY OF GUADALUPE CHURCH; ST. JUDE INTERNATIONAL SHRINE, NEW ORLEANS, LA

The Oblates of Mary Immaculate were invited by the archbishop of New Orleans in 1918 to administer St. Louis Cathedral and the mortuary chapel. They accepted and upon coming, renamed the chapel Our Lady of Guadalupe. The chapel is co-located with The International Shrine of St. Jude. The shrine "honors Saint Jude the Apostle, known as the patron for impossible cases." (Shrine brochure, 2012) According to the New Orleans City Guide published in 1938, "To the right of the church entrance is the Shrine of Our Lady of Lourdes, a miniature copy of the grotto of Our Lady of Lourdes, at Lourdes, France." (p. 302) The official Shrine website history link confirms the grotto was built by Father Bornes, OMI in 1924. (Website, 2012

Pilgrims visiting this grotto will find evidence of gratitude in the form of plaques and other ex votos permanently attached to the grotto walls.

L'EVECHE – ST. JOHN THE EVANGELIST CATHEDRAL, LAFAYETTE, LOUISIANA

An historical brochure about the cathedral confirms that the Diocese of Lafayette was erected in 1918 and the first bishop was Bishop Jules Jeanmard. Next door to the cathedral in Lafayette, a replica shrine of the Lourdes grotto was erected in the yard at L'eveche, which is French for bishop's residence in 1924. The brochure states this shrine "…reflects Bishop Jeanmard's devotion to the Blessed Virgin."

ST. BRIDGET CHURCH, LAWTELL, LOUISIANA

Next to St. Bridget's Church in Lawtell, is a grotto to Our Lady of Lourdes which was originally erected in 1927 by Father Maurice G. Veekmans according to a plaque mounted on the grotto. This grotto was then restored in 1998 by Father Daniel R. Picard in memory to Mr. and Mrs. Joseph Evans Savoy Sr.

THE GROTTO AT GRAND COTEAU, LOUISIANA

Grand Coteau is an historic city especially well known for the presence of The Jesuit Spirituality Center at St. Charles College and the beautiful St. Charles Borromeo Church located there. According to the parish website:

> "St. Charles Parish was established in 1819. It is the third oldest parish in the Diocese of Lafayette, pre-dated only by the church in St. Martinville and St. Landry of Opelousas." … On March 19, 1879, the cornerstone of the new church building was put into position and blessed."[19]

The grotto is among the largest I have seen. It is solidly constructed having been built by seminarians who gave up recreation time to build the grotto.

One should no longer be surprised to find connections between Archbishop Perche' and yet another grotto. Since the time Archbishop Perche' consecrated the Archdiocese, his love and devotion to Our Lady of Lourdes and the spreading of the message of Lourdes must have been forever on his mind and his lips. Research confirms that the archbishop was in Grand Coteau, although admittedly before the grotto was built.

[19] Website. (2012) St. Charles Borromeo Church. Retrieved May 5, 2012 from http://www.st-charles-borromeo.org/.

"...A consolation of 1878 was the two-month stay of Archbishop Napoleon Joseph Perche' at Coteau, which he referred to as "the most precious and most serene days of my life." (p.94)[20]

Trent Angers is the author who provides us with confirmation of when the grotto was constructed. The grotto is immense. Covered in vines and set in a clear opening between the church and the college, it is accessible also from the retreat center and is just a short walk from an historic cemetery.

"...The following year, 1928, was highlighted by the building of a grotto honoring Our Lady of Lourdes, just behind the college." (Angers, p. 84)[21]

Bonnie T. Barry offers more details about this grotto in her 1987 book entitled For The Greater Honor And Glory of God – *St. Charles Borromeo Catholic Church, Grand Coteau, LA.* In the chapter titled The Grotto is Built, Bonnie's research reveals:

Early Picture of Grotto – Photo courtesy of Archives of the New Orleans Province, Society of Jesus, Loyola University Monroe Library

"In 1926, a beautiful addition was made to the grounds behind the rectory. On a tract of land belonging to the St. Charles College, a replica of the original Grotto of Our Lady of Lourdes in France was constructed by the Jesuit Scholastics, in honor of the Blessed Mother...

[20] Dawes, D. and Nolan, C. (2004) Religious Pioneers Building the Faith in the Archdiocese of New Orleans.
[21] Angers, T. (2005) Grand Coteau The Holy Land of South Louisiana.

The Grotto project began on May 20, 1926, with the blessing of the ground by Father E. J. Bernard, S.J. and was completed by February 11, 1928, the Feast of Our Lady of Lourdes. According to one of the builders of the Grotto, Father Joseph Malloy, S.J., a foundation was laid and the brick column which supports the statue of the Blessed Mother was erected. Next, a network of gas pipes, screwed together and twisted at various angles to form a mountain-looking formation, was added and overlaid with sturdy wire. Finally, the whole structure was covered with heavy consistency cement, and the statues of the Blessed Mother and Bernadette were put into their proper places. These statues had originally been at St. Stanislaus College in Macon, Georgia; however, when that school was gutted by fired, the statues were transferred to the St. Charles College. Hence, their appearance on the shrine in Grand Coteau. In 1930,

a cement altar replaced the original wooden one inside the shrine, and an exquisite white

Cararra marble panel depicting the Last Supper was positioned on the front of the altar. It was a donation of J. Martial Lapeyre.

For many years, May devotions were held on a regular basis at the Grotto by the Jesuits. Today, re remains, a favorite spot of visitors, retreatants, and parishioners for prayer and meditation." (pg. 40)[22]

An interesting observation is made about the place on which Bernadette is situated. A close inspection of the concrete slab reveals it is actually a tombstone for Caliste Marks. This man was born May 22, 1835 and died October 16, 1860. It is an unknown mystery as to why this tombstone would be the base for the statue of St. Bernadette.

ST. LEO THE GREAT, NEW ORLEANS, LOUISIANA

St. Leo the Great Parish was first established in 1920 by Father Vincent Prats. For many years, he said Mass in a rail car. Despite this meager beginning, Father Prats eventually bought some property and built a temporary church. In 1925 he erected a school and finally on Sunday, October 6, 1930 "at the height of the Depression, the Church of St. Leo the Great was dedicated." (Gurtner, p. 84) In a book written by Roger

[22] Barry, Bonnie T. (1987) For the Greater Honor and Glory of God. Andrepont Printing Company, Inc., Opelousas, LA

Baudier, K.S.G. entitled St. Leo the Great Parish – A History of the Parish, compiled for the Silver Jubilee in 1945, we find an approximate date as to when the grotto was added.

"Father Prats had planned a shrine in honor of Our Lady of Lourdes, and when the church was built, the foundation for the shrine was laid, but lack of funds prevented its completion. When the church was finished, a generous Catholic woman, devoted to Our Lady of Lourdes, noted the unfinished grotto, and gave Father Prats a check for $1,000 to enable him to complete the project, which was undertaken at once." (Baudier, p. 23)

When the grotto to Our Lady of Lourdes was finished is not clear, but since the church was completed and dedicated in 1930 and the grotto was started promptly thereafter, we can assume it was probably completed shortly after in 1930 or 1931.

A visit to this church reveals this beautiful grotto that once had running water. Bernadette is simple yet beautiful and holds a candle in her left hand.

MT. CARMEL ACADEMY, NEW ORLEANS, LOUISIANA

The Mt. Carmel website, www.mcacubs.com posts an article written by Greyson Bordelon, Class of 2012, entitled *Campus ministry holds rosary in the grotto* posted October 11, 2011. Mt. Carmel has also hosted a Virtual Lourdes Experience offered by Marlene Watkins, foundress of the North American Lourdes Volunteers. During that experience, all of the students processed to the lovely grotto while saying the rosary. There is a plaque on this grotto which indicates it was erected "In loving memory of our Father & Mother Mr. & Mrs. Samuel T. Gately, 1930". (Gregoire, 2009)

HOLY ANGELS ACADEMY, NEW ORLEANS, LOUISIANA

The Sunday, February 4, 1934 edition of The Times Picayune States issued a report about the recent construction of a grotto to Our Lady of Lourdes at Holy Angels Academy. The article was titled *Archbishop Shaw Will Bless Grotto* and read as follows:

> "Archbishop John W. Shaw will bless a grotto of Our Lady of Lourdes recently erected on the campus of the Holy Angels academy, 3500 St. Claude Avenue, at 3:30pm February 11, official of the academy announced Saturday. The public is invited to the ceremony." (p. 10)

This grotto was built 76 years after the apparitions and blessed on the anniversary of the first apparition. Visitors to the campus will immediately notice the large grotto prominently located on the campus grounds. The grotto is a genuine replica of the grotto in France with

statues of Bernadette and Our Lady. A small altar is located to the left of the apparition scene which is noticeably different from the Grotto of Massabielle but the presence of a place to enter with the altar inside reminds one of the original grotto.

The statue of Bernadette is one that is unique among those discovered throughout the research of this topic. In this depiction of Bernadette, there is a candle held out in her right hand with the flame very close to the fingers and hand holding it. Her left hand is raised and at the time I took this picture, flowers had been placed in that hand.

Bernadette carried candles to the grotto beginning with the third apparition. During the seventeenth apparition, a doctor (Dr. Douzous) was there to witness the flames touching her hands but without any affect upon inspection. In the chapter entitled *A Flame Between Two Hands – Seventeeth Apparition, April 7, 1858*, The Wonders of Lourdes records the event as follows:

"...The young seer, as usual, had brought to the grotto a thick holy candle that she had planted in ground. To keep the wind from blowing it out, she took the slender flame between her hands. Immersed in her contemplation, she did not notice that the fire was licking at her palms. "Do something! The girl is going to get burned!" a witness implored. With an imperious gesture, the doctor quieted the murmurs and kept the well-intentioned from intervening. Bernadette did not seem to suffer. The physician's heart beat wildly. Perhaps he had finally witnessed his supernatural phenomenon. When young Bernadette returned to consciousness, the doctor dashed ahead, took her two hands, and attentively scanned their palms. There was nothing. These little hands did not bear the slightest trace of a burn..." (pgs. 76-77)

There is no way to know what the artist who made this interpretation of Bernadette with this small candle was trying to portray. But, if he was trying to indicate the flame may have touched only her right hand, this version would be inconsistent with the account in the 150th Anniversary Edition published by Magnificat in 2008.

ST. ANN SHRINE, NEW ORLEANS, LOUISIANA

In Roger Baudier's 1939 book, The Catholic Church in Louisiana, he tells us of another Grotto of Lourdes that was erected at St. Ann Shrine.

> "...In 1926, the Holy See raised the Confraternity of St. Ann to the dignity of an Archconfraternity, as the center for affiliated confraternities of the United States. In 1927, plans were made for the erection of a great Basilica of St. Ann,...the rest of the square was bought...a magazine, St. Ann's Herald – was founded...In 1936, a replica of the Grotto of Lourdes was built by Father Badeaux on the ground adjoining the rectory, as a center for devotion to St. Ann and to the Blessed Mother." (Baudier, p. 562)

This application of the grotto at the National Shrine of St. Ann was also somewhat unique when compared with other stated reasons for erecting a grotto. This grotto includes a replica of Lourdes but it includes others as well.

While the grotto is authentic with Our Lady in the niche to the right above the grotto opening, and the grotto itself open and able to be entered with an altar; we do not see Our Lord in the opening. Instead, we find St. Ann and the child Mary. There is no statue of Bernadette and the Crucifix stands above the grotto. Although the grotto appears with the texture of a rocky cave, the color of this grotto today does not evoke the sense of the color of stone or rock as found at the grotto of Massabielle. At one time, this grotto was surrounded with lush green trees and shrubs creating an atmosphere of reverence and serenity.

CENTER OF JESUS THE LORD, THE FORMER MONASTERY FOR THE DISCALCED ORDER OF CARMELITES FROM 1877 – 1971 – NEW ORLEANS, LOUISIANA

A visit to the soon-to-be relocated Center of Jesus the Lord reveals another attractive monument to Our Lady of Lourdes. The story behind this monument eluded this researcher. A sign on the front of it simply reads "Donated in Memory of Louis and Mary L. Caillouet."

ROSARYVILLE SPIRIT LIFE CENTER, PONCHATOULA, LOUISIANA

In 1989, Rosaryville issued "Rosaryville – God's Kaleidescope", "...a publication created for the fiftieth anniversary of Rosaryville." This history reveals that "...Sister Mary Catherine Delaney, O.P., the Superior General of the Dominican Sisters..." purchased the property in 1939 for $6,000 from the Spanish Fathers. This publication documents in stories and pictures the many events that occurred among the Sisters, Friars, students, retreatants and visitors. It is an interesting pictoral history that includes many photos of the replica of the Lourdes grotto on the property.

Upon acquiring the property, the sisters wasted no time in demonstrating their devotion to Our Lady of Lourdes. In a short informal history brochure, the grotto story is revealed. The grotto replica was built in 1940 using the remaining stones of Founders Hall. The statue of the Blessed Virgin was donated by Mr. Joseph Elmer and the statue of Bernadette was donated by Mr. W. Delaney. The replica was the project of Sister Mary Ignatius Maurin who was an arthritic invalid. She painted cards and made other items to help pay for the cost of the replica. The Kaleidescope book contains many photographs which include the replica over the years. On the grounds in front of this replica, many experienced faith, recreation, prayer and relaxation over the past 72 years.

ST. PETER'S COLLEGE, NEW IBERIA, LOUISIANA

According to their official website, The City of New Iberia "...is proud to share its rich history and culture with you. Here in the heart of Cajun country, French, Spanish, Native American and African American cultures have blended together to create something unlike anything found anywhere else..."(Website, 2012) Our Lady of Lourdes was made a part of this Cajun culture with a replica of the Grotto of Lourdes built in the Historic District of New Iberia. The city website provides the following historical account of the grotto:

"This replica of the Grotto of Lourdes was erected in 1941 on what was the campus of St. Peter's College, a boy's school operated by the DeLaSalle Christian Brother. The grotto is a solid construction of cement and Louisiana marble and resembles the Grotto of Our

Lady of Lourdes. It contains a statue of Our Lady of Lourdes and Bernadette...was

originally erected in grateful memory of the pioneer families of New Iberia and in gratitude to God for His abundant blessing on the Teche country. It was rededicated in 1967 by a grateful community to the Veterans of Foreign Wars from New Iberia, who died in the service of their country...The grotto is shaded by a live oak tree estimated to be over 150 years old." (Website, 2012)

NOTRE DAME SEMINARY, NEW ORLEANS, LOUISIANA

Another beautiful grotto was constructed on the serene grounds of Notre Dame Seminary on Carrollton Avenue in New Orleans. The Times-Picayune reported the events on May 14, 1943 under the article title *Lourdes Grotto Replica Erected – Shrine at Notre Dame Seminary Dedicated.* The article captured the story like this:

> "As kneeling seminarians sang "Immaculate Mother" a replica of the Grotto of Lourdes which they had built of discarded concrete and pieces of stone was dedicated to the Virgin Mary Thursday afternoon at Notre Dame Seminary by Archbishop Joseph Francis Rummel.
>
> Last December 8, feast of the Immaculate Conception, a tube containing a statement of establishment written by the seminarians was sealed in the half-completed grotto. With faculty members and friends gathered at the shrine for the dedication. Seminarians heard the Very Reverend Michal J. Larkin, S.M. rector of the seminary read a copy of the document.
>
> "With the co-operation of generous benefactors, we students of Notre Dame Seminary, under guidance of our rector and the supervision of the Rev. Robert Ripp, S.M., have gladly sacrificed our recreations to build with our own hands this Grotto of Lourdes, for

the greater honor and glory of God and as a pledge of our love and devotion to our Immaculate Queen and Mother." It said in part.

Courage to Be Renewed

"We don't expect miracles at our modest replica of the Grotto in Lourdes, which we built because we wanted our Blessed Mother a little nearer to us, but who knows. It is certain that here many battles will be won: many will leave this shrine with renewed courage." Presenting the shrine in the name of the faculty and students of Notre Dame to the archdiocese of New Orleans, the rector thanked Archbishop Rummel for his gracious approval of the plan and his financial assistance: J. H. Kessels, who designed the structure; Lionel Favret who supervised construction; and the Right Reverend August J. Bruening pastor of Our Lady of Good Counsel church who contributed the statue of the Blessed Virgin which stands in a high niche of the Grotto. He asked that a prayer be said for the Rev. Godfrey Frohn, late pastor of St. Henry's church, who gave $500 shortly before his death to help build the shrine.

Archbishop Speaks

In accepting the shrine and dedicating it to Our Lady of Lourdes, Archbishop Rummel expressed pleasure in the fact that the shrine stood ready for dedication after more than a year of labor at the exact time when the archdiocese is celebrating its 150th anniversary; and in the month set aside for paying tribute to the Virgin Mary. "I dare say the miracles performed at this shrine will be more spiritual and moral than physical." The archbishop said. "I know that students, faculty and their friends will never come to this sacred spot without finding comfort and consolation."

Acting as deacon to the archbishop was Father Ripp, faculty member of Notre Dame and as sub-deacon, Marcel Fourcade, seminarian. The Rev. Robert Stahl, S.M. led the singing of the hymns by the seminarians during the ceremonies." (Times-Picayune, p. 21)

History of the Grotto at Notre Dame Seminary.

The following passages are from Mark S. Raphael's History of Notre Dame Seminary. New Orleans, LA: Notre Dame Seminary, 1997.

"...World War II Years September 1, 1939-October 25, 1945 Seminary life at Notre Dame remained largely unaffected by the beginning of what would become known as World War II. In fact, when the Most Reverend James Walsh, Superior General of the Maryknoll Foreign Missionaries visited Notre Dame on April 14, 1940, he told the seminarians that he felt so confident that missionaries would be respected by the Imperial Japanese Army that he ordered the 550 Maryknoll missionaries in the Pacific to remain at their posts. The ordinations took place as usual in May of 1940, on Tuesday, February 13, 1940, Fr. O'Meara gave an illustrated lecture on Lourdes, and the seminarians were allowed to attend the Jesuit-Behrman football game..."

(Raphael, p. 86)

"Determined to continue growth of the seminary in the wake of the Eucharistic Congress, the seminarians undertook a project that was to occupy them for the next three years, the construction of a grotto to the Blessed Mother. The idea was inspired by O'Meara's illustrated lectures on Lourdes, which he shared with the seminarians on Tuesday, February 13, 1940. Fr. Larkin presided at the ground breaking ceremonies on February 19, 1941. The design was drawn up by Jack Kessels and the materials were donated by Lionel Favret, the team who would later construct St. Joseph Hall, but as much work as possible was performed by the seminarians under the direction of Rev. Robert Ripp, the school bursar. The grotto was intended to be a smaller replica of the grotto at Massabielle, Lourdes, where the Blessed Mother appeared to Bernadette Soubirous in 1858. It took far longer to construct than anyone anticipated at the outset, but it would be completed in May of 1943, and remains virtually unchanged to this day."

(Raphael, pgs. 86-87)

"The seminary did enjoy a brief moment of forgetfulness from the war on Thursday May 13, 1943, when the newly completed grotto was dedicated to Rummel. The completion of the grotto happened to coincided with the Sesquicentennial of the Archdiocese of New Orleans, so Fr. Larkin made a virtue out of coincidence by making the grotto the gift of the seminary to the Archdiocese for the occasion. The ground breaking, it will be recalled, had taken place on February 19, 1941. The whole structure, an attempt at a smaller version of the famous Lourdes Grotto, contained 33.5 cubic yards of concrete, 234 sacks of mason's mix, 71 sacks of cement, 3 sacks of lime, and the foundation slab contained 16 cubic yards of concrete. Rev. Robert Ripp, the faculty member who had most closely supervised the student labor on the project, was said to have swelled with pride for weeks after the dedication ceremonies.

The grotto project was a fitting completion to the nine year tenure of Fr. Larkin, who learned at the end of May, 1943, that he was to be made pastor of St. Michael in Wheeling, West Virginia, and that he was to be replaced as rector of Notre Dame by Rev. Daniel O'Meara." (Raphael, p. 95)

During a visit by Pere' Regis-Marie de la Teyssonniere to New Orleans for a meeting of the North American Lourdes Volunteers, it was arranged by Pere' Regis-Marie to donate to the Notre Dame Seminary a rock which had been taken from the Grotto of Lourdes in France. This rock was presented to the Rector, Father Jose' Lavasita after the seminarians participated in a virtual Lourdes Experience and then participated in a rosary procession from the seminary to the grotto. At that time, each was afforded the opportunity to venerate a relic of St. Bernadette as well.

ST. PHILOMENA CHURCH, LABADIEVILLE, LOUISIANA

Revered Jules Berthault pastor of St. Philomena Church "…had a special devotion to the Blessed Virgin under the title of Our Lady of Lourdes…"[23] A history of that parish was written in a parish book and supplied to this writer by photocopy. In have inserted the pictures supplied to me by the parish secretary, Carolyn. The history of this grotto reads as follows:

The Grotto of Our Lady of Lourdes, a replica of the one in Lourdes, France. It was built under the direction of Father Jules Berthault, pastor, who gathered the rocks for it and carried them in his car. Rosary devotions, May crownings, and processions carried on for many years were external manifestations of a deep and cherished friendship which the parishioners felt for Mary.

Photo of Parish Article about Grotto

> "…Father Berthault, a native of France, had seen and admired the many shrines and grottoes there, and had the desire to erect one…at St. Philomena Convent. The large structure was finally built in 1949…and rocks used were parts of an old concrete highway. A large statue of the Blessed Virgin Mary was situated as a shrine in the rocks while a smaller statue of St. Bernadette was arranged in the front of the grotto. Every morning during the month of May, Fr. Bertault would assemble the children in front of the grotto for devotions, and at some given times, the adults would gather ther the recitation of the rosary." (p.6)[24]

[23] The Times Picayune. (1975) p. 18. Fr. Berthault Rites Monday
[24] St. Philomena Parish History.

Photo of Lourdes Replica 2012

A picture supplied by the parish secretary shown here, states that the pastor "gathered the rocks for it and carried them in his car."

Today, a replica of the grotto of

Lourdes still stands in this parish, but it is not the original grotto. Another grotto was built in 1996 and is similar in appearance to the original.

SACRED HEART ORPHANAGE – CABRINI HIGH SCHOOL, NEW ORLEANS, LOUISIANA

At 3400 Esplanade Avenue, passersby can spot a Lourdes monument prominently featured on the lawn behind Cabrini High School and near Holy Rosary Church. This monument was erected in 1951 and like many of the Lourdes replicas we have in New Orleans, gratitude is the basis for this monument.

On June 23, 1951, The Times Picayune reported the story under the title *Dedication of Grotto Set Today on Orphanage Lawn – Bishop Caillouet to Bless the Structure*. This monument has something special contained within.

"A new grotto on the front lawn of the Sacred Heart orphanage...will be dedicated to the Immaculate Conception...following Benediction of the Most Blessed Sacrament...The

Most Rev. L. Abel Caillouiet, auxiliary bishop of New Orleans and pastor of Holy Rosary church…The orphanage is conducted by the Missionary Sisters of the Sacred Heart, founded by St. Frances Xavier Cabrini.

Photo by The Times-Picayune.
GRANITE IS USED FOR GROTTO
Stone from Lourdes, France, is in niche.

Times Picayune Photo of Replica in 1951

The grotto was built at a cost of $1,600, a gift of Mr. and Mrs. Joseph De Luca, who made a promise to build a grotto in honor of the Immaculate Conception if their son returned safely from World War II.

The grotto is built of granite donated by the Wholesale Granite Company of New Orleans, Joseph Ridolfo, New Orleans' contractor and two helpers did the work, which was started last fall.

A feature of the grotto is a stone from Lourdes, France, which is placed under the waterfall in the niche." (Times-Picayune, p. 8)

The Bernadette statue in this structure is like

others we see in the area - her right hand clasping a rosary to her body while her left hand is extended. I have found no accounts in which Bernadette actually brought flowers to the grotto, instead, she carried candles. Below is a photograph taken in 2012 of the structure as it appears now.

Present day photo of replica near Cabrini High School and Holy Rosary Church

HOLY CROSS HIGH SCHOOL - GROTTO BLESSED - NEW ORLEANS, LOUISIANA

The Saturday, September 10, 1955 edition of The Times Picayune alerted readers to the dedication of the new Holy Cross High School and blessing of the Lourdes grotto which had been built there. This edition provided some anticipatory details about the some of the unique aspects of the grotto:

Church Dignitaries Stand Near New Grotto

— Photo by The Times Picayune

AMONG THOSE ATTENDING the blessing and dedication of the new Holy Cross High school building Sunday were (from left) Brother Reinald Duran, headmaster; the Very Rev. W. Patrick Donnelly, president, Loyola university; the Most Rev. Joseph F. Rummel, archbishop of New Orleans; the Rev. Walter J. Higgins, pastor, Sacred Heart of Jesus church; Brother Ephrem O'Dwyer, provincial, Brothers of the Holy Cross; the Rt. Rev. Msgr. Henry C. Bezou, archdiocesan superintendent of schools.

Times Picayune Photo of 1955 Grotto at Holy Cross High School

"...Blessing of Grotto. Also included in the ceremonies will be the blessing of the Lourdes Grotto, recently completed on the campus quadrangle...The Lourdes Grotto, one of the largest in the nation, was begun in October, 1954, as a Marian Year project and is a copy of the one at Massabielle in Lourdes, France. It is 16 ½ feet high, 18 feet deep and 60 feet wide. The five-foot statue of St. Bernadette in the kneeling position was sculptured in Italy from Carrara marble...The grotto will be illuminated at night by lights on the statue, within the cave, and on the surrounding grounds by wrought iron lamps. Before the grotto is an "M" shaped walk of broken marble set in red cement. Future Marian processions and devotions on the campus will wind their way to the Lourdes Grotto..." (p. 8)

The dedication and blessings occurred on Sunday, September 11, 1955 and were reported in The Times Picayune on September 12th.

"...In addition the school's new Lourdes grotto was blessed by the archbishop...The blessing was followed by dedication ceremonies at the grotto...Archbishop Rummel told those gathered before the grotto that the dedication of the new school exemplified...great strides Catholic education in America had made..." (p. 12)

A visit to the old Holy Cross High School campus today reveals that the grotto is no longer there.

OUR LADY OF LOURDES CHURCH, ERATH, LOUISIANA

In October of 1955, another grotto to Our Lady of Lourdes was erected at the church parish bearing the same name. The plaque affixed to the groto reads:

"A NOTRE BIEN-AIME' PASTEUR PERE JUSTIN MIRATE SES PAROISSIENS LE 9TH OCTOBRE, 1955"

POOR CLARE MONASTERY, NEW ORLEANS, LOUISIANA

A visit to the Poor Clare Monastery at Henry Clay and Magazine Street in New Orleans reveals that they have a grotto to Our Lady of Lourdes also. In 1877, Archbishop Perche' invited the Poor Clares into his diocese when many dioceses were disinterested in contemplative orders favoring instead those who could care and educate the immigrant populations. (Dawes, Nolan pgs. 300 – 301)

As with almost every grotto discovered in this research, there is a story and again we should not be surprised to learn that Perche's influence was involved at some point. This story however, predates this grotto. In the book entitled Religious Pioneers – Building the Faith in the Archdiocese of New Orleans, Dorothy Dawes and Charles Nolan present the story of Sister Marie Melicere Perret (1888 – 1982) which was written by Sister Rita Marie Hickey, OSC.

For much of her life, Marie was known as Sister Mary Magdalen of the Sacred Heart of Jesus. Only after the second Vatican Council did she return to using her baptismal name, Marie Melicere Perret. At an advanced age, she told a story about her childhood. She was one of ten children; her father was the manager of a plantation in Edgard, LA. He died and shortly after her youngest brother also died. Marie also became sick soon after these untimely deaths. She refused to eat and her mother became more worried. Marie's mother had told her that Our Lady of Lourdes saved her life. Marie's uncle had recently been to Lourdes and Marie revealed this story:

> "...When Melicere became ill, her uncle had just returned from the famous French shrine. He brought her mother a bottle of Lourdes water and promised Sophie that if she put a drop on Melicere's tongue every day for nine days, she would be cured and returned to health. On the ninth day, Marie Melicere stole her mother's cabbage. She always felt very special when her mother told this story, and she never forgot it..." (Dawes, Nolan pg. 300)

It seems that whenever cabbage was served to eat at the convent, this story was told to great interest and amusement.

The monastery prioress, Sister Charlene Toups believes this grotto was built in the mid 1950's. Today, the grotto is beautifully groomed and in a delightfully serene garden. Every grotto has something unique about it and this one does not disappoint. In the pedastal of the statue of Our Lady of Lourdes is a bottle of Lourdes water cemented into the base.

ANGOLA PRISON, ANGOLA, LOUISIANA – LOURDES GROTTO ERECTED

Among the most interesting stories found in this research is that of the Lourdes grotto built by prisoners at Angola. The Times Picayune of Wednesday, February 12, 1958 ran a story called *Angola Grottos Blessing Held – Archbishop Rummel at Dedication.* On February 11, 1958, the 100th anniversary of the first apparitions in Lourdes, "A grotto, built by inmates of the state penitentiary at Angola, was dedicated to Our Lady of Lourdes and was blessed by Archbishop Joseph Francis Rummel here Tuesday." (p. 20)

> "The shrine, built with contributions from inmates...was begun several years ago...Inmates worked on the project during their free time...The Rev James Fennigan, chaplain at the time the grotto was begun, said the inspiration for the shrine came from a man "who was once a bad, bad boy..." The Archbishop "...told the...inmates, visiting clergy, officials...that "the grotto of Lourdes at Angola will serve as an inspiration for years to come to all who pass this way...the sacrifice of the men to build the shrine "is a manifestation of unanimity of purpose and harmony of concentration on one great worthwhile ideal." (p. 20)

Archbishop Joseph Francis Rummel – Visited Lourdes

Only a few years before formally blessing the two grottos mentioned above, Archbishop Rummel visited Lourdes, France and the grotto of Our Lady of Lourdes in 1949. The Times Picayune carried a brief mention of the visit while he was en route to Rome.

Archbishop Rummel Visits France's Grotto of Lourdes

ST. LEO THE GREAT CHURCH, LEONVILLE, LOUISIANA

As a result of the devotion Howard Champagne and his family have to the Blessed Virgin, Louisiana is blessed to have a grotto shrine built in the early years of the 21st century. In an article written by Trevis R. Badeaux entitled *Built as a blessing Leonville man builds grotto to honor the Blessed Mother and his late wife of 46 years* in the Sunday Advertiser on August 7, 2007 the story of this magnificent tribute was shared. This writer had the privilege to interview Mr. Champagne who kindly sent me brochures, the newspaper article and photographs to include in this book. Mrs. Sarah Champagne passed away on December 14, 2003 from ALS; she and Mr. Howard were married 46 years and had nine children. Mr. Howard said they prayed the family rosary every night since 1964. He attributes many graces and blessings to the Blessed Mother and the practice of praying the nightly family rosary. Mr. Champagne constructed and dedicated this grotto in memory of his wife. This grotto was completed and blessed on Saturday, December 1, 2007 just months before the 150th anniversary of the apparitions in Lourdes. Present at the dedication was Mr. Champagne's son, Father Michael Champagne.

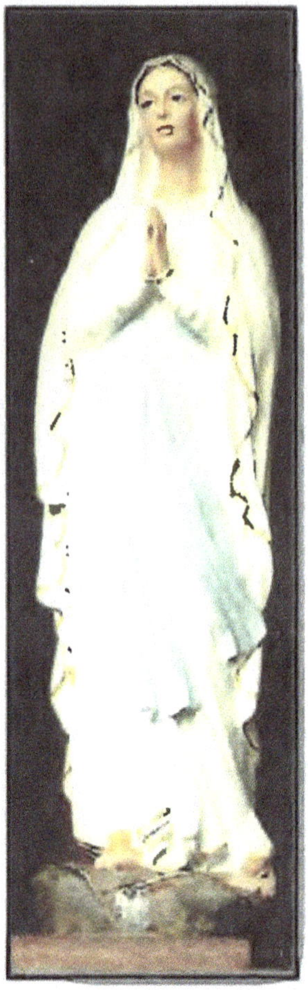

The shrine has one of the most beautiful statues of Our Lady of Lourdes. Anyone who visits this shrine would be pleased with the lovely expression on her face. This grotto is preceded by a walkway that is lined with stations depicting the mysteries of the rosary. The altar inside this grotto is a place from which the Mass has been offered.

The brochure, titled *A Labor of Love*, describing this shrine can be obtained through St. Leo the Great Church in Leonville, LA. This brochure contains a photo of many pilgrims visiting the shrine and praying to Our Lady in this serene grotto. Mr. Champagne is quoted in the article by Badeaux as saying "...This is a dream I had for a long time...I get no credit for this. If we can just bring a few souls to Jesus, every penny of it is well spent." (Badeaux) The brochure also provides readers with a guide for praying the rosary.

As Pere' Regis-Marie so aptly stated in the foreword of this book, "...It is the story of a meeting with Our Lady of Lourdes. It is the story of a meeting which changes the life of someone, because this meeting opens to others through the witness and charity rooted in a simple prayer. It is a meeting which contains a treasure, but this treasure is only accessible when shared." Mr. Champagne has shared his faith, meeting and story with many providing them with the opportunity to change lives and experience the charity Jesus has to offer through his Mother.

Statues and Stained Glass

For some churches, the Lourdes apparitions were and still are remembered not by a grotto, monument or shrine, but simply by beautiful statues or stained glass windows. These statues are generally placed in a prominent space on church properties. As with other replicas, many have stories and offer some insight into the devotion to Our Lady of Lourdes or the desire to have a given replica made part of a parish church, garden or altar.

ST. ALPHONSUS CHURCH, NEW ORLEANS, LOUISIANA

A nomination form was submitted by St. Alphonsus Church located at 2045 Constance Street, New Orleans to have this church placed on the register of National Historic places and reveals the church is now referred to as the St. Alphonsus Art and Cultural Center. The church was constructed between 1855 and 1857. On page 12 of the nomination form details about a stained glass window read as follows:

> "...The stained glass windows at St. Alphonsus Church have always been considered to be one of its most important artistic treasures. The first of these to be placed in the church were the two round-headed ones in the upper wall of the apse, flanking the high alter. *The Annals* for February 26, 1889, record their installation:
>
>> Today the scaffolding-needed for the purpose of putting up two stained-glass windows in the sanctuary-was taken away. The pictures give universal satisfaction. Messrs. Benzingers had them made at Munich, Bavaria. One

> window represents the Sacred Heart of Our Lord, the other our Lady of Lourdes. Each costs $200. Some people say that the pictures are too small-others would wish the borders to be a little darker. As soon as the parties who subscribed for the memorial windows in the body of the Church will have paid up-then only will the stained-glass memorial windows be ordered.

Apparently the subscribers for the memorial windows did pay promptly, for the windows for the body of the church were ordered and arrived on October 30, 1890...The *Annals* record that by December 1890, "...the beautiful windows of St. Alphonsus are now permanently fixed." (NHL nomination form pg. 12)

During a visit to this beautiful church, it was learned that a Lourdes Grotto had been in place in a side garden of the church for years. Confirmation comes from Anne Rice in her book entitled *Called Out of Darkness – a spiritual confession*. In this part of her book, Ms. Rice was telling a story about a friend named Kitty.

> "...Kitty had a great glowing generosity of spirit very like her mother, and she remains in this memory of mine nestled among the flowers and near to the Grotto of the Virgin, a large stone edifice, in which the Blessed Mother stood with arms out, appearing to the kneeling figure of St. Bernadette. No Catholic school existed in those days that didn't have a grotto, with the Virgin and St. Bernadette. We all knew the Virgin had appeared to St. Bernadette in Lourdes, France, and that there was a great miraculous shrine there where people were constantly healed by the powerful waters that had sprung from the earth at the command of the Virgin to Bernadette..." (Rice, pg. 54)

Ms. Rice certainly relates the truth about the widespread knowledge "all" had regarding Lourdes, the Blessed Virgin and the miraculous apparitions to Bernadette in Lourdes. In knowing of these events and the subsequent miracles, the people of New Orleans embraced devotion to Our Lady of Lourdes, the messages of Lourdes and for decades did a marvelous job in handing down to generations of children the meaning and importance of these events.

ST. PATRICK'S CHURCH, NEW ORLEANS, LOUISIANA

Thirty years after Perche' consecrated the Archdiocese to the Sacred Heart of Jesus and Our Lady of Lourdes, in 1904, which was also the golden anniversary of the declaration of the dogma of The Immaculate Conception, two statues were donated to St. Patrick's Church on Camp Street. The Times Picayune article referred to the statues as "Marble Masterpieces of Our Lady of Lourdes and the Sacred Heart…" The article recorded an "…interesting and impressive ceremony…" in which the church "…was filled to its utmost limit by a very large concourse of people witnessing the solemn benediction, dedication and acceptance of two marble statues…"

STATUE OF THE SACRED HEART. OUR LADY OF LOURDES.

Times Picayune Photos of Statues in 1904

Could it be that the people who donated the two statues were aware of these consecrations and the related Arch confraternities? Is it possible that in 1904 both consecrations were alive and well and being faithfully carried on by Catholics of that era? Once the statue of the Sacred Heart had been blessed and dedicated, "...the reverend fathers next crossed over to the other side of the sanctuary rail and halted in front of the statue of Our Lady of Lourdes...which occupies a position to the left, or on the epistle side of the altar. This statue was donated...by Mr. and Mrs. Charles Schutten in thanksgiving for spiritual favors conferred upon them by God...then the solemn ceremony of blessing and dedication took place, while the choir sang the Hymn to Our Lady of Lourdes..." (Times Picayune, 4/11/1904) This statue was carved by Italian artists in Cavara and was reported to be "...noble and majestic...clad in flowing draperies and in the exact pose she assumed when she appeared to Bernadette..." These statues can be found in St. Patrick's Cathedral today. They are still as beautiful as the day they were presented more than 100 years ago.

St. Patrick's Church has a beautiful stained glass window depicting the apparitions at Lourdes. With assistance from the Historic New Orleans Collection reference associate, information about this window is made available.

Photo of Stained Glass Window at St. Patrick's Church depicting apparition

"...Sam Wilson's 1992 booklet St. Patrick's Church of New Orleans indicates that, following the 1915 hurricane, the Emil Frei Art Glass Company of St. Louis Missouri created and installed much of the existing stained glass, including a memorial window Miss Celanire Correjolles donated in honor of her late mother, depicting the apparition at Lourdes." (Wilson)

OUR LADY OF GOOD COUNSEL CHURCH, NEW ORLEANS, LOUISIANA

In the September, 2001 Edition of Preservation in Print, Volume 28, Number 7, Patty Andrews provides some details about the stained glass window depicting an apparition at Lourdes in her article entitled *The Majesty of Stained Glass*:

"Our Lady of Good Counsel Catholic Church on Louisiana Avenue is distinguished...The structure dates to 1894; though the stained glass was added in the 1920's...The portrayal of St. Bernadette's vision of Our Lady of Lourdes is rarely seen in New Orleans." (Andrews, pg. 12)

Photo taken by and used courtesy of Brian Plauche

The Good Shepherd Parish Website adds an additional detail:

"..The present brick church was dedicated on January 21, 1894. Its stained glass windows were crafted by Emil Frei Company and tell the story of the relationship of Our Lady and Christ..." (2012)

There may be more stained glass windows in New Orleans depicting Our Lady of Lourdes or the apparitions at Lourdes but the three windows described are the only ones this researcher was able to locate.

OUR LADY OF PERPETUAL HELP, KENNER, LOUISIANA

Our Lady of Perpetual Help Church in Kenner, LA also has a lovely replica of the

Grotto of Lourdes in the courtyard outside the main entrance to the church.

ST. STEPHENS CHURCH, NEW ORLEANS, LOUISIANA

In the garden on the side of St. Stephens Church, two pretty statues can be found resting quietly in the shade. Although, Bernadette actually looked up to Our Lady from the lower left of the grotto toward the niche which was in the upper right, the positions do not matter when viewing the scene at this majestic church.

It may be that the statue of Bernadette actually came from another church. A small plaque attached to the base of this statue reads:

"In memory of Father Frohn Donated by the Hussey and Krinkie Family."

On Good Friday, a short history of the Church of St. Henry was being shared with visitors to that church. That history reveals that Father Godfred Frohn was the pastor at St. Henry from 1936 until his death in 1941. I think it is reasonable to conclude this statue of Bernadette was possibly at St. Henry's and subsequently moved to St. Stephens or it is the mate to the Our Lady of Lourdes statue that was donated by the pastor of Our Lady of Good

Engraved plaque on Bernadette Statue

Counsel to Notre Dame Seminary with a request to remember the recently deceased Father Frohn in prayer.

ST. EDWARD THE CONFESSOR, METAIRIE, LOUISIANA

Two authentic statues stand in a garden on the side of St. Edward the Confessor Church in Metairie, LA. This garden replica has a plaque in the front that says why the garden is there:

> "In gratitude to Our Lady of Lourdes, the students and graduates of St. Edward the Confessor School dedicate this garden to Sister Mary de Lourdes Charbonnet for her years of devoted service to our school and parish community."

A recently confirmed story reports that these statues were previously located at Annunciation Church in New Orleans and relocated to St. Edwards after that church was closed. We have previously mentioned the grotto in the side garden known as the Annunciation Garden earlier in this record.

PERSONAL SHRINES AND STATUES

The article from 1936 is entitled, *Shrines Placed in Many Gardens of New Orleans – Perhaps No U.S. City Has So Many Out-of-Door Sacred Statues* was written in The Times Picayune by Lady Banksia on October 11, 1936. In it, she describes the propensity of New Orleans residents to erect beautiful shrines and statues "…In the most unexpected places…partly concealed leafy recesses will discover an illuminated grotto, often with the figure of a white dove hovering above the image of Our Lady of Lourdes…" (pg. 2)

Times Picayune Photo of Grotto Garden

This article featured one particular garden and shrine that was erected by Mrs. Harry B. McClosky, 2916 St. Charles Avenue in New Orleans. In fact, a picture of that beautiful grotto with a statue of Our Lady of Lourdes was displayed in the paper that day. (pgs. 2 & 10)

While driving around the city exploring all the places where grottos exist, we happened past another statue of Our Lady of Lourdes. She was placed on a tall pedestal in the front of a vacant lot near the corner of St. Ferdinand and Royal streets in New Orleans. It is as if

Our Lady solemnly stands guard over this neighborhood patiently waiting for passersby to take notice.

CHAPTER 9

LOURDES CONSECRATION AND CONFRATERNITY EXPERIENCED THROUGH LECTURES, ASSOCIATIONS AND JUBILEE CELEBRATIONS

Experiencing Lourdes from Afar – Lectures, Photographs, Altars, Miniatures

The devotion to Our Lady of Lourdes was not confined to church altars or large grotto replicas. In the February 1, 1874 edition of The Morning Star and Catholic Messenger, we read of the Very Rev. J. M. Gartner visiting New Orleans with a large number of relics from Europe as well as "…a very excellent Panorama of the Grotto and Church of Our Immaculate Lady of Lourdes, both of the interiors and of the surrounding, including the pool outside of the railing of the Grotto, from which the miraculous water of Lourdes is bottled, that has wrought so many renowned cures in the United States…" (pg. 3)

The same paper carried an article on February 15, 1874 entitled A *Miniature Grotto of Lourdes*. An anonymous author reported "…that a pious lady of our city had caused to be brought from France a statue representing the blessed apparition seen at Lourdes…" (pg. 4) The author was pleased to find a "…small chapel fitted up for its reception..." The author felt as though he had "journeyed to France" upon entering the room of the private residence. He captures the beauty of the statue in his description but also more than that…"This statue, carved as it is by the hand of man, fashioned out of perishable materials, still carries the soul beyond this earth and speaks to it of eternal destinies…is at once a lesson and a prayer..It teaches us the ineffable mystery of the Incarnation…" (pg. 4)

It is learned from a November 22, 1909 article that Rev. F. C. McGarry, C.S.C. "…delivered an interesting lecture…entitled *"Lourdes and Its Wonders,"* in St. Vincent de Paul's School…" The account of the lecture reports that a large attended "...the beautiful discourse" and enjoyed "the illustrations." "The pictures included the town of Lourdes…the grotto showing the niche where the Blessed Virgin appeared." The article reported that Father McGarry told the crowd of the history of Bernadette, the apparitions and the subsequent miracles that occurred. He brought numerous pictures which "…showed the great devotion of the earnest pilgrims from far off lands, and the piety of natives of Lourdes alike, and the lecture and pictures were a beautiful and impressive sermon on Catholic devotion to the Mother of God." (Times Picayune, 11/22/1909)

A very small announcement appeared in The Times Picayune on May 22, 1910 telling its readers that a lecture on Lourdes would be given at the Annunciation Hall on Marais Street "…for the benefit of the fund for the rebuilding of the Holy Cross Convents, Lake Charles, LA…" Rev. McGarry also delivered this lecture.

The Times Picayune under date of June 17, 1924 reported a story entitled *"Church to Present Benefit Film Show…"* In the convent hall of St. Maurice's church a film called "The Mystery of Lourdes…a moving picture in six reels…" (pg. 9) was shown and sponsored by the Ushers' Society. The article reported that "…The claim is made that it is the only moving picture ever produced in the world famous village of Lourdes…" (Times Picayune, 6/17/1924, pg. 9)

In 1925 James Louis Small delivered a lecture on Lourdes at St. Ann Church on Ursuline Avenue. It was described in The Times Picayune on March 7, 1925 as a "…illustrated lecture on "Lourdes." Small was "widely known as a writer and lecturer and formerly secretary with the Knights of Columbus…" Those who attended must have been well pleased because there were "…more than sixty slides in the set shown…" Many of them were "…specially made for this talk, which is the result of the speaker's personal ten days' visit at the shrine." (pg. 21)

Courtesy of Times Picayune - Ad displaying the 3 piece set.

Many years later, in 1959, shortly after the 100th anniversary of the apparitions, Maison Blanche advertised a 3-pc set of the Lady of Lourdes Grotto which sold for $39.95. (Times Picayune, 4/29/1959, pg. 29)

Maud O'Bryan, Want Ad Reporter wrote a column in The Times Picayune on February 9, 1962 when she reported that a sound and color film of the Grotto of Lourdes was going to be presented by Father Anselmo Sanniola, American chaplain to the Grottos of Lourdes France. Father Sanniola was the guest of His Excellency Most Rev. L. A. Calliouet at the time. The film was to be shown at Holy Rosary auditorium on Esplanade Avenue. The admission to this event was free but "...good-will offerings are to be accepted toward the debt on new St. Pius X Basilica at Lourdes..." She went on to report "...Mrs. G. L. Pattison...Archdiocesan Council of Catholic Women, states that St. Pius X Basilica is the second-largest church in the world after St. Peter's of Rome. It is completely underground, can shelter more than 22,000 pilgrims in the event of inclement weather during huge processions. "The film about Lourdes is fascinating." Mrs. Pattison adds." (pg. 11)

Organizations

While uncovering the many details revealed in this research, numerous organizations which were founded in order to carry out good works in the name of Our Lady of Lourdes were discovered. Newspapers contained references to meeting dates, elected officers, various fund raisers that were being conducted and religious events that were celebrated. Unfortunately, this research was unsuccessful in finding the genesis of any of these organizations, their rules, founding documents or whatever became of them. This work would be incomplete, however if these organizations were not mentioned by name as it is likely that many were founded for the purpose of carrying forward the Arch Confraternity which had begun in 1874. The list is:

Association of Our Lady of Lourdes

Our Lady of Lourdes Sodality

Confraternity of Christian Doctrine of Our Lady of Lourdes

Third Order of Mary of Our Lady of Lourdes

Altar Society of Our Lady of Lourdes

Society of Our Lady of Lourdes

Our Lady of Lourdes Holy Name Society

Our Lady of Lourdes Circle

SILVER JUBILEE OF THE ASSOCIATION OF OUR LADY OF LOURDES

One article recognizing the 25th anniversary of the Association of Our Lady of Lourdes contains interesting details about the purpose and faithfulness of this organization and its members.

The Times Picayune reported on the silver jubilee of the Association of Our Lady of Lourdes in their August 13, 1900 edition. The lengthy article read in part:

> "...Association...kept its silver jubilee yesterday in a beautiful and appropriate manner. The association was organized August 8, 1875, by Rev. Father Borias, of the Sacred Heart church. Its objects were the spiritual and material assistance of the members, and especially their relief in time of sickness...
>
> Never once during all the years since organization has the association failed in its faithful and earnest work and pledges...The celebration took the form of an anniversary mass and

dinner. The mass was celebrated at 10 o'clock at the St. Louis cathedral, of which the society has been for the past quarter of a century one of the parish associations...

At 10 o'clock, as the cathedral bells chimed solemnly forth, the ladies entered, one of the members bearing aloft the beautiful banner of Our Lady of Lourdes wreathed around with white roses...All in all, it was a most charming celebration, and many were the hopes expressed that the society might live to celebrate its golden anniversary..." (Times Picayune, 8/13/1900)

Certainly, if all the organizations were founded and implemented as this one was, surely, Archbishop Perche' would have been proud and Our Lady of Lourdes would have blessed the membership for carrying out the message and works of Lourdes with such charity and devotion.

The Jubilee Years

When Archbishop Napoleon Joseph Perche' consecrated the Archdiocese to Our Lady of Lourdes and thereafter requested and received Papal approval to enroll the entire archdiocese into the Arch Confraternity, he must have contemplated the legacy to which he gave life. In his twilight years, this Frenchman who adopted and loved Louisiana, must have wanted to leave her under the strong protection of Our Lady of Lourdes in union with her divine Son, the Sacred Heart of Jesus for many generations to come.

In fact, as the evidence suggests, devotion to Our Lady of Lourdes was so strong among the faithful of South Louisiana that many enrolled in the arch confraternity, participated in sodalities and societies, erected grottos, prominently displayed statues and regularly attended lectures and other events which enlightened and motivated the attendees. This did not last a decade or two; – this devotion became part of the fabric of Catholic Marian devotion in South

Louisiana for almost 100 years. In 1914, The Times Picayune ran a story about the debate for and against building a "spacious chapel for Our Lady of Prompt Succor". At the conclusion of that article the proponent for the chapel concluded his argument by stating – "...Only in a year will be celebrated the centenary of her victory at Chalmette. Shall we not at that time see a shrine where thousands may come to ask her favors, where the devotion to Our Lady of Prompt Succor may grow to the proportions and in popularity with that of Our Lady of Lourdes?" (Times Picayune, 1914) More than forty years since the archdiocese had been consecrated to Our Lady of Lourdes had passed but still, no other devotion as yet compared. Devotion was especially pious in the jubilee years when anniversaries of the declaration of the dogma or the apparitions were celebrated.

THE 50TH ANNIVERSARY OF THE DOGMA OF THE IMMACULATE CONCEPTION

The declaration of Pope Pius IX was commemorated by none other than the Ursulines on December 8, 1904. The Times Picayune article stated "...throughout the Catholic world, and with a unison which Catholicity alone can produce, there arose one grand hymn of praise in honor of Mary Immaculate..." (Times Picayune, 12/12/1904)

The scene was vividly described by the unknown author:

> "...the day was one of unusual splendor in the display of religious magnificence. The chapel had been gorgeously decorated for the occasion, the sanctuary and altar of Our Lady especially presenting a most beautiful picture of incandescent lights, waxen tapers, golden sprays, graceful potted ferns and sweet-scented flowers...In the Convent annals the day will ever remain a memorable one for many reasons, among others that of having

witnessed two imposing religious ceremonies – the blessing of a newly-built rustic chapel dedicated to Mary Immaculate, under her titled of Our Lady of Lourdes…This chapel, situated in the rear of the shady pecan grove, contains a fac simile of the grotto of Lourdes itself, and the building is a pretty little structure.

Courtesy of Ursuline Convent Collection Archives

"…At 3 o'clock, the community…gathered…and...marched in procession to the rustic chapel…formed a graceful circle…while the two reverend fathers proceeded to the ceremony of the blessing of the building. On the way…the "Litany of Our Lady" was sung, and on the way back the ever-sweet strains of the "Ave, Maris Stella" re-echoed through the Convent grounds…" (Times Picayune, 12/12/1904)

The ceremonies that day concluded with the Convent choir singing "Je Suis l'enfant de Marie" and solemn benediction of the Most Blessed Sacrament. Eleven girls were received into the Sodality that day. Miss Lea Waguespack read the consecration to the Blessed Virgin and was thus accepted as a child of Mary. Surely, this was one of the most reverent and heavenly celebrations among all those that were carried out throughout the world that year. The structure above has an M and a V at the top with a cross on the peak. It is likely this structure housed the grotto referred to in the article.

THE 50TH ANNIVERSARY COMMEMORATED – SPECTACULAR EVENTS

HIS EMINENCE, CARDINAL GIBBONS.

Times Picayune Photo of Cardinal Gibbons

The site of the 50th anniversary of the apparitions at Lourdes took place at the Church of Our Lady of Lourdes on Napoleon Avenue and was celebrated by Cardinal Gibbons according to a Times Picayune report. This event was grand by all accounts and was celebrated as a triduum of Masses in honor of the golden anniversary of the apparitions. Cardinal Gibbons visited New Orleans annually to see his brother the Honorable John T. Gibbons. On the occasion of his visit in 1908, he was asked to celebrate this anniversary with the faithful of New Orleans. The Times Picayune article from February, 1908, was entitled *His Eminence, Cardinal Gibbons on His Annual Visit. – Welcomed at Depot by Crowd of Admiring Friends. Will Participate in Our Lady of Lourdes Jubilee.*

> "...Mr. Harry McEnorny then stepped forward in behalf of the parishioners of the Church of Our Lady of Lourdes, presented the Cardinal with an invitation to attend the opening ceremonies of the triduum in honor of the apparition at Lourdes. The invitation was a

parchment scroll, signed with the seal of the Church of Our Lady of Lourdes in gold, and with the Cardinal's colors attached..."

The letter is too rich not to cite in its entirety. The letter and the Cardinal's acceptance of the invitation demonstrate the great affection the people of New Orleans had for Our Lady of Lourdes and the importance they placed on a celebration of this anniversary with utmost reverence and solemnity.

OUR LADY OF LOURDES CHURCH.

Times Picayune Photo by L. E. Cormier of Our Lady of Lourdes Church

"Your Eminence, In behalf of Rev. Father Kavanaugh and the people of the Parish of Our Lady of Lourdes, we come to extend a most earnest invitation to America's distinguished Ambassador of Christ to lend the dignity of his presence to the celebration of the golden jubilee of the apparition of the Blessed Virgin Mary to Bernadette at Lourdes, in France, which event will be solemnized next Sunday, Feb. 9, at the hour of 10 a.m., in the Church of Our Lady of Lourdes.

"We will know that the Prince of Holy Mother Church comes to our "delightful city" for rest and recuperation, yet we are impelled to intrude upon the privacy of that annual visit because of our great desire to show every honor to the Mother of our Church, and to make an exposition of the love and devotion which the people of New Orleans cherish for the Prime Minister of the Lord in these United States.

"We beg of Your Eminence to come to us, to the baby parish of this great archiepiscopal see, revitalized and splendidly brilliant under the illumined leadership of His Grace, Archbishop Blenk, whose desire it is to show your sacred person every respect and consideration.

"If you will honor us in our little frame church, parish school and rectory, combined all within the one, will be encouraged to some day in the near future give way to giant structures, all for the greater glory of God, and for the edification of people of greater New Orleans, who are loyal in their love for your distinguished person."

Times Picayune Picture of Kavanagh

In response to this sincere and reverent invitation, the Cardinal accepted. This article concluded with a summary of the upcoming golden jubilee events.

"...The opening celebration next Sunday at the Church of Our Lady of Lourdes, which will begin at the 10 o'clock mass, has by the Cardinal's generous acceptance of the invitation to be present acquired a new dignity. The Cardinal of America, the Archbishop of New Orleans, the Auxiliary Bishop and the Abbot of the Benedictines, together with about thirty of the city's clergy, will form an imposing array of distinguished ecclesiastics on this jubilee celebration of the little Church's paternal feast, which will be an event in the parish long remembered." (Times Picayune, 2/1908)

For three days straight, the city newspaper covered this story and these ceremonies devoting considerable space to the coverage. The February 10, 1908 edition of <u>The Times Picayune</u> carried a multi-column story titled *Cardinal and Archbishop Honor the Celebration –*

Of the Semi centennial of the Miracle of Our Lady of Lourdes. – Little Church Honored by Great Catholic Gathering – Presentation of Statue Will Lead to Reproduction of Famous Grotto.

"...The church was filled to its utmost capacity when the mass was begun...It seemed that the rainy weather did not prevent a very large attendance of faithful Catholics...the church...handsomely decorated, revealing as the principal adornments the colors of the Pope, the Cardinal and the Archbishop...

Times Picayune Picture of the Bicentennial Celebration at Our Lady of Lourdes Church

As the cortege of church dignitaries...entered the church, there was sung a hymn by a choir of male voices – some of the gentlemen of the parish and the boys of the school – under the direction of Mrs. M. E. Dunn. The singing of the mass was exclusively Gregorian...

Rev. Leslie J. Kavanagh was the celebrant of the solemn high mass...Archbishop Blenk read the Gospel of the day and then announced his text for his sermon "my soul doth magnify the Lord; because he that is mighty has done great things to me, and holy is his name....This is the canticle of the Blessed Mother, as recorded in the first chapter of St. Luke. We are assembled here...under circumstances of dignity and splendor, with the august present of the Prince of the Church, our dearly-beloved Cardinal Gibbons; and we are met for the purpose of honoring her whom he that is mighty has made great.

The focus that day was on Our Lady of Lourdes, The Immaculate Conception and "...Then the Archbishop drew a most fervent picture of the life of the Blessed Virgin, her purity, her spotless soul, her Immaculate Conception, her divine maternity, and spoke of her as the highest, grandest and absolutely spotless figure in the whole history of the world of womanhood. "Think of her, my dearly beloved, as the Mother of God, the Mother of Jesus Christ, and the majesty of her glory, and you will exclaim, with Massillion, "God alone is great."

"With divine generosity God has clothed the Holy Mother with Infinite glory and greatness, and she has constantly sent out abundant graces to her children, the faithful Catholics, and she is constantly sending out messages to them. My dear children listen to her voice. Avoid sin, love Jesus, venerate the Mother of God and try to be GOOD STRONG CATHOLICS and also to be good citizens, obedient to the laws." (Times Picayune, 2/8/1908)

The day was absolutely breathtaking by all accounts – the Cardinal, the Archbishop, numerous clergy and a new parish church filled to capacity with Catholic faithful, all there to share in the celebration of the Holy Mass – the ultimate purpose of Our Blessed Mother – to bring Gods children to her Divine Son.

On February 11, 1908, page 7 of that edition of The Times Picayune ran an account of the second day of the solemn triduum declaring it "...was marked with most gratifying attendance..." On this evening the litany of the Blessed Virgin was chanted, the rosary was recited and the male choir sang "appropriate hymns." On this evening Father Kavanagh was assisted by a Jesuit priest, Rev. J. O'Shanahan who delivered a sermon which "...was listened to with deep attention." The account of this sermon read in part:

> "...the history of the Catholic Church is the history of the glories of Mary. Her name is linked with that of Jesus, as she was found with the Master at Bethlehem, in Egypt, at Nazareth, in Jerusalem, in the temple and at the foot of the cross. She was present at his glorious ascension. Mary was the coredemptor with Jesus for the world, because she as the mother of the Man-God consented to his final sacrifice, so that the human race might be saved...The learned Jesuit then gave some interesting data about St. Bernard and his devotion to the Blessed Mother and conclude with an earnest appeal to the people to always cultivate an ardent and abiding devotion to the Virgin Mary." (pg. 7)

The article concludes by stating that it was expected many would take communion this day because a "large number of parishioners were in the confessionals last evening..."

This conclusion may cause some readers to reflect on reception of Communion today. How do we feel today about the state of souls and receiving Communion? Do those of us receiving Communion today use the same standard for reception of the Eucharist as those who received the sacrament of Communion then? The solemn reverence the faithful of the early 20th century demonstrated in attending and celebrating this golden anniversary of the apparitions at Lourdes is inspiring and thought provoking for anyone reading or learning about it today.

The article covering the final day of the triduum was titled *"Our Lady of Lourdes Celebration Ends – With Another Great Gathering of Clergy and Laity; - ... Analyzing the Miracle and Its Potent Purpose. – A Procession With Lighted Candles One of the Stirring Scenes at closing..."*

This article provided a short summary of the events over three days:

"...The solemn Triduum...was concluded last night in most appropriate and interesting manner...Rev. Leslie Kavanagh...made a great success of the three days' celebration. The opening ceremonies on Sunday were graced with the presence of Cardinal Gibbons...Archbishop Blenk, and they spoke to the large congregation such words as cannot be forgotten...and...preached a sermon on the Immaculate Conception and Our Lady of Lourdes that will be long remembered.

...The church was crowded to its utmost capacity...was resplendent with myriads of lights and the most beautiful and conspicuous object was the statue of the Blessed Mother, over the main altar, encircled with tiny electric globes, and seeming to smile upon the vast assemblage..."

"...The sermon was preached by Very Rev. Father Smith, S.M...God always chooses the poor and the lowly to manifest his power and his glory...Smith said that such events...are within the province of God to show at certain critical periods of the world the prestige and the divine origin of the Catholic Church. It was about that time that the wave of naturalism was sweeping over France and gradually reaching other countries...therefore the Lord permitted the miraculous vision...and it was triumphantly proven that the wonderful incident was true..." (Times Picayune, 2/12/1908)

The golden jubilee was celebrated in a marvelous and grand manner over three days in the Church of Our Lady of Lourdes on Napoleon Avenue. However, across town, another jubilee celebration also occurred on February 11 at St. Joseph's Academy by the residents there.

"...At 6 o'clock...all assembled within the convent chapel, where Rev. Thomas Delaney, the Chaplain, delivered a very eloquent and pathetic sermon on the subject...A procession was...formed from the Chapel to the Grotto of Our Lady of Lourdes, which stands beneath the overshadowing branches of a gigantic magnolia in the center of the convent yard. There all stood in admiration before the vision of beauty that burst from the Grotto. Twelve electric stars shone over the head of the statue of Our Lady of Lourdes, and case a bewitching radiance through and around the shrine. Roses, pink and white, were spread in rich profusion around the feet of the statue and among the vines that creep here and there over the grotto, which is itself a masterpiece of rural beauty and the only one of its kind in the South. It was planned by Father Delaney some years ago, and has proved to be a shrine for many afflicted.

"...Around the scene of beauty and faith the rosary was chanted by the sisters and their pupils...On the way to and from the grotto there rose from over 400 voices the "Immaculata" and the "Ave Maria." (Times Picayune, 2/12/1908)

The Picayune Guide of 1904 confirms that the grotto was constructed at that time. It reports as follows:

"...At the corner of St. Philip and Galvez Street, is St. Joseph's Convent, for the education of young ladies. The beautiful old grounds and quaint building are deserving of a visit. Within the grounds is a handsome fac simile of the famous Grotto of Lourdes..." (pg. 64)

Most will never witness the kind of pageantry described in the articles about the Triduum except, perhaps, in one place on this earth and that is Lourdes. Reading these accounts may provoke thoughts about Archbishop Perche'. Thirty five years earlier, he had consecrated the Archdiocese of New Orleans to Our Lady of Lourdes. It is easy to picture him smiling from above on the scenes unfolding in New Orleans in celebration of this momentous jubilee.

Might he also wonder what happened to the strong devotion to Our Lady of Lourdes and what has become of the act of consecration which Perche' invoked in 1873? Clearly, the Catholics of the Archdiocese of the late 19th century and early 20th century, tightly embraced Our Lady and the message of Lourdes – can this devotion be renewed to its former glory today? The 50th jubilee was not the end of Lourdes in New Orleans; it was a stop along the way.

THE 75TH ANNIVERSARY RECOGNIZED

Devotion to Our Lady of Lourdes was very much alive in 1933, 75 years after the apparitions in Lourdes. The year began in New Orleans with a celebration commemorating the apparitions and ended with Pope Pius XI canonizing Bernadette a saint on December 8, 1933. The Magnificat publication, The Wonders of Lourdes recorded a portion of the event as follows:

> "*...We declare and define as a Saint the Blessed Marie-Bernard Soubirous and inscribe her in the catalog of Saints, ruling that her memory shall be piously celebrated in the Church Universal on April 16th every year, the day of her birth to Heaven...*" (pgs. 244-245)

Earlier that year, the Sunday edition of The Times Picayune ran an article titled *Lady of Lourdes Program Planned – New Orleans to Observe 75th Anniversary of Apparition.* By the time this anniversary came to pass, the center of activities for Our Lady of Lourdes had moved to the church which was built in her honor. The article served notice to readers:

> "The 75th anniversary of the Feast of Our Lady of Lourdes will be observed in New Orleans February 11 at 8 a.m. with a solemn high mass at Our Lady of Lourdes church, 4423 LaSalle street, the Right Reverend L. J. Kavanagh, pastor, announced

Saturday...The Very Reverend John E. Wickham...will deliver the sermon...choosing as his topic, "Mary, the Mother of God.""

"...The feast will be preceded by a novena in honor of Our Lady of Lourdes...It was on February 11, 1858, Father Kavanagh explained Saturday, that the first apparition of Mary Immaculate to Blessed Bernadette occurred at Lourdes, France...Since that time multiple and various have been the miracles wrought, the priest said, both at the shrine at Lourdes and at shrines which have been dedicated to Our Lady of Lourdes throughout the world. "Were there a publication of all the cures wrought and heavenly favors granted," Father Kavanagh said, "the books printed would materially increase a good-sized library and reveal to many much which they have hitherto not known." (pg. 2)

1958 – 100 YEARS

Sadly, by 1958, there was little evidence of grand celebrations to mark the 100th anniversary of the apparitions of Our Lady of Lourdes to St. Bernadette in Lourdes. One of the most impressive commemorations my research uncovered was the building of the grotto at Angola Prison in 1958 and the blessing of it by the Archbishop.

The feast was also commemorated by Rev. Albert J. Coburn, O.P., who conducted a "...solemn novena..." This novena was referred to as the "winter novena of St. Ann, and that year it was "...offered in homage to Our Lady of Lourdes, in observance of the Jubilee Year of Lourdes..." (Times Picayune, 2/15/1958, pg. 11)

On June 29, 1958, the Metropolitan Council of Holy Name Societies, sponsored a rally known as "A Holy Name Rally" and consisting of The Holy Name men from 33 parishes. These men first assembled and St. Mary's Italian Holy Name Society began the procession and was charged with the responsibility of carrying a statue of Our Lady of Lourdes, "...in whose honor the rally is to be dedicated." (pg. 16) The rally marched from St. Mary's on Chartres then onto St. Louis Cathedral by way of Decatur. The procession was led by a sound truck which assisted in leading the processors in the recitation of the rosary. This procession ended at the Cathedral with a Mass and Solemn Benediction. (Times Picayune, 6/21/1958, pg. 16)

100 YEARS – GROTTO AT ST. MICHAEL THE ARCHANGEL IN CONVENT, LOUISIANA

Although the 100th anniversary appears to have passed with minimal celebration, Joseph A. Lucia of The Times Picayune Upriver Bureau covered the story in Convent of the 100th anniversary in his February 22, 1976 story of "...what is believed to be the first grotto erected in the United States to Our Lady of Lourdes..." (pg. 6)

The Centennial Mass of Thanksgiving was celebrated that day by Bishop Joseph V. Sullivan of Baton Rouge and the homilist was the "...Very Rev. Joseph Buckley, S.M. who was a former superior general and former provincial of the Society of Mary, the order which since 1863 has been in charge of St. Michael's church parish, the first Marist foundation in the United States. The 1976 article provided some interesting details about this grotto:

> "...the original grotto is completely preserved to the present day and is still under the supervision of priests of the Society of Mary...Since its dedication on Easter Sunday – April 17 – in 1876, which history records as a day the church could barely hold all the people who attended the event, the grotto has been visited daily by Catholics in this section and by countless person and pilgrimages from practically every state in the nation and many foreign countries.

"...The grotto...is one of the many erected throughout the world to Our Lady of Lourdes. It was built two years before the death of Bernadette on Dec. 12, 1878 and only 18 years after the apparitions. The same year that the grotto at St. Michael's was dedicated, a great basilica was built upon the rock at Massabielle in Lourdes." (pg. 6)

The article concluded by providing a new detail regarding the connections between Lourdes, Bernadette and South Louisiana. Lucia reported that "...Bernadette was canonized as a saint on the Feast of the Immaculate Conception December 8, 1933. The postulator for her cause at Rome was a Marist priest, the Rev. Jules Grimal, who spent many years in the United States and frequently visited the Marist Fathers in St. James Parish. " (pg. 6)

The Everlasting Covenant

Death is not the end but a prelude.
Life on earth is but interlude
between mortal time we spend here
and immortal joy to appear.
Sometimes the facts our minds elude.
Still, in moments of quietude,
we speak to God in solitude
and understand. We should not fear
Death is not the end.
Sometimes our earthly cares delude
our minds and hearts so to occlude
Christ's covenant, yet still adhere
to the Word which we hold so dear.
Our loved ones live. We should not brood
Death is not the end.

CHAPTER 10

PASSING ON TO THE OTHER WORLD

19th Century Incorruptible Saints and Pilgrims – "The Other World"

Before the end of the 19th century, those who were the central figures in the events surrounding the apparitions at Lourdes and spreading the devotion around the world and in New Orleans would pass over to "the other world" where Our Lady of Lourdes promised Bernadette happiness. The priest, the Pope, the Saint and the Archbishop – all key Pilgrims courageously journeying into the story of Lourdes and being touched in such a way as to act upon the promptings of the Spirit which was undoubtedly at work in each of them.

ABBE' DOMINIQUE PEYRAMALE

The parish priest who had at first disbelieved Bernadette but eventually became her most ardent supporter died on September 8, 1877. His death went unrecognized in the New Orleans newspapers insofar as my research was able to uncover. For many, he will be forever the person who was first touched by understanding of what Bernadette was experiencing and the wise guardian of the story which he placed in the hands of Henri Lasserre. In both cases, he became a foundation on which both Bernadette and the miracles of Lourdes could rest for support and right counsel.

Abbe' Peyramale - Wikipedia

BLESSED POPE PIUS IX – INCORRUPT

Pope Pius IX (May 13, 1792 – February 7, 1878), born Giovanni Maria Mastai-Ferretti, reigned as Pope of the Roman Catholic Church from his election in June 16, 1846, until his death more than 31 years later in 1878. Pius IX was elected as the candidate of the liberal and moderate wings on the College of Cardinals, following the pontificate of arch-conservative Pope Gregory XVI. Initially sympathetic to democratic and modernizing reforms in Italy and in the Church, Pius became increasingly conservative after he was deposed as the temporal ruler of the Papal States in the events that followed the Revolutions of 1848. (Wikipedia)

REACTION OF THE ARCHDIOCESE OF NEW ORLEANS

Incorrupt Body of Pope Pius IX - Website ListVerse

The column read **IN MEMORIAM.-** *Yesterday's Celebration Commemorative of the Death of Pio Nono. – A Display to be Remembered. The High Mass at the Cathedral and the Procession Along the Streets. – The Speeches and the Resolutions.* When Pope Pius IX died The Times Picayune ran an article that occupied 12 full columns in its paper on February 21, 1878. The paper recorded his death on February 7, 1878 and extensively covered the services conducted by Archbishop Napoleon Perche' that day. The article described the scene, the catafalque[25], the services, the music, the streets, the procession, Jackson Square and the many speeches which were offered that day. Mr. Chas. Gayarre read a preamble and resolution which stated in part:

---

[25] Catafalque is **1.** A decorated platform or framework on which a coffin rests in state during a funeral.
2. *Roman Catholic Church* A coffin-shaped structure draped with a pall, used to represent the corpse at a requiem Mass celebrated after the burial. http://www.thefreedictionary.com/catafalque

"...The history of the Pontificate of Pius the Ninth is particularly signalized by three great events under whose influence the world still palpitates in anger, or in joyous assent. The dogma of the Immaculate Conception, the final affirmation of the belief that had floated for ages over the sea of Catholic tradition, like those nebulae in the vault of Heaven which to the naked eye seem to be faintly illumined mists, but which to telescopic vision resolve themselves into a cluster of globes of light. It teaches the faithful that, among the other granted prerogatives of divine grace, the Mother of our Saviour was exempted from the original curse and conceived without a stain of sin; thus exalting us through one of our race and encouragingly showing us to what degree of purity our sinful nature may rise through the merits of Jesus Christ..." (Times Picayune, 2/21/1978)

This lengthy article offered a window into the past in terms of the affection Louisianans held for the Pope for many years. In fact, this support was reduced to writing in a resolution which read in part:

"...On the 16th of March, 1848, the following joint resolution of the Senate and House of Representatives was signed by Gov. Johnson, and a copy forwarded to the supreme pontiff:

Act of 1848

Be it resolved by the Senate and House of Representatives of the State of Louisiana in General Assembly convened. That the General Assembly of Louisiana have witnessed, with admiration and delight, the noble efforts of Pope Pius IX to reform ancient abuses and to promote the happiness of his people; that his conduct has endeared him to every lover of constitutional freedom; the we hail him as the instrument destined by Divine

Providence to accomplish the political regeneration of Italy; that the people of Louisiana more ardently cherish the hope that his exertions in the great cause of liberal principles may surmount every obstacle, triumph over every opposition and defeat the machinations of despotisms until they find a concerted, a universal and an enthusiastic response from the emancipated millions of renovated Italy.

Be it further resolved, etc. That the Governor of this State be requested to transmit a copy of the above resolutions to Pope Pius IX…." (Times Picayune, 2/21/1878)

SAINT BERNADETTE OF LOURDES, INCORRUPT –JANUARY 7, 1844 – APRIL 16, 1879

St. Bernadette was born Bernadette Soubirous in Lourdes, France. From February to July 1858, she experienced eighteen apparitions of "a Lady." Despite initial skepticism from the Roman Catholic Church, these claims were eventually declared to be worthy of belief after a canonical investigation. After her death, Bernadette's body remained "incorruptible", and the shrine at Lourdes went on to become a major site for pilgrimage, attracting millions of Catholics each year. (Lourdes Website, 2012)

Bernadette Soubirous - Picture from Official Lourdes Website

Some important dates in the history of Bernadette are recorded on the official Lourdes website:

- "1907: The opening of the process for Beatification completed in 1909.
- 1909: 22 September, the first exhumation of the body of Bernadette. The body is found completely intact.
- 1913: 13 August, Pope Pius X allows the introduction of the Cause for Beatification.

- 1919: 3 April: 2nd exhumation to identify the body.
- 1923: 18 November, Pius XI declares the heroic virtues of Bernadette.
- 1925: 18 April, 3rd exhumation. The body is still intact. 14th June, the Beatification of Bernadette, by Pope Pius XI in St. Peter's Rome. 18 July, the body of Bernadette is places in a shrine, her face and hands are covered with a light film of wax. 3rd August the shrine is transferred from the Novitiate to the Chapel of the Convent of Saint-Gildard.
- 1933: 8 December, Feast of the Immaculate Conception, Bernadette is canonised by Pope Pius XI.
- 1958: The Centenary of the Apparitions in Lourdes. 4½ million pilgrims visit Lourdes.
- 1979: The Centenary of the death of St. Bernadette" (Lourdes Website, 2012)

This research did not uncover any newspaper accounts of the death of Sister Marie-Bernard in New Orleans or any other Louisiana newspapers. It is not surprising there would be no mention of Bernadette in local newspapers. She never wanted to be the center of the story. Bernadette's life ended in great pain and suffering quietly in Nevers, France. Undeniably, Bernadette embraced the words spoken to her by the Blessed Virgin – that she didn't promise to make her happy in this world but in the next.

ARCHBISHOP NAPOLEON JOSEPH PERCHE' – JANUARY 10, 1805 – DECEMBER 27, 1883

Archbishop Perche' was known throughout the United States by reason of not only his long and successful priesthood and time as Archbishop of the Archdiocese of New Orleans, but also because he had founded a well-respected Catholic newspaper, Le Propagateur. He was so well know in fact that the New York Times recorded his illness in an article carried in that newspaper on May 12, 1882 and titled *Archbishop Perche Very Ill.*

> "New Orleans, May 11 – The venerable Archbishop Perche, of this Roman Catholic diocese, is dangerously ill, and it is not believed he can live many days." (p. 5)

The Archbishop lived for several months thereafter although in a weakened state. On December 26, 1883, The New York Times ran another article entitled *Archbishop Perche Dying. Forty-six years in the service of his church in this country.*

> "New-Orleans, Dec. 25 – The venerable Archbishop Napoleon Joseph Perche of this Roman Catholic diocese is dying. He cannot live many hours longer. The doctors have done all they could for him and have given up...He was a man of great energy, far-seeing judgment and great eloquence, and his many charitable acts endeared him to the people, among whom he labored with zeal and fidelity..." (NYT, 1/26/1883)

The New York Times continued daily to follow the developments regarding Perche's illness and impending death. On December 27, 1883 the story read – *Archbishop Perche Dying.*

Picture of the Tombstone for Archbishop Napoleon Joseph Perche' mounted to the right of the main altar at St. Louis Cathedral, New Orleans, LA

"New Orleans, Dec. 26. – The Most Rev. Napoleon Joseph Perche, Roman Catholic Archbishop of New Orleans, received the last sacraments of the church this morning in the presence of his coadjutor, the Right Rev. Bishop Francois Leroy; the Vicar-General, The Rev. G. A. Rouxel; the Rev. Dr. Chasse, Chancellor of the diocese, and several priests and representatives of the Catholic community. He gave his blessing and benediction to those at his bedside. He retained consciousness up to 1 o'clock today, when he dropped into a semi-comatose condition, and his final dissolution is not many hours off." (NYT, 12/27/1883)

The final coverage of The New York Times was solemnly presented:

"The Late Archbishop Perche. New Orleans, Dec. 28. – The body of the late Archbishop Perche' was embalmed and early this morning laid in a catafalque in the Church of St. Mary, adjoining the Archiepiscopal residence, on Charters street, where it has been visited by thousands of the faithful, who manifested their grief in sobs and tears...The body will be conveyed directly to the cathedral, only five squares, and placed in the vault under the altar. Archbishop Elder, of Cincinnati, has been selected to perform the chief religious service at the burial, which will occur on Wednesday next." (New York Times, 12/29/1883)

"Funeral of Archbishop Perche...Jan. 2. – The obsequies of the late Archbishop Perche', which took place here to-day, were of a very imposing character. The procession included, in addition to the Catholic clergy, the State and city officials; military, the various Catholic societies, the Sisters of Charity and Mercy in charge of the inmates of the Catholic asylums here, and a great concourse of citizens. St. Louis's cathedral, where the ceremonies were held, was draped with funeral emblems and inscriptions. The Right

Rev. F. X. Leray, who succeeds the deceased prelate, officiated at the cathedral, assisted by clergy from this and other States." (New York Times, 1/3/1884)

After his death, Richard Clark wrote a book called Lives of Deceased Bishops in the United States in 1888. In it he reviewed the life and works of Perche'. Although other works have been written about Perche', little is written about his devotion to Our Lady of Lourdes or the work he accomplished in spreading that devotion in South Louisiana. Clark, perhaps writing so close in time to Perche's death, is among the few authors who recorded this aspect of Perche's life and work.

> "...In 1873 he erected and inaugurated, with appropriate and solemn religious ceremonies, a fine monument in honor of Our Lady of Lourdes in his metropolitan Church, and founded a Confraternity to perpetuate this devotion, and to be affiliated to the Arch-Confraternity of Lourdes. His circular on this subject is characteristically eloquent and devout..." (Clark, pg. 366)

Will Perche' receive the recognition he deserves for his many and varied accomplishments? Or...will recognition elude him perhaps because he offered his support in the cause of the South during the Civil War; or because, during his time as Archbishop, great debt was accumulated against the Archdiocese of New Orleans which was not eliminated for many years to come? I have come to admire Perche' for a life well spent in the service of the Catholic Church, the Sacred Heart of Jesus, Our Lady of Lourdes and St. Joseph. He was a man fully human yet fully devoted to the service of the many people under his spiritual leadership.

Archbishop Perche' and Pope Pius IX are memorialized in New Orleans on the front of one of the oldest churches in the City – St. Joseph's Church on Tulane. Above the main entrance are two medallions – one for Pope Pius IX and the other for Archbishop Perche'. (St. Joseph

Catholic Church - A Brief History n.d.) It should be recalled that Pope Pius declared St. Joseph's Feast Day when Perche' was in Rome to receive the Pallium. Their paths crossed numerous times throughout the tumultuous 19th century; it is a privilege to see them honored prominently on this church in our city.

Medallion of Pope Pius IX and Archbishop Napoleon Joseph Perche' on the front of St. Joseph's Church on Tulane Avenue in New Orleans, LA

LOURDES, ST. BERNADETTE AND AL COPELAND

The 150th anniversary of the apparitions was commemorated in 2008 for the entire year. Many pilgrims journeyed in that year to Lourdes. It was my first time there and so too, was it the first time for Al Copeland. Anyone likely to buy this book is also likely to know Al Copeland. Al Copeland, the famous New Orleans restaurateur, was born February 2, 1944 and died of cancer on March 23, 2008. Before his death, he journeyed to Rome and also to Lourdes. The website, www.catholic.net carried a story written by Brother Stephen Dardis, LC and entitled *He Must Have Done His First Fridays – Good News reflection on Divine Mercy*. In this article we learn of an encounter Al Copeland experienced while in Rome:

> "…Weeks before what might have been a lamentable occasion, Al had asked for a trip to Rome, as he put it, to "get things right with Jesus." The priest who organized the trip remembers that, at one moment following the Mass in St. Peter's, the millionaire, his face disfigured from cancer, sat attentive in his wheelchair, listening to a woman kneeling beside him. She kept kissing his hand while praying the Rosary with him. The priest could not see the woman's face, but Al was evidently moved. "Tears were rolling down his face," the priest recounted, "and I knew that Al was 'getting right with Jesus.'"
>
> Only a week before, Lourdes had commemorated the 150th anniversary of the apparitions of the Blessed Virgin Mary to St. Bernadette. To celebrate the occasion, the Holy Father had granted a special Plenary Indulgence. Al sought a profound healing, and the priest suggested a pilgrimage to the famous shrine, aware of its miracles both of soul and body. Following a brief flight in the Copeland jet, they entered the town of Lourdes. Posters of St. Bernadette were everywhere. "But, that's her, isn't it?" asked the millionaire anxiously. "Yes, that's Bernadette, the girl whom the Blessed Mother appeared to in…" "No, no; that's the woman I was talking with in Rome, right?" Those riding in the car sat silent and dumbfounded. "We learned later that, on that very day, February 18th, France was celebrating the Feast of St. Bernadette, which normally falls a week earlier." For those present, the coincidence was just another confirmation of God's closeness during those moments. Following the healing baths and with time running out before the return to Rome, a determined and visibly moved Al Copeland managed to fulfill the rather

complex requirements of the Lourdes Plenary Indulgence. His death followed only weeks later." (Dardis)

This story touched the lives of many people who read or heard about it. It is impossible now to know for sure what Mr. Copeland experienced in Rome; however, the effect of this account reassures me that, indeed, death is not the end.

THE MESSAGE OF LOURDES – ENFLAMING THE MESSAGE AGAIN

In a matter of a few short years, the authentic messages of Lourdes were spread worldwide and were especially embraced and revered in the Archdiocese of New Orleans. Early in this book, I quoted one of the nuns who witnessed Soeur Marie-Bernard's profession of vows as saying that Bernadette was only good for "blowing embers into flame". What a magnificent purpose Bernadette made of a seemingly inconsequential task. For many years, the devotion to Our Lady of Lourdes and more importantly the messages Our Lady asked Bernadette to share, have lain dormant in our area. Many my age and younger know very little about Lourdes. Should this history assist Bernadette by enflaming a renewed devotion to the messages of Lourdes, Our Lady of Lourdes and most importantly the Gospel message of Our Lord, Jesus Christ, to current and future generations particularly in Louisiana, the purpose of this work would be achieved. May God be pleased with this servant's imperfect effort which has all been for the honor and glory of God!

The Love Maker

Easy-flow river

What goes around comes around

Crescent City love

Afterthoughts

In 1856 in a small town in Southern France, the poor Soubirous family was relocating from the comfort of their home to a vacant cachot in Lourdes, France. Born 100 years later in 1956 and for most of my life I had limited knowledge of this family or the young peasant girl, Bernadette Soubirous, who was destined to be a saint. Upon entering the story of Lourdes, I joined the millions of people who had entered before me and became linked to the millions more who will come in the future. For those who experience Lourdes, it is as if the grace and privilege of experiencing heaven on earth is a gift in this otherwise challenging life. This research confirms many in Louisiana entered the story of Lourdes decades before my consciousness was raised and left a legacy for us to uphold.

When Archbishop Perche' caused his archdiocese to enter the story of Lourdes he was cooperating with the Blessed Virgin's eternal purpose of introducing his flock to Mary's Son, Jesus Christ. At the same time, Perche' was encouraging, through this devotion, faith in the miraculous healing that occurs when we experience the Gospels through the message of Lourdes. In reality, Lourdes is the geographic location where God allowed the manifestation of the Blessed Virgin to be revealed on earth to a single human being. Those privileged few who were present with Bernadette during the apparitions, were given a special grace of seeing the glow of ecstasy on the face of the young girl – they are witnesses to divinity and history. The effect of this manifestation has been that millions of people throughout the world have made pilgrimage to Lourdes looking for and experiencing healing – looking for and finding answers – searching for and sometimes finding the Divine. The New Testament is filled with stories of Jesus healing people with all manner of illness. But perhaps more importantly, Jesus is the humble servant who came to meet people where they are in their lives. Upon journeying to Lourdes, one sees in the pilgrims there, the humanity and brokenness of us all. One also sees the capacity of humanity for hope and love and charity in service to others.

We learn that Lourdes is a physical location on earth, but it is also a spiritual place in our hearts and our souls. Like Bernadette, who left the grotto and never returned we can journey to Lourdes in spirit. Every time we choose to serve rather than be served; every time we pray for sinners; every time we offer penance for our own sins as well as those of others in hope for the conversion of sinners, we are in truth, journeying to Lourdes because we are carrying out the message of the Gospels through the instructions the Blessed Virgin gave to Bernadette at Lourdes.

In this way, the message of Lourdes in any age is timeless because the message of Jesus Christ in the Gospels is timeless. In many ways, Lourdes is a reflection of heaven on earth. In Lourdes, angelic choirs of people sing praise; prayer is constant; participation in the Sacraments is ever present including the Sacrament of Reconciliation and Holy Eucharist. Healing of all kinds takes place there – physical, mental, emotional, and perhaps most important, spiritual. The Church in Lourdes is Universal. It seems that every language on earth is spoken there; people from every continent journey there. In Lourdes, the Universal Catholic Church is the shared purpose, the common value; all peoples harmonize in praising The Holy Trinity in song, prayer, procession, sacrifice, service, penance and blind faith.

In spirit, people of any age in any place can choose to enter the story of Lourdes and participate fully in the Paschal Mystery and the message of Lourdes – prayer, penance and conversion. This is true of New Orleans, Louisiana and our country. To re-ignite the message of Lourdes is to experience heaven on earth through sacrifice, prayer, and service to others.

Now

Now I sit and wait, on my guard
For my next assignment from the Lord.
Each one I've received before
I've fumbled. I may get no more.
I hope He knows I tried real hard.

All my efforts seemed untoward,
Lacking strength, like a house of card,
Like a wave breaking before the shore.
Now I sit and wait.

I always rushed in, a vanguard,
Too confident of my regard.
I look upon my life's closed doors
And hope to open just one more.
My sword is sheathed. Now, see me Lord,
Now I sit and wait

Acknowledgements

This book would not have been possible without the inspiration of The Holy Spirit and support of friends and family.

In thankfulness to the Blessed Virgin, Our Lady of Lourdes; this work is done in gratitude for graces received and in hopeful anticipation of a favor granted – all honor and glory to her Divine Son, Our Lord Jesus Christ.

To Pere' Regis-Marie de la Teyssonniere I offer my sincere gratitude for igniting within me a genuine love for Our Lady of Lourdes and the story into which 19th century New Orleanians, led by a French Archbishop, entered. I was pulled into that historical story of Lourdes and at the same time, realized my own entry into the story along the way.

To my family, who listened to my stories, entertained my pilgrimages, and showed interest in my pursuit of this book – I am grateful to each of you for the support you provided. Among my family, my father – Edgar Desforges, patiently endured all of my discoveries; he listened with interest like only a father can do – dad, you have been my comfort and my strength for many years. To my sister, Nancy Hughes, thank you for being the person who first introduced me to Lourdes; none of my journey would have been possible without you.

For the poems in this book I acknowledge and thank my mother posthumously. My mother, Joy Rittler Desforges, wrote poetry most of her life. In her own right, my mother was an accomplished poet. I have included some of her poems as introductions to various parts of this work. Mom, I hope you are looking down on this work with love; your poetry has added immensely to the story of Lourdes.

To my friends Barbara and Randy Roth, I am indebted for the continuous encouragement they provided. Barbara has been THE person who has journeyed with me; has supplied her own knowledge of the City, the Churches, the history and fearlessly accompanied wherever our journey led us in search of the true story about the devotion to Our Lady of Lourdes in the Archdiocese of New Orleans.

To Claitor's Publishing for taking a leap of faith in agreeing to publish this book written by a novice, first-time author; thank you for your guidance in the production of the book and your support during the writing of it.

To the following people who have comforted me, inspired me, helped me with research, talked with me about writing books and offered me advice. I remain forever grateful:

The Discalced Carmelite Nuns and Mary, Spouse of the Holy Spirit Order of Carmelite Discalced Secular, Covington, LA – for their prayers, encouragement and support

Sister Alicia Lau and the Sisters of Saint Francis, Honolulu, HI – for their compassion, hospitality, love and prayers

Mary Jane Zeringue and the Little Flock Prayer Group, Destrehan, LA – for unceasing prayers

Anne Gisclard, my dear friend – for reading early drafts and providing valuable feedback

Marlene Watkins and the North American Lourdes Volunteers

William Kevin Cawley, Archivist, University of Notre Dame Archives – for help with research

Megan Albritton, Archdiocese of New Orleans – for help researching archdiocesan archives.

Father William Greene – for his inspirational work on Archbishop Perche'

Charles E. Nolan - for taking the time to speak with me

Annie Howat – French teacher at St. Charles Borromeo, Destrehan, LA for translating documents.

Mary Lou Eichorn and the Historic New Orleans Collection, New Orleans, LA

Mary Lee Berner Harris, Curator, Ursuline Convent Collection Archive and Museum, New Orleans, LA

Mary Lee Eggart, Baton Rouge, LA – for producing the map

Joan Gaulene – Archivist, Jesuit Collection, New Orleans, LA

John and Kathleen DeMajo – for permission to use their photos

Candy Brunet – Associate Archivist, Diocese of Lafayette, LA

Carolyn - St. Philomena Parish, Labadieville, LA

Robert Pedesco, Parishioner, St. Leo the Great Church

Brian Plauche, BPNolaphotographs, New Orleans, LA

Sister Charlene Toups, Prioress, Poor Clare Monastery, New Orleans, LA

Doug Parker, Times-Picayune, New Orleans, LA – in gratitude for permission to use photos

Julie DeLaune – Sacred Heart Church, Morgan City, LA

St. John the Evangelist Cathedral Parish Employees, Lafayette, LA – for sending photos of their grotto

Linda Ibert – St. Alphonsus Volunteer, New Orleans, LA

Howard F. Champagne – St. Leo the Great, Leonville, LA

LaVerne Parfait – Rosaryville Spirit Center, Ponchatoula, LA

Appendices

APPENDIX I

PERCHE' PASTORAL LETTERS - OCTOBER 12, 1873

PASTORAL LETTER

OF HIS GRACE, THE ARCHBISHOP OF NEW ORLEANS, ANNOUNCING THE INAUGURATION OF THE MONUMENT ERECTED IN HONOR OF OUR LADY OF LOURDES, IN THE METROPOLITAN CHURCH OF NEW ORLEANS.

NAPOLEON JOSEPH, *by the grace of God and favor of the Holy See, Archbishop of New Orleans, Prelate of the Papal Household, Assistant at the Pontifical Throne, Roman Count, etc. To the clergy and laity of our Diocese :*

Health and Benediction in Jesus Christ Our Lord.

Beloved Fellow-Laborers of the Clergy and Dear Brethren of the Laity :

Our Catholic population, always so remarkable by a most ardent devotion towards Mary, the Immaculate Virgin, the Mother of God, and the Queen of Angels and men, has been for

— 2 —

a long time deeply moved at the recital of the wonderful miracles constantly performed at the Grotto of Lourdes, a place sanctified some sixteen years ago by the apparitions of the Blessed Virgin. On several occasions, pious members of the Clergy and Laity have manifested to us the wish, that the devotion to our Lady of Lourdes should be established in our Diocese in a public and solemn manner; and as this wish coincided with the inclination of our own heart and our filial love to that good and tender Mother, we have determined to erect in the Chapel of the Blessed Virgin of our Metropolitan Church a monument, which, in recalling as much as possible the Grotto of Lourdes, will transmit to those who will come after us an enduring memorial of our tender devotion towards her, who said of herself: *I am the Immaculate Conception.**

The Feast of the Immaculate Conception, which is celebrated on the 8th of December, being a feast of obligation for all the Catholics of the United States, and being moreover the patronal feast of the whole country, is naturally the most appropriate day for the inauguration of the monument of our Lady of Lourdes; it is the day we have selected for this ceremony; and by this solemn inauguration we intend placing in a special manner the city and Diocese of New Orleans under the powerful and maternal protection of the Immaculate Mother of God.

Conformably to the words which she herself uttered in her apparitions at the Grotto, we shall beseech her to retain the arm of her Divine Son, so justly raised against us; and to obtain for us that spirit of penance which alone can disarm the justice of the Lord; and in order that our prayers may be more favorably heard, we shall make to him the sacrifice of our extravagance, follies, vanities, and sensual inclinations, and immoderate love of pleasure, and of all other evil habits which have drawn upon us the chastisements of heaven, and prepared for us, more than any other cause, the ruin of our beloved country.

We shall ask her to procure for the just the courage and firmness so necessary in these evil days to persevere unto the

* Words of the Blessed Virgin to Bernadotte.

end, and to obtain for the sinner the grace of conversion, as well as for our wandering brethren the happiness to return to the only true Church, out of which there is no salvation.

As for us, we shall thank her from the bottom of our heart for the striking Catholic progress, which manifests itself more and more in our Diocese, and which we mainly attribute to her powerful intercession; we shall beg of her to keep it up, and develop it more and more; for it is our sweetest consolation in the midst of the trials and pains, which it has pleased Almighty God to send us. But at the same time, we shall beg of her, to have pity on our dear Louisiana, now so severely tried, and to avert all those evils by which we see her so miserably oppressed, and against which all human efforts seem to be entirely powerless; we shall beg of her to restore to us our ancient prosperity, promising her at the same time, to make a better use of it, than we have in the past.

You see, Beloved Brethren, that it is our dearest interest to unite our prayers on this solemn occasion, and being prostrated at the feet of that Mother of Mercy, to send forth to her our most earnest supplications, that we may move her, and obtain from her that she may look upon us with eyes of compassion, filling our souls with hope and life.

Alas, among those we are now addressing, more than one will likely refuse to listen to our voice, or take notice of our appeal; nay more, several will perhaps answer us only by their impious sneers and injurious blasphemies. We shall pray for them particularly, Dear Brethren; we shall ask for them, through the intercession of Mary, those powerful graces which open the eyes the most obstinately closed against light, those graces that soften the hardest hearts, and incline wills to good, in order that we may all, after celebrating the praise of the Immaculate Virgin on earth, deserve to contemplate and praise her in heaven, with her blessed Son, to whom belongs all glory forever and ever.

We, therefore, after invoking the holy name of God, have ordained, and do ordain as follows:

1.—The inauguration of the Monument erected in our

— 4 —

Metropolitan Church in honor of our Lady of Lourdes will take place on Monday, the 8th of December, which is the Feast of the Immaculate Conception, in the afternoon, at an hour to be hereafter designated.

2.—It is our desire that all the clergymen, who will be able, should attend this ceremony.

3.—In all the Churches and Chapels of the Diocese, there will be on that day benediction of the Blessed Sacrament, followed by the singing of the *Te Deum*.

4.—A Triduum of Prayers and public instructions will take place in our Metropolitan Church, during the three days which will precede the inauguration.

5.—We grant an indulgence of forty days to all the faithful who, visiting the Chapel of our Lady of Lourdes, will recite three Hail Marys, to honor the mystery of the Immaculate Conception. They can gain this indulgence, as many times each day, as they visit the Chapel, during the Triduum, the day of the Feast, and its octave. After the octave, they can gain it only once a day.

6.—It is our intention to establish in our Metropolitan Church a Confraternity of our Lady of Lourdes, which will be affiliated to the Arch-Confraternity of Lourdes; the persons who may wish to become members of it may from this time give their names to the Rev. Vicars of the Cathedral.

This our Pastoral Letter will be read, in each Church, at the parochial Mass, on the Sunday immediately following its reception.

Given at New Orleans, on the Feast of the Maternity of the Blessed Virgin Mary, Sunday, October 12th, 1873.

† NAPOLEON JOSEPH,
Archbishop of New Orleans.

By order of the Archbishop,

G. Raymond, V. G.
Secretary Chancelor.

APPENDIX II

PERCHE' PASTORAL LETTER – MARCH 25, 1874

52

PASTORAL LETTER

OF

HIS GRACE, THE MOST REV. ARCHBISHOP OF NEW ORLEANS, PREPARATORY TO THE CONSECRATION OF THE ARCHDIOCESE AND THE PROVINCE OF NEW ORLEANS TO THE SACRED HEART OF JESUS.

Napoléon Joseph, *by the Grace of God and favor of the Holy Apostolic See, Archbishop of New Orleans, Prelate of the Papal Household, Assistant at the Pontifical Throne, Roman Count, etc.,*

To the Clergy and Faithful of our Diocese.

Health and Benediction in our Lord Jesus Christ.

Dearly Beloved Co-Laborers and Brethren :

Coeval with the Church is the Devotion to the Most Sacred and Adorable Heart of our Lord and Savior Jesus Christ. The Cross is its origin. From out the material Heart of Jesus,

— 2 —

which the lance of the Roman Soldier opened, burst the remnant of that Precious Blood, the very last drop of which, our Divine Savior was willing to shed, that we might be cleansed, and our souls purified from every sinful stain. This material Heart of Jesus, an Object as worthy of our adoration as it is meet for our homage, was but an external expression of that infinite love, with which, the Son of God, from eternity, hath loved us. It was a sensible manifestation of that boundless, Incomprehensible Mercy, the Divine Whisperings of which, prompted Him, not alone to demean Himself in the assumption of our lowly nature, but even to so elevate that nature, as to make it the embodiment of His own Divine Being. For, from the union of both natures, the Divine and the human, springs but one and the same Person, the Adorable Person, Jesus Christ, True God and True Man.

As Eve, in the beginning, grew, beneath the Plastic Hand of the Almighty, out of the flesh, drawn from Adam's side, while he lay buried in the deep, mysterious slumber, into which the Lord had cast him, so did the Church, the Immaculate Spouse of Christ, spring from the Adorable Heart of her Divine Bridegroom, as He, sleeping the sleep of death, hung upon the Wood of the Cross. On His ever Sacred and Adorable Heart, has the Spotless Bride of the Lamb, our Mother in the order of Grace, from Her very dawn, fixed Her gaze, directed Her hopes and centred Her affections. For she knew that this ever Sacred and Adorable Heart is an undying fire, whose light, while it illumines and warms, at the same time enlivens and quickens; that this Heart aglow with love, is a furnace as fiery, as it is inexhaustible, and in the flames of which the world is incessantly enveloped; nay, that this ever Sacred and Adorable Heart, whose richness is as infinite as Its Mercy, is the ever-teeming Fount, whence flows the Sacramental Grace, that inundates our spiritual being, and that regenerates, transforms and vivifies our souls. For she always perfectly knew, neither has She ever ceased to impress on her children's minds, that this ever Adorable Heart of Jesus is the Sacred Spring, whence streams out upon the creature, every manifestation of the Divine Mercy, be its object the Material or the Spiritual, the Natural or the Supernatural; that It is the Fount of every Grace and Blessing, which we enjoy here below, as it is of the Eternal Happiness and Glory, of which we hope to be sharers, in the Kingdom of the Blessed.

The Devotion, therefore, to the Sacred Heart has its reasons in the very essence of the Church, of whose existence as of whose vitality it is a condition.

But the Works of the Creator are ever characterized by a perfect order and precise adaptation to the time; He has judged it meet that this Devotion to His ever Sacred and Adorable Heart should follow Creation's law, which is the law of progress; as also, that it should unfold itself in the time, at the place, and through the instrumentality of those, whom He, in His Eternal Decrees, hath chosen to be its propagators. And when the period, which He, in His wisdom, hath appointed for its manifestation, had dawned, France, so frequently styled the "Heart of Christendom" and the "Centre of Catholicity" was the Land of His choice.—The century, which He chose, was one of Religious decay and Spiritual debasement. It was one, in which men's higher, and nobler, and loftier aspirations were materialized, even paralyzed, by the infidelity and corruption with which the world was deluged.

And the instrument, which He selected to be its originator, was not a man, remarkable among the world's great ones, either by the splendor of his position, the brilliancy of his talent, or the extent of his influence. It was a poor, humble, lowly virgin, Blessed Margaret Mary, buried in the seclusion of the cloister, hidden beneath the shadow of the Sanctuary, whose thoughts hovered round no other object, whose heart beat in unison with none other, save the ever Sacred and Adorable Heart of her Crucified Lord. "*In Him hath she disposed, her heart to ascend by steps.*" And the nearer she approached that Adorable Heart, and the oftener she looked down into Its

— 4 —

hidden, mysterious depths, the readier was that humble virgin to develop the Devotion to the Sacred Heart of Jesus in every region in Christendom, that thus she might realize the words of the prophet-king: "*Man shall come to a deep Heart, and the Lord shall be exalted.*

Catholic France soon re-echoed the voice of Blessed Margaret Mary of Paray-le-Monial. Her Bishops, those ever vigilant Sentries, on guard on the Watch-Towers of Israel, to warn and to avert the threatening danger, hearing the low, dull, yet distant rumbling of that storm, which would soon burst upon the Church and upon Society, hastened to mail their flocks with the armor of the Sacred Heart and to consecrate them to the ever Adorable Heart of Jesus. And, certain it is, that to her Devotion to the Sacred Heart must France attribute her preservation of her ancient faith, despite that furious tornado, before which swept, as chaff, her social institutions so deeply embedded in her soil.

But the French Revolution, apparently Impiety's last essay, was on the contrary but the forerunner of those storms, which, during the present century, continually attempt the Church's destruction, and Society's overthrow. Now, indeed, are really verified the words of the Psalmist. In their anger "*have the Gentiles raged, and the people devised vain things. The Kings of the earth stood up, and the Princes met together against the Lord, and against His Christ.*"

Let us burst, say they, *the chains* which fetter our liberty—our unbounded liberty of thought, of word, of action, *and cast aside Their yoke*—the yoke of Faith, Morality and Conscience.

Groundless indeed, Dearly Beloved Brethren, are our fears, should we be craven enough to conceive any, for the safety of that Church, whose life is indestructible, because the principle of Its being is immortal, and of whose victory in Her present, as Her every other conflict, whether past or to come, there rests upon our minds not a shadow of doubt. "*He, who dwelleth in the Heavens scoffs at the abortive assaults of His enemies.*"—Their puny efforts He ridicules, and He, in His own good time, will speak to them in His Wrath, and upon their guilty heads will fall the terrible chastisements, which they have so justly merited. Yet to Us, Dearly Beloved, it is a source of no less inexpressible sorrow, when We behold so many souls, ransomed by the Blood of Jesus Christ, treading in Satan's rebellious wake, thus hazarding their every hope of salvation and exposing themselves to the risk of eternal association, and exile with him for Eternity. Could We, Dear Beloved, be but idle spectators of the trials and sufferings of that holy and illustrious Pontiff, to whose guidance Providence has so wisely entrusted His Church's Government during those troublous days? Not only is He forcibly robbed of His Patrimony, but even *dastardly* insulted by the serfs of a faithless, perfidious government, nay inhumanly outraged, and violently persecuted by the minions of the thankless, iniquitous, sacrilegious Sardinian. In almost every country in Europe, in Germany, in Switzerland and Italy, the Church is the butt of a legalized persecution, which is the most refined manifestation of their hypocritical phrensy. Where persecution is not the order of the day, insult, outrage, injury and calumny the very vilest, a persecution, the more to be feared, because it is the more insidious, holds the sway. In language the very lowest, and to interpretation the most senseless are the Truths of Our Holy Religion exposed. Our works of charity misrepresented — even falsified. In short, nothing which the genius of man can devise, has been left untried, that the Church might appear, in as odious and ridiculous a light as possible, to the eyes of men—an object worthy of the hatred, and deserving the contempt of an enlightened century. As its greatest enemy, its very bitterest foe, hostile to its every development, ever retarding its onward progress, do the Satellites of the Demon, present to the world the Church of Jesus Christ. And yet it is that Church, which cloisters within Her pale children of every nation and of every people, of every clime and of every tongue. It is She, the inexhaustible treasures of whose maternal heart, are so profusely lavished upon Her children. It is

— 6 —

She, who consults their every true wish, procures their every happiness, supplies them with the only real, imperishable Goods of this life, that they may attain and possess the Eternal Ones of the life to come. The words of the Apocalypse would, in Our day, D. B., seem to have found their fulfilment. Satan is *unfettered ; he has seduced the nations, which are spread over the four quarters of the earth. He composses the* CAMP *of the Saints—The Holy City*, but to desolate and lay it waste, and even, if possible, to bury it in ruins. Patient, indeed, D. B., is the Lord, because He is eternal. Yet, at His nod, His enemies will disappear faster than smoke before the wind, than the wax before the fire, and then shall "*the just feast and rejoice before God, and with gladness shall they be delighted.*" But it is Ours, D. B., to hasten, by our prayers and supplication to the Throne of Grace, the speedy dawn of this much wished-for day. In the present crisis, D. B., the Faith of Christendom welling-up, by an innate, and voluntary expression, from the depth of Her children's hearts, casts its eyes upon the Sacred Heart of Jesus. In the fathomless recesses of that Adorable Heart, have Her children ever been certain of finding light in their darkest hours, fortitude in their severest conflicts, and strength and consolation in their heaviest afflictions. The Consecration of the various Dioceses to the Sacred Heart of Jesus was but the manifestation of their Faith in the Heart of their Divine Redeemer, as it was the realization of their long-cherished hopes, and ardent aspirations. Thus, D. Beloved, has even the malice of the Church's enemies, been the unwilling instrument of unfolding Her children's unwavering fidelity, and ever-increasing Devotion to the Heart of their Adorable Savior.

The Hierarchy of the United States, as remarkable for their zeal for the Church's growth, as for their Devotion to its Head, could not but feel that love for the Sacred Heart with which the heart of Christendom was yearning, and to which It was everywhere giving expression. Province after Province, Diocese after Diocese, in these States, has been laid at the feet of Jesus, to be united the more closely to His Adorable Heart. And we, Dearly Beloved, eminently Catholic, sprung from catholic parents, children of a catholic soil, in which Faith and Civilization have ever been a twin; we, through whose veins courses the best blood of France and of Ireland, of Italy, of Spain and of Germany; we, so diverse in origin, yet forming but one, grand, Glorious, Religious, Catholic Whole, now, do We intend to consecrate, in the most solemn manner possible, Our Diocese and Our Province to the Sacred Heart of Jesus.

Therefore, seeing, Dearly Beloved, that the pilgrim spirit of the Middle Ages has been revived in our days, considering that the Sovereign Pontiff has granted Plenary Indulgences to the faithful who are visiting Paray-le-Monial, the centre of the Devotion to the Sacred Heart, and Lourdes, the choice Grotto of Mary Immaculate; and knowing that we are unable, almost every one of us, to visit those Miraculous Sanctuaries, We have asked and obtained from His Holiness, Pius IX, a favor, the bestowal of which proves his paternal interest in our regard. And not only for Our Diocese, but for all the Dioceses of the Province, We besought that favor, the acceptation of which depends on each of Our Venerable Brethren for his own Diocese.—This privilege consists in the fact, that Pius IX has granted Plenary Indulgences in the same degree, and, in the same manner, to the Novena of Pilgrimages, which We herein prescribe, and subject to the conditions, which We hereby append, as He has to the very Pilgrimage of Paray-le-Monial and of the Grotto of Lourdes.

During the nine consecutive Sundays below named, and in the various Churches, which We add thereto, the Faithful of Our Diocese should visit the Church which We name on the day of its Pilgrimage, and to recite therein the prayers which We indicate below. In Our Suffragan Dioceses, both as to the Church which the Faithful should visit and as to the prayers, that they are to recite, the expressed will of their respective Bishops is the Rule by which they are to abide. In country parishes the

— 8 —

parochial church shall be the church of the Pilgrimage. The members of Religious Communities will visit, the specified number of times, their Community-Chapels. Those, who will not be able to make the Novena entire, should, at least, make six of the visits, with the privilege of reciting, at their homes, the prayers for the remaining three. On Sunday, 14th June, the Sunday within the Octave of the Sacred Heart, the Novena will close in Our Metropolitan Church, and on that day also, both Our Arch-Diocese, and Our Province will be consecrated to the Sacred Heart of Jesus.

This Novena of Ours, Dearly Beloved, links us to that Pilgrim band—Our brethren in the Faith, and portion of which will soon leave Our city for the Shrine of Mary Immaculate and the Tombs of the Apostles. Prostate at the feet of Christ's Vicar, they will tender Our undying love for His Holiness, and Our unswerving Devotion to the Successor of St. Peter. The precious boon of His Blessing He will bestow, not alone upon them—kneeling at His feet, but also upon Us and upon Our Province. To Us, Dearly Beloved, a more suitable preparation, for Our Grand Solemn Act of Consecration, is hardly conceivable.

And, Dearly Beloved, in that Solemn Hour, when the Catholics of Our Diocese, and Our Province will be laid at the feet of Our Crucified Lord, let Our prayers at that moment, be the genuine expression of hearts truly consecrated to His. Let Us so completely incorporate ourselves in His Adorable Heart, that that Heart may throb with a ready response for what petition soever we address to Him for HIS Greater Glory, the immediate triumph of His Church, and the sanctification of Our own souls, that when Our earthly Pilgrimage is ended, we may be enabled to see, love, bless, and possess Him for eternity.

Therefore, after having invoked the Holy Name of God, and after having asked and received the counsel of our Venerable Suffragans, the Bishops of Our Province, We have ordained, and do hereby ordain, that which is hereinafter prescribed:

1o.—The Consecration, both of Our Arch-Diocese and Our Province, to the Sacred Heart of Jesus, will take place, in Our Metropolitan Church, on Sunday, 14th June, the Sunday within the Octave of the Feast of the Sacred Heart of Jesus.

2o.—A Novena of Pilgrimages, preparatory to this Consecration, will commence on Sunday, 19th April, and will be continued for nine consecutive Sundays, terminating on Sunday 14th June, the day on which the Pilgrimage will be closed, and the Dioceses consecrated.

3o.—In Our Metropolitan City the Pilgrimage will be made to the Churches We designate below, and in the order that We hereby prescribe.

1o.—St-Mary's—Chapel of the Archbishop, Sunday, 19th April.

2o.—Church of the Immaculate Conception, Jesuits, 26th April.

3o.—St-Mary's—German, 4th District, Redemptorists, Sunday, 3d May.

4o.—Church of the Nativity of B. V. M., Carrollton, Sunday, May 10th.

5o.—Church of the Holy Name of Mary, Algiers, Sunday, May 17th.

6o.—Church of Our Lady of the Sacred Heart, Sunday, May 24.

7o.—Church of the Annunciation, Sunday, May 31st.

8o.—Church of Our Lady of Ready Help and St. Maurice, June 7th.

9o.—Cathedral-Church, Sunday, June 14th., the day as aforesaid, on which the Pilgrimage will be closed and the Act of Consecration made.

4o.—Every Church, to which the Pilgrimage is to be made, may, on the Sunday of its Pilgrimage, be visited at any time, either in the fore or in the afternoon. But, in the afternoon, at an hour to be hereinafter designated, there will, in the above-named Churches, be exercises suitable to the Pilgrimage, viz: 1o. Sermon. 2o. The singing or the re-

— 10 —

cital of prayers prescribed. 3o. Lastly, Benediction of the Most Blessed Sacrament. In fine, lest anything that would tend to the Solemnity of the Pilgrimage should be omitted; lest any means that might increase the Piety and strengthen the Faith of the Pilgrims, be left untried, We hereby permit the *Solemn Exposition* of the Most Holy Sacrament, throughout the entire day of each Church's Pilgrimage.

5o.—The prayers, either to be sung or recited, are the Psalm *Miserere*, the *Parce Domine* trice, and to the usual versicles, and prayers for the Benediction of the Most Holy Sacrament are to be added the versicle: "*Domine, non secundum peccata nostra facias nobis*," and the prayer: *Exaudi, quæsumus Domine, supplicum preces.*" Those who are unable to read, when they are incapable of joining in the public exercises, will recite five *Paters*, and *Aves*.

This Our present Pastoral must be read at the Parochial-Mass, on the first Sunday after Easter, or on the Sunday which immediately follows Its Receipt.

Given at New Orleans, on the Feast of the Annunciation of the B. V. M., on this 25th day of March, 1874.

† NAPOLEON JOSEPH.
Archbishop of New Orleans.

By order of His Grace,

G. RAYMOND, D. D.,
Vicar General and Chancellor.

APPENDIX III

ARCHDIOCESE OF NEW ORLEANS COLLECTION

Invoice for two statues

1873 Sep. 9
Wapler, C.: Paris, (France)
to Archbishop (Napoleon Joseph Perché): New Orleans, (Louisiana)

An invoice amounting to $956.25 for two statues, one of Our Lady of Lourdes and one of Bernadette, shipped to (Perché), care of Am. Lutton, on the steamer Missouri.

Facture de deux Caisses Statuaire achetées d'ordre et p.r compte de Monseigneur l'Archevêque de la Nouvelle-Orléans, et expédiées à Mr Am. Fulton par Steamer "Missouri"

Liverpool 9 Septembre 1873.

1 Caisse.

1 N. D. Lourdes 2m / Carton décor extra riche jeu de fonds s/ la robe et sur le voile. 600

1 Caisse.

1 Bernadette pour d.: décor simple. 900

800

Escompte 10% 80

720

Commission d'achat 5% 30 750

... Emballage ... 180

Note de frais de Paris au Havre

Transport	10 90
Permis droits Statistique	1 30
Ports de lettres	1 50
Commission	4
Ass. de 1000 p. 1% et Police	11 50
Connaissements. Timbre	2 40
	30 65
Timbre & frais de Paris	10.

30. 70.

Légalisation de Facture. 13. 50

Total Fr. 906.90.

Paris le 9 Septembre 1873

C. Mazolery

APPENDIX IV

Receipt of payment for work on altar

1873 Nov. 1
Perché, N(apoleon) J(oseph), Archbishop of: New Orleans, (Louisiana)

One year from date Perché promises to pay George Soulier 600 piastres for work done at the Cathedral (of St. Louis) on the altar of Our Lady of Lourdes and the altar of St. Francis Assisi. (Reverse): Soulier acknowledges the receipt of payments in 1873 and 1874

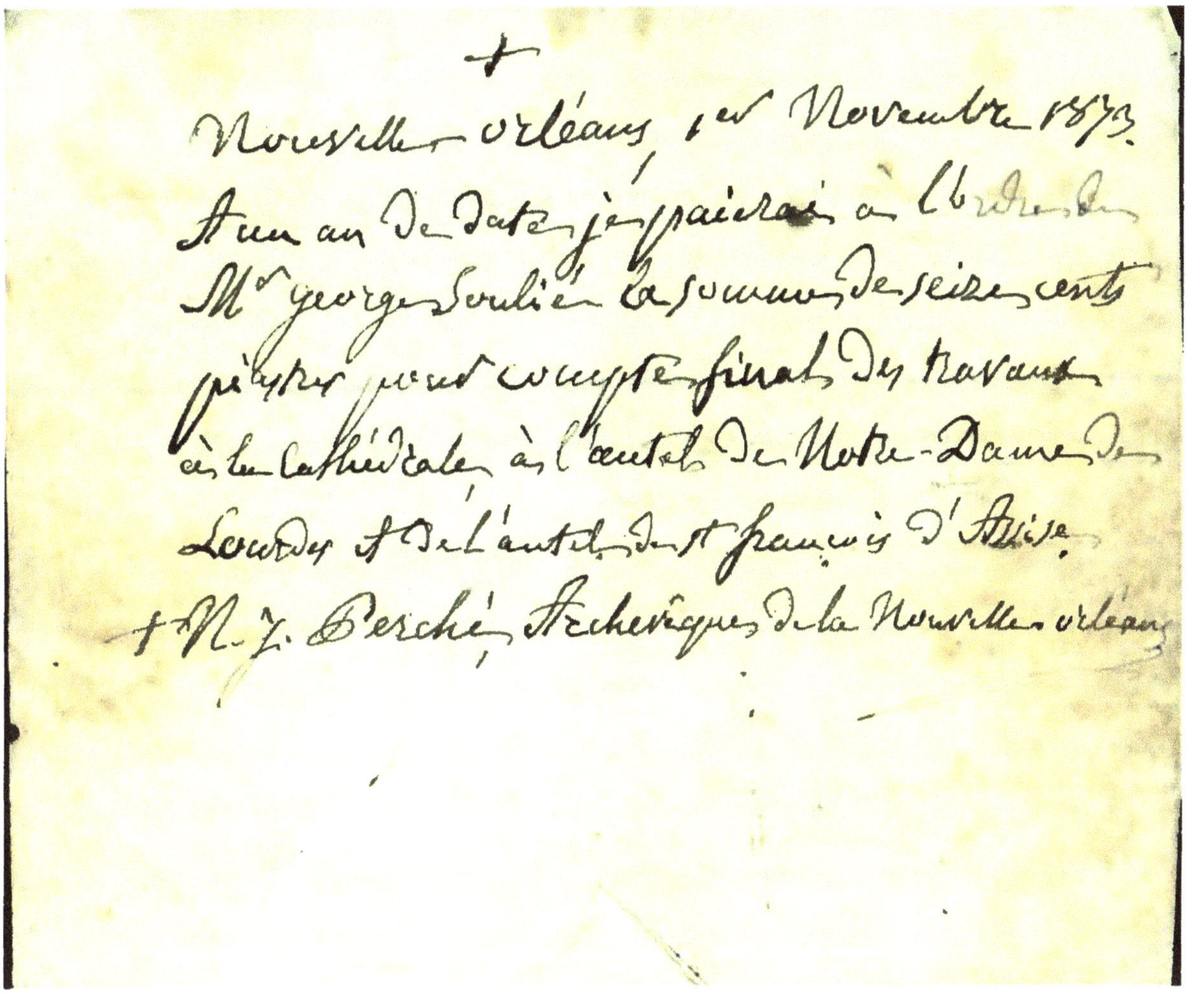
+
Nouvelle orléans, 1er Novembre 1873.
A un an de date je payerai à l'ordre de
Mr George Soulié la somme de seize cents
piastres pour compte final des travaux
à la Cathédrale, à l'autel de Notre-Dame de
Lourdes et de l'autel de St François d'Assise.
+ N. J. Perché, Archevêque de la Nouvelle orléans

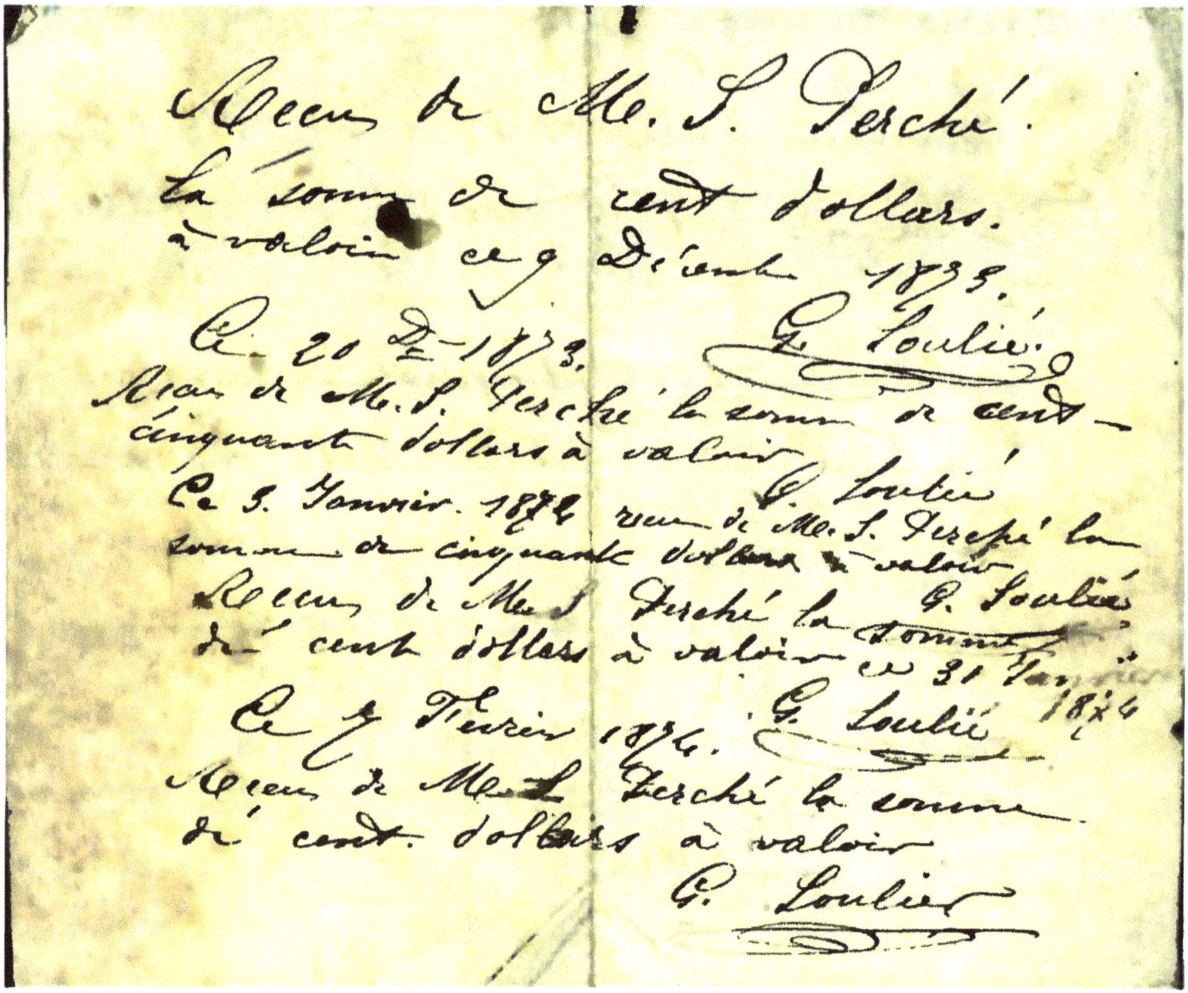

Reçu de Me. S. Perché
la somme de cent dollars.
à valoir ce 9 Décembre 1873.

Ce 20 Xbre 1873. G. Soulié

Reçu de Me. S. Perché la somme de cent-cinquante dollars à valoir

Ce 5. Janvier 1874 G. Soulié

reçu de Me. S. Perché la somme de cinquante dollars à valoir

Reçu de Me. S. Perché la somme de cent dollars à valoir ce 31 Janvier 1874 G. Soulié

Ce 7 Février 1874. G. Soulié

Reçu de Me. S. Perché la somme de cent dollars à valoir

G. Soulié

APPENDIX V

Bill for two statues

1873 Dec. 9
Lutton, Am.: New Orleans, (Louisiana)
to Archbishop N(apoleon) J(oseph) Perché: (New Orleans, Louisiana)

A bill for two statues: Our Lady of Lourdes and Bernadette, $307.74. Paid, Dec. 10, 1873.

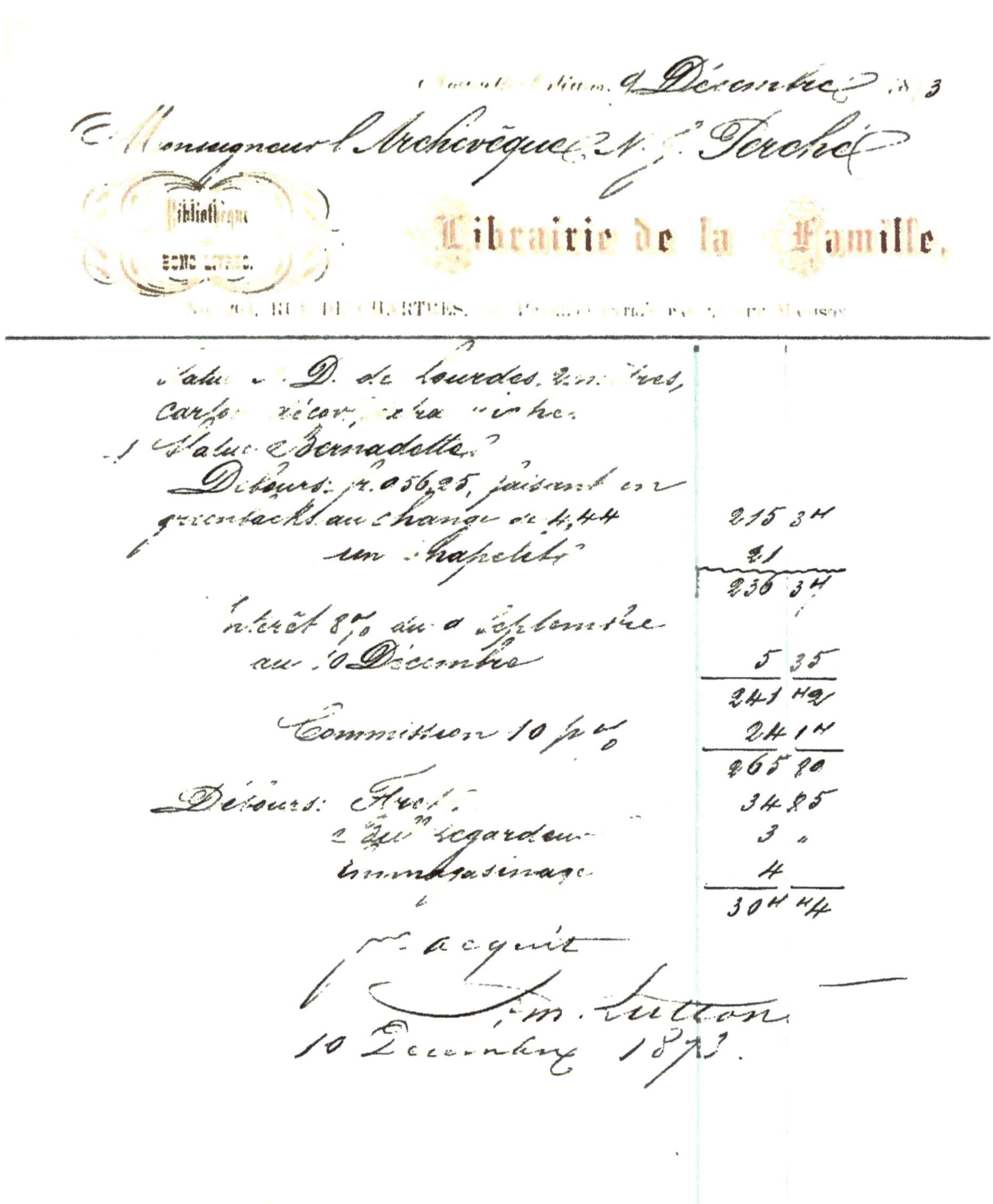
Nouvelle-Orléans, 9 Décembre 1873

Monseigneur l'Archevêque N. J. Perché

Bibliothèque des Bons Livres. Librairie de la Famille.

No. 201, Rue de Chartres, [illegible]

Statue N. D. de Lourdes, 2 mètres, carton décor, extra riche.	
1 Statue Bernadette	
Déboursé: fr. 956,25, faisant en greenbacks au change de 4,44	215 37
1 un Chapelet	21
	236 37
Intérêt 8% du 9 Septembre au 10 Décembre	5 35
	241 72
Commission 10 p%	24 17
	265 89
Déboursé: Fret	34 85
2 [illegible] garde	3 "
Emmagasinage	4
	307 74

Pour acquit

[illegible] Sutton

10 Décembre 1873.

APPENDIX VI

Handwritten petition for enrollment in Confraternity and response

1874 Jan. 25
Simeoni, Father John, Secretary of the Sacred Congregation of Propaganda: Rome, (Italy) to Archbishop Napoleon Joseph Perché of: New Orleans, (Louisiana)

(This is a petition from Perché which is answered on the back). (Perche) asks the Holy Father that his Confraternity of Our Lady of Lourdes which he was erected in his cathedral be affiliated with the Confraternity in Lourdes itself. The superior of the missionaries at Lourdes tells him that they can make such an affiliation only among the churches of France. Therefore he applies to the Holy Father for this affiliation. Also since many pastors of churches in his diocese also ask for affiliation both in his see city and in other cities he asks that they too obtain this affiliation. The faithful of the diocese have always had great devotion to Our Lady, especially in her title of the Immaculate Conception and have erected in his cathedral a magnificent statue of Our Lady of Lourdes. (On the back of this letter written by Perché in his own hand is the letter of Simeoni in which he states that in the audience of January 25, 1874, Pope Pius IX gave the privilege of the affiliation to the confraternity not only in the cathedral but also in the parish churches of the diocese with the indulgences and privileges thereby attached. (Attached: a copy of Simeoni's letter.)

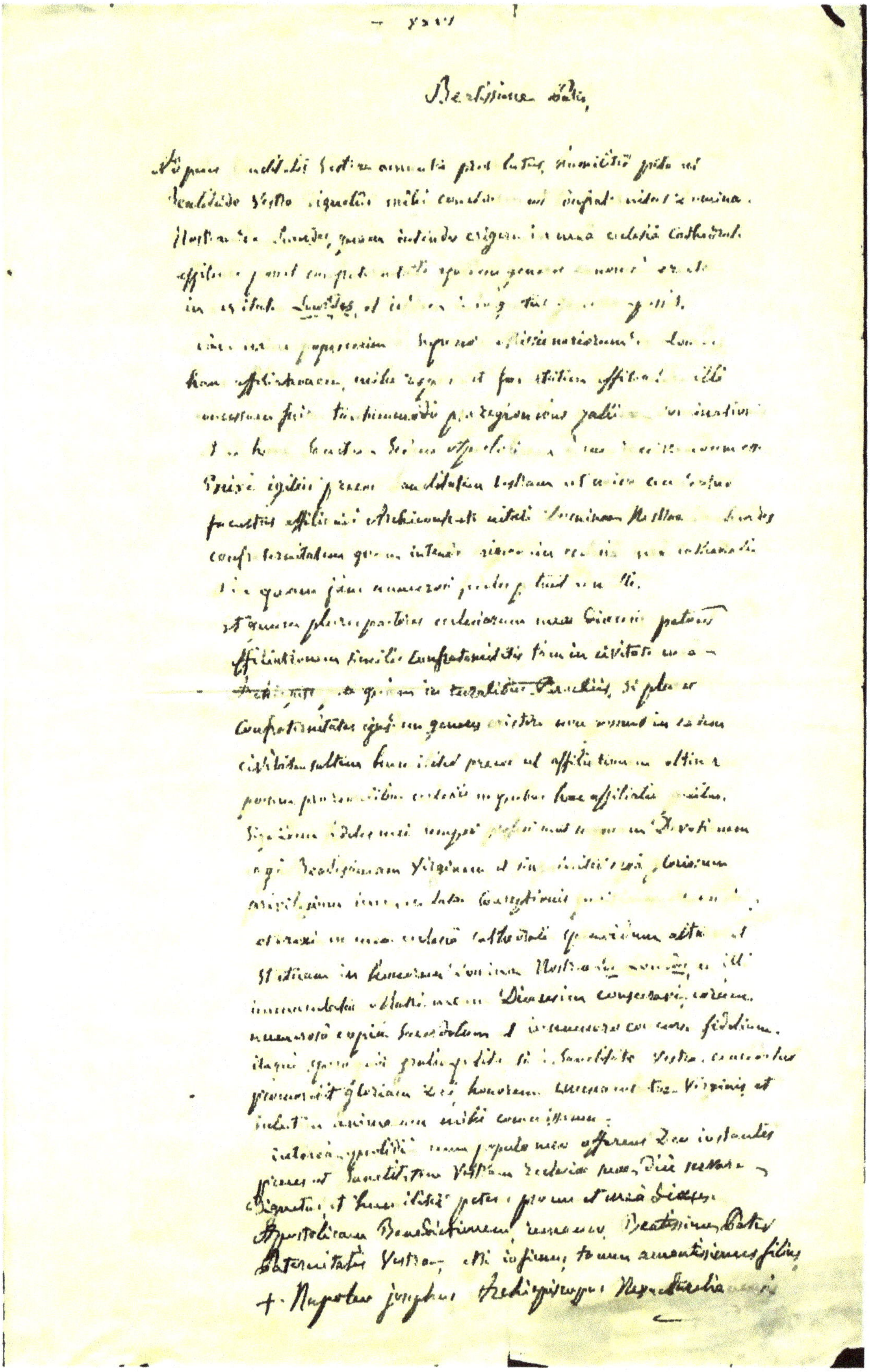

Beatissime Pater,

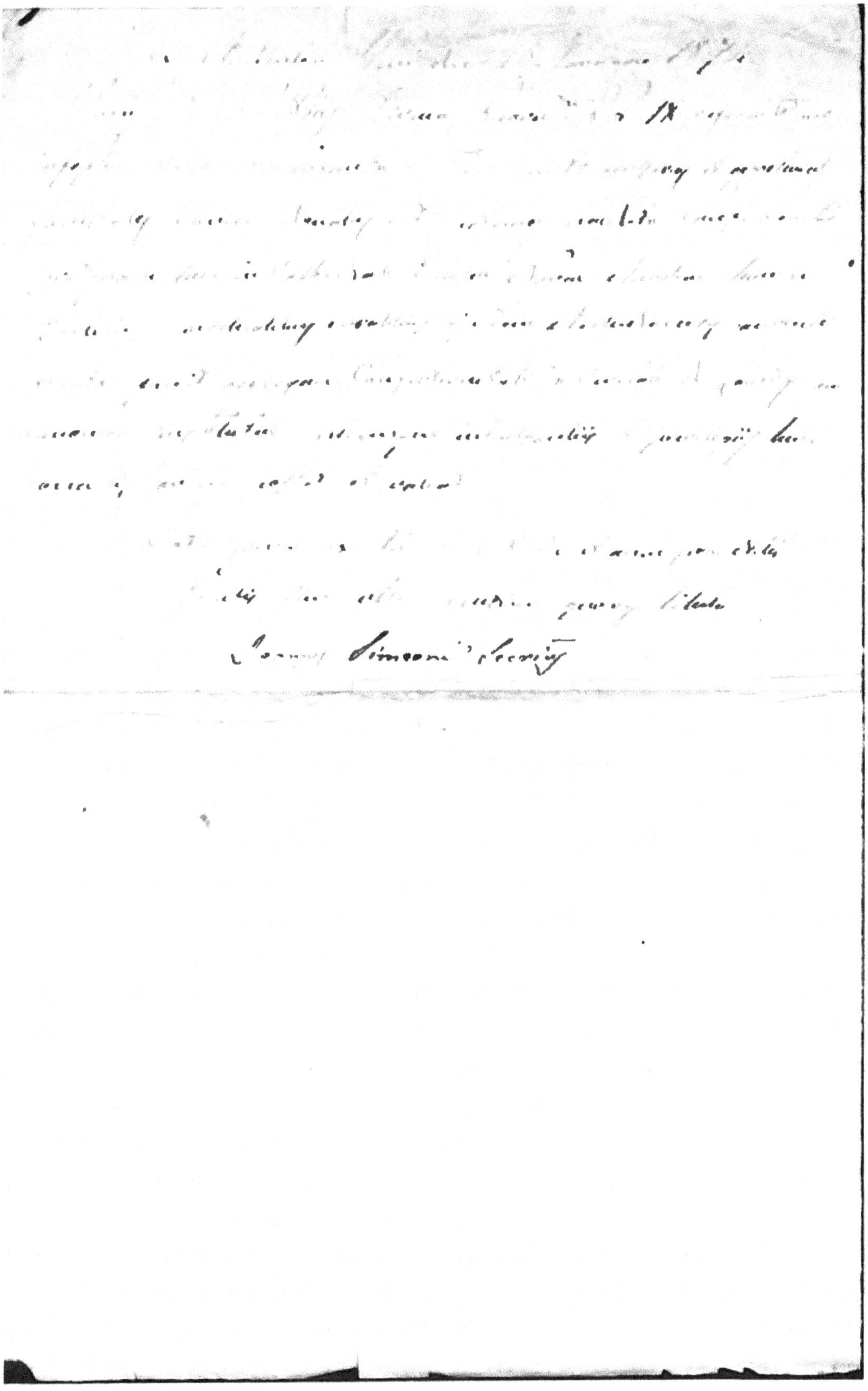

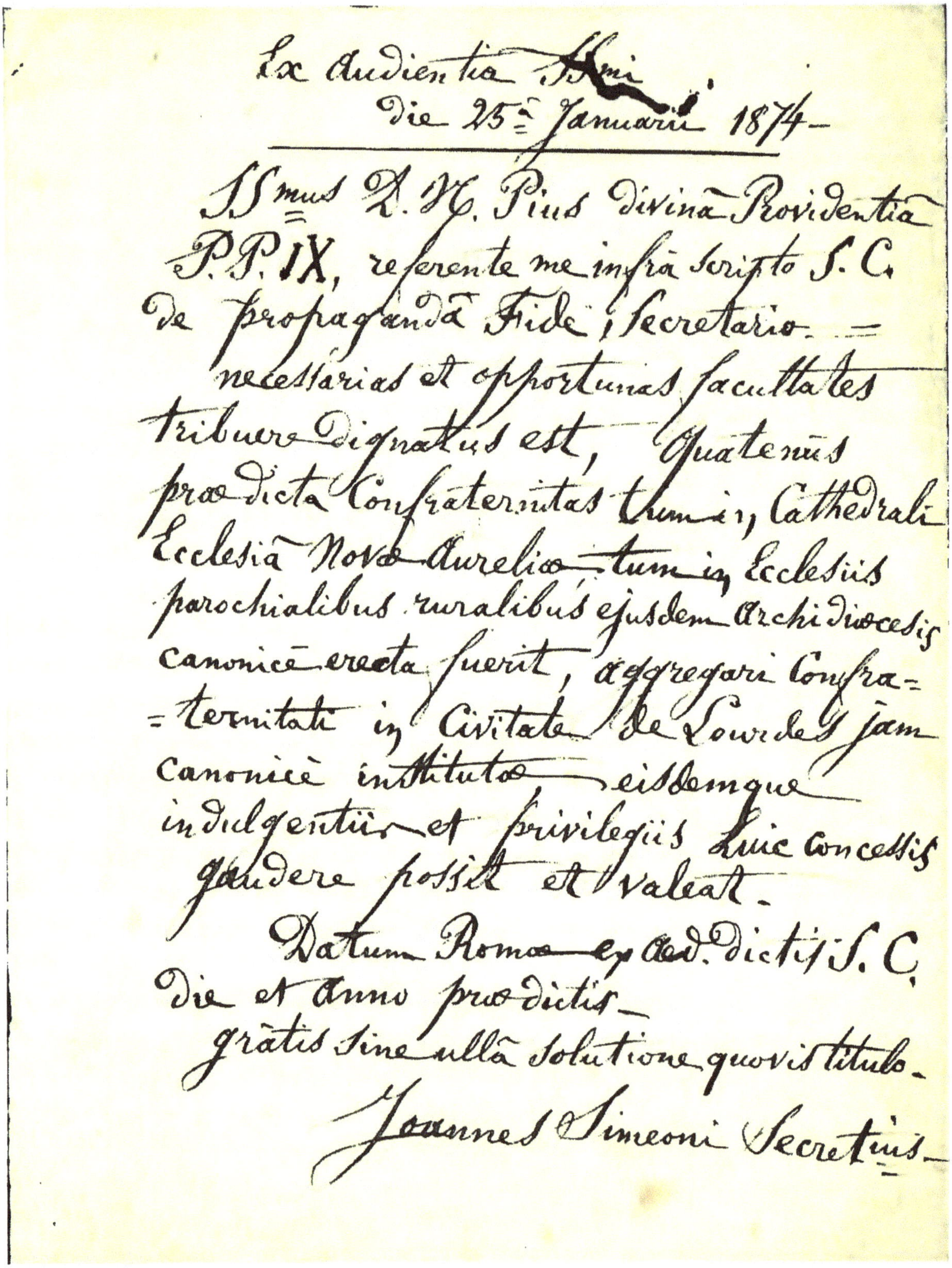

Ex Audientia SSmi
die 25a Januarii 1874

SSmus D. N. Pius divina Providentia P.P. IX, referente me infrascripto S. C. de propaganda Fide, Secretario —
necessarias et opportunas facultates tribuere Dignatus est, Quatenus prædicta Confraternitas tum in Cathedrali Ecclesia Novæ Aureliæ tum in Ecclesiis parochialibus ruralibus ejusdem Archidiœcesis canonice erecta fuerit, aggregari Confraternitati in Civitate de Lourdes jam canonice institutæ, eisdemque indulgentiis et privilegiis huic concessis gaudere possit et valeat.

Datum Romæ ex Aed. dictæ S. C. die et Anno prædictis.
gratis sine ulla solutione quovis titulo.

Joannes Simeoni Secretarius

APPENDIX VII

Letter to Archbishop Perche' in Lourdes, France

1876 Jun. 10
Brand, Eugénie: New Orleans, (Louisiana)
to Archbishop (Napoleon Joseph) Perché: Lourdes, (France)

Since Perché's departure death has made many empty places in their family. After the death of Father (Victor) Jamey there died her uncle, Anatole Jamey; her aunt, Mrs. Pauline Ingouf; Lucie Trahant; Trahant's uncle, Flor Boudreaux - the brother of Marie Trahant; and, finally, their grandmother whose good example will accompany them always. She asks Perché to pray to Our Lady of Lourdes to give her enough health to work for her children. Since the birth of her last daughter she has been confined almost constantly to bed. She has had several doctors, including Dr. (Charles) Faget, all of whom say that the only remedy is a very dangerous operation. Others have added that a new pregnancy would endanger her life. She has 4 children living: Paul (Brand), Francis (Brand), Marie (Brand), and Claire (Brand). Sabin (Brand) is still at Donaldson; he comes two days each month. Papa is well but Celina is not

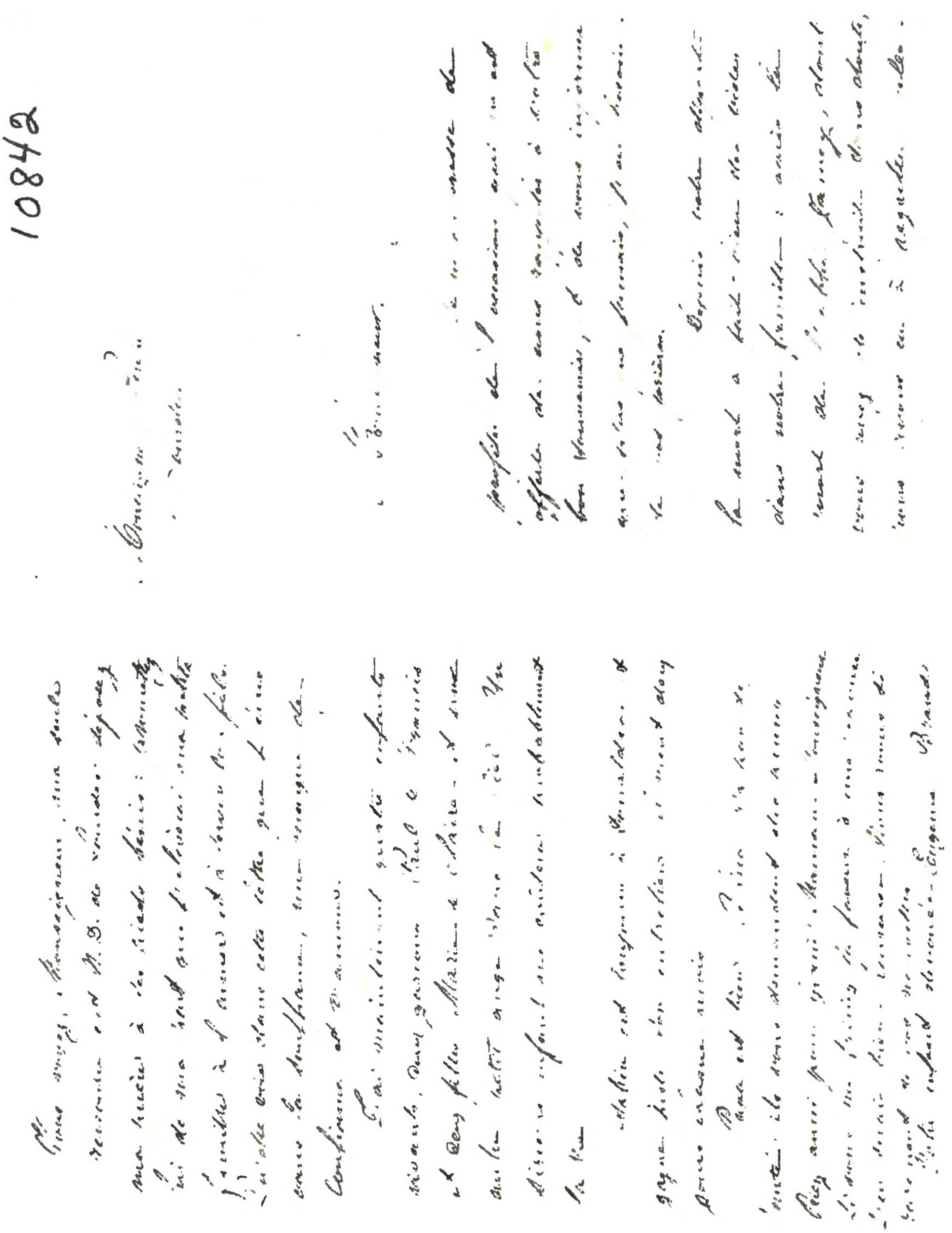

[illegible] 13 [illegible] 1876.

10842

Monseigneur [illegible]
[illegible] Lourdes

Monseigneur,

Je m'empresse de profiter de l'occasion qui m'est offerte de vous rappeler à votre bon souvenir, et de vous informer que plus que jamais, [illegible]

Depuis notre dernière [illegible] la mort a fait bien des vides dans notre famille : ainsi la mort de l'abbé Fa[illegible], dont vous avez été instruit sans doute, nous avons eu à regretter celle [illegible]

Vous voyez, Monseigneur, ma seule ressource est N. D. de Lourdes. déposez ma prière à ses pieds bénis : [illegible] de ma [illegible] ma petite famille à l'amour et à servir son fils. [illegible] dans cette lettre [illegible] une marque de confiance et d'amour.

J'ai maintenant quatre enfants vivants, deux garçons Paul et François et deux filles Marie et Claire, et un autre petit ange dans le ciel. Un dixième enfant [illegible] probablement la vie.

[illegible] est toujours à [illegible] et gagne juste son entretien [illegible] pour chacun [illegible]

Paul est bien [illegible]
Priez aussi pour [illegible] Monseigneur [illegible]
Votre enfant dévouée Eugénie Brands

de mon oncle Anatole [illegible], de tante Pauline (Mme Pigeon) de Lucie Trahant, de son oncle Flor Boudreau (le frère de Maria Trahant) et enfin une mort qui nous a causé un véritable chagrin, celle de notre chère grand maman qui nous a quittés le lendemain de l'Ascension.

Vous ne sauriez vous imaginer, Monseigneur, combien nous avons à remercier Dieu de la grâce d'une mort si édifiante. [illegible] toujours.

Maintenant, Monseigneur, je viens [illegible] celle [illegible] qui est de vous demander de prier [illegible] pour ma tante [illegible] de santé [illegible] pour mes chers enfants. Depuis [illegible] ma dernière fille (à [illegible] Patronage de St [illegible]) [illegible] au moment [illegible]. Voilà trois mois que [illegible] continuellement et à chaque fois une faiblesse me force à abandonner la leçon. Quant aux soins de la [illegible] il n'y faut [illegible] abandonner depuis quatre mois. [illegible] plusieurs médecins, entr'autres le Dr [illegible] une opération bien dangereuse [illegible] une nouvelle grossesse serait bien à craindre

Bibliography

A Century of Prayer 1885 - 1985. New Orleans: St. Clare Monastery, 1985.

A History of the Archdiocese of New Orleans. *Archdiocese of New Orleans.* 1888 - 1918. http://www.archdiocese-no.org/history/century.htm (accessed January 16, 2012).

Academy of the Sacred Heart. *Grotto Moves to Rosary Chapel Yard.* August 17, 2011. http://www.ashrosary.org/news.aspx?id=19 (accessed June 25, 2012).

Andrews, Patty. "The Majesty of Stained Glass." *Preservation in Print. Volume 28. Number 7*, September 12, 2001: 12.

—. "Preservation Resource Center of New Orleans." *Preservation Resources Center of New Orleans.* September 2001. http://www.prcno.org/programs/preservationinprint/piparchives/2001%20PIP/September%202001/12.html (accessed May 16, 2012).

AngelPig at AngelsWeb. *Old New Orleans Churches - 1897 - 1917.* 1997 - Present. http://www.storyvilledistrictnola.com/churches_nola.html (accessed June 24, 2012).

—. *St. Louis Cathedral - 1718.* 1997 - Present. http://www.storyvilledistrictnola.com/stlouis_cathedral.html (accessed June 24, 2012).

Angers, Trent. *Grand Coteau The Holy Land of South Louisiana.* Lafayette, LA: Acadian House Publishing, 2005.

Arceneaux, Reverend Chester C. "Cathedral of St. John the Evangelist." *Cathedral of St. John the Evangelist.* Lafayette: Church, September 2010.

Archbishop Napoleon Joseph Perche'. "Archbishop Napoleon J. Perche' to Archbishop John Purcell, 17 November 1871." *Archdiocese of New Orleans Collection, II-5-e, Archives of the University of Notre Dame.*

Badeaux, Trevis R. "Built as a blessing." *The Advertiser*, December 2007.

Banksia, Lady. "Shrines Placed in Many Gardens of New Orleans - Perhaps No City Has So Many Out-of-Door Sacred Statues." *The Times Picayune*, 11 October, 1936: 2.

Barry, Bonnie T. *For the Greater Honor and Glory of God - St. Charles Borromeo Church - Grand Coteau, LA.* Opelousas, LA: Andrepont Printing Company, 1987.

Baudier, Roger. *The Catholic Church in Louisiana.* New Orleans, LA: Reprinted 1972 by Louisiana Library, Association Public Library, 1972.

Behold this Heart Which Has So Loved Men. *Behold this Heart Which Has So Loved Men.* 2012. http://www.acfp2000.com/Sacred_Heart/Sacred%20Heart.html (accessed January 16, 2012).

Bodin, Elaine B. "THE FIRST HUNDRED YEARS: 1882-1982THE CENTENNIAL OF CATHOLIC EDUCATION IN "IMPERIAL" CALCASIEU." *THE FIRST HUNDRED YEARS: 1882-1982THE CENTENNIAL OF CATHOLIC EDUCATION IN "IMPERIAL" CALCASIEU.* September 1982, 1982. http://library.mcneese.edu/depts/archive/ftbooks/catholic%20education.htm (accessed July 23, 2012).

Bordelon, Greyson. *Mt. Carmel Academy - Campus ministry holds rosary in the grotto.* October 11, 2011. http://www.mcacubs.com/cf_news/view.cfm?newsid=74 (accessed June 25, 2012).

Bourgeois, Lilliam C. *Cabanocey. The History, Customs and Folklore of St. James Parish.* Gretna, LA: Pelican Publishing, 1976.

Brand, Eugenie. "Letter of June 10, 1876 from Eugenie Brand of New Orleans to Archbishop Napoleon Joseph Perche', Lourdes, France." *Collection, VI-2-o, Archives of the University of Notre Dame.*

Brother Stephen Dardis, LC. "He Must Have Done His First Fridays." *www.catholic.net.* March 2008. http://www.catholic.net/index.php?option=dedestaca&id=706# (accessed July 11, 2012).

C.S.W.: Rome, (Italy). "C. S.W. to Archbishop Napoleon Joseph Perche', 1 April 1871." *Archdiocese of New Orleans Collection, VI-2-o, Archives of the University of Notre Dame.*

Catholic News Agency. *Catholic News Agency.* February 20, 2012. http://www.catholicnewsagency.com/news/journalist-chronicles-a-day-in-the-life-of-pope-benedict/ (accessed May 11, 2012).

Chambon, Rev. C. M. *In and Around the Old St. Louis Cathedral of New Orleans.* New Orleans, LA: Phillipe's Printery, Exchange Place, 1908.

Clark, Richard Henry. *Lives of Deceased Bishops of the Catholic Church in the United States, Vol III.* New York, NY: Richard H. Clark, Nos. 49 & 51, 1888.

Collins, Andrew. "Moon Handbooks New Orleans: Including Cajun Country and the River Road." *Google Books.* February 27, 2007. http://books.google.com/books?id=3CDGQinECFgC&pg=PA301&lpg=PA301&dq=Lourdes+in+19th+century+New+Orleans&source=bl&ots=7mM8kY1MEH&sig=dCPEbqnB1k9ifZuwCDu52XZ_7Hs&hl=en&sa=X&ei=C_tST-mNAY_qtgeeiYyXBA&ved=0CCQQ6AEwATge#v=onepage&q=Lourdes%20in%2019th%20centu (accessed May 11, 2012).

Corson, Dorothy V. *Spirit of Notre Dame - A Cave of Candles.* 2001. http://nd.edu/~wcawley/corson/cors016.htm (accessed February 1, 2012).

Currier, Charles Warren. *A Centennial History of the Discalced Carmelites in the United States.* Baltimore: John Murphy and Company, 1890.

Dawes, D. and Nolan, C. *Religious Pioneers Building the Faith in the Archdiocese of New Orleans.* New Orleans: Archdiocese of New Orleans in cooperation with the Religious Community of Archivists of Greater New Orleans, 2004.

Delair, M. "M. Delair to Archbishop Napoleon Joseph Perche', 19 December 1880." *Archdiocese of New Orleans Collection, VI-3-b, Archives of the University of Notre Dame.*

—. "M. Delair to Archbishop Napoleon Joseph Perche', 28 December 1879." *Archdiocese of New Orleans Collection, VI-3-a, Archives of the University of Notre Dame.*

Denton, Father Anthony. *The Birds Will Sing Blogspot.* June 2, 2010. http://thebirdswillstillsing.blogspot.com/2010/06/pope-benedict-xvi-at-lourdes-grotto-in.html (accessed May 6, 2012).

Dolors, Sister Mary of the Seven. "Sister Mary of the Seven Dolors to Archbishop Napoleon Joseph Perche', 11 April 1871." *Archdiocese of New Orleans Collection, VI-2-o, Archives of the University of Notre Dame.*

Duncan, R. C. "A Condensed History of New Orleans - America's Most Interesting City." In *A Condensed History of New Orleans - America's Most Interesting City*, by R. C. Duncan. New Orleans, LA: Garrett County Press Reprint Edition 2010, 1920's.

Encyclopedia Americana. *Encyclopedia Americana: a library of universal knowledge, Vol. 20.* Albany, NY: A. B. Lyon, 1922.

Evans, Mills. "New Orleans The Carnival City of America." *Motor Age*, February 24, 1916: 10.

Father Tagh Tierney, O.C.D. *Bernadette of Lourdes and the Carmelite Connection 1858 - 2008.* 2008. carmelitedigest.com/Update_to_Website_Fall_2008.doc (accessed January 31, 2011).

Find a Grave. *Find a Grave.* 2012. http://www.findagrave.com/cgi-bin/fg.cgi?page=gr&GRid=62689482 (accessed January 29, 2012).

Freeman's Journal. "The Water of the Grotto of Lourdes." *The Morning Star and Catholic Messenger*, May 4, 1873: 5.

Good Shepherd Parish St Stephen Church. *Good Shepherd Parish St Stephen Church.* 2012. http://goodshepherdparishnola.com/content/view/1/2/ (accessed May 16, 2012).

Green, Harry. *Immigrant Ships Transcribers Guild SS France.* December 7, 1876. http://www.immigrantships.net/v9/1800v9/france18761207.html (accessed May 11, 2012).

—. *Immigrant Ships Transcribers Guild SS France.* March 8, 2008. http://www.immigrantships.net/v9/1800v9/france18761207.html (accessed July 21, 2012).

Greene, Father William Lemuel. *Antoine Blanc - 1792 - 1860 Fourth Bishop and First Archbishop of New Orleans.* Baton Rouge: Claitor's Publishing Division, 2008.

—. *Spicing Ecclesiastical Gumbo The Life of Napoleon Joseph Perche' Third Archbishop of New Orleans 1805 - 1883.* Baton Roug, LA: Claitor's Publishing Division, 2012.

Gregoire, Sister Therese. *ancestry.com - Leonard E. Gately of New Orleans, LA.* April 9, 2009. http://boards.ancestry.com/surnames.gately/121.2/mb.ashx (accessed June 25, 2012).

Hawley, Carrie Moss. "Mind Volume 15. Faith as a Law of the Universe." *Google Books.* February 27, 1905. http://books.google.com/books?id=sV8DAAAAYAAJ&pg=PA386&dq=Our+lady+of+lourdes+altar+at+St.+Louis+Cathedral&hl=en&sa=X&ei=Gl56T-LUNIOTtweR7sXYBA&ved=0CF4Q6AEwBg#v=onepage&q=Our%20lady%20of%20lourdes%20altar%20at%20St.%20Louis%20Cathedral&f=false (accessed May 11, 2012).

History of Annunciation Church. "History of Annunciation Church." *History of Annunciation Church.* http://www.neworleanschurches.com/annunciation/history.htm (accessed April 7, 2012).

Huber, Leonard V. *Creole Collage: Reflections on the Colorful Customs of Latter-Day New Orleans Creoles.* Lafayette, LA: Center for Louisiana Studies, University of Southwestern Louisiana, 1980.

Immaculate Conception Parish. *Immaculate Conception Parish. Jesuit Church. The History of the Jesuits in New Orleans.* May 11, 2012. http://jesuitchurch.net/parish_history.htm (accessed Mary 11, 2012).

Jessie Poesch, Professor Emerita. "National Historic Landmark Nomination." *United States Department of Interior, National Park Service.* May 12, 1996. http://pdfhost.focus.nps.gov/docs/NHLS/Text/73000872.pdf (accessed June 24, 2012).

John and Kathleen DeMajo. *Our Lady of Lourdes Catholic Church.* July. http://www.neworleanschurches.com/ollourdes/lourdes.htm (accessed July 17, 2012).

katrinafilm. *www.zomobo.net.* April 14, 2007. http://zomobo.net/play.php?id=78bc5252GE (accessed July 5, 2012).

Kemseke, Fr. Horacio Brito and Fr. Mark. "With Bernadette Praying the Rosary - Theme for 2012." © *Imprimerie de la Grotte / Sanctuaires Notre-Dame de Lourdes - Impression eurL Basilique du rosaire - Octobre 2011 - Photos VINCeNT.* October 2011. © Imprimerie de la Grotte / Sanctuaires Notre-Dame de Lourdes - Impression eurL Basilique du rosaire - Octobre 2011 - Photos VINCeNT (accessed May 12, 2012).

Kendall, John. *History of New Orleans.* Chicago and New York: The Lewis Publishing Company, 1922.

Lareum, Lucy. "The Pilgrim at Lourdes." *The Times - Richmond, VA*, April 23, 1893: 16.

Lasserre, Henri. *Notre Dame de Lourdes.* Paris, France: Victor Palme, 1876.

latinmass1983. *Tracitional Catholic.* May 9, 2017. http://traditionalcatholicism83.blogspot.com/2007/05/blessed-pope-pius-ix.html (accessed January 16, 2012).

Laurentin, Rene'. *Bernadette Speaks A Life of Saint Bernadette Soubirous In Her Own Words.* Boston: Pauline Books & Media, 2000.

Lisa. *Are We There Yet?* November 28, 2011. http://arewethereyet-davisfarmmom.blogspot.com/2011/11/feast-of-st-catherine-of-laboure.html (accessed January 16, 2011).

List Verse. *List Verse.* August 21, 2007. http://listverse.com/2007/08/21/top-10-incorrupt-corpses/ (accessed October 1, 2011).

Lourdes-France.org Site Internet des Sanctuaries Notre-Dame de Lourdes. *Lourdes-France.org Site Internet des Sanctuaries Notre-Dame de Lourdes.* 2012. http://www.lourdes-france.org/index.php?goto_centre=ru&contexte=en&id=414&id_rubrique=414 (accessed May 16, 2012).

—. *Lourdes-France.org Site Internet des Sanctuaries Notre-Dame de Lourdes.* 2012. http://www.lourdes-france.org/index.php?goto_centre=ru&contexte=en&id=416&id_rubrique=416 (accessed February 1, 2012).

—. *Lourdes-France.org Site Internet des Sanctuaries Notre-Dame de Lourdes.* 2012. http://www.lourdes-france.org/index.php?goto_centre=ru&contexte=en&id=417&id_rubrique=417 (accessed January 31, 2012).

—. *Lourdes-France.org Site Internet des Sanctuaries Notre-Dame de Lourdes.* 2012. http://www.lourdes-france.org/index.php?goto_centre=ru&contexte=en&id=417&id_rubrique=417 (accessed January 31, 2012).

—. *Lourdes-France.org Site Internet des Sanctuaries Notre-Dame de Lourdes.* 2012. http://www.lourdes-france.org/index.php?goto_centre=ru&contexte=en&id=415&id_rubrique=415 (accessed January 31, 2012).

Lucia, Joseph A. "Grotto at St. Michael's Observing Centennial." *The Times Picayune*, February 22, 1976: 6.

Lutton, Am. "Am. Lutton to Archbishop Napoleon Joseph Perche', 9 December 1873." *Archdiocese of New Orleans Collection, VI-2-o, Archives of the University of Notre Dame.*

Magnificat. *The Wonders of Lourdes.* Mame-Paris: Pierre-Marie Dumont, 2008.

Maud O'Bryan, Want Ad Reporter. "Grotto of Lourdes Sound and Color Film." *The Times Picayune*, February 9, 1962: 11.

New York Times (1857 - 1922)ProQuest. "Archbishop Perche Dying." *New York Times (1857 - 1922)ProQuest*, December 27, 1883: 1.

—. "Archbishop Perche Dying." *New York Times (1857 - 1922)ProQuest*, December 26, 1883.

—. "Archbishop Perche Dying: Forty Six Years in the Service of His Church." *New York Times (1857 - 1922)ProQuest*, December 25, 1883: 1.

—. "Archbishop Perche Very Ill." *New York Times (1857 - 1922)ProQuest*, May 12, 1882: 5.

—. "Funeral of Archbishop Perche." *New York Times (1857 - 1922)ProQuest*, January 3, 1884: 5.

—. "The Late Archbishop Perche." *New York Times (1857 - 1922)ProQuest*, December 29, 1883: 1.

Nolan, Charles E. *Cathedral-Basilica of St. Louis, King of France.* New Orleans, LA: Editions du Signe, 2009.

Nolan, Dorothy Dawes and Charles. *Religious Pioneers - Building the Faith in the Archdiocese of New Orleans.* New Orleans: Archdiocese of New Orleans in cooperation with the Religious Community Archivists of Greater New Orleans, 2004.

Pasquier, Michael. *Fathers on the Frontier: French Missionaries and the Roman Catholic Priesthood in the United States 1789 - 1870.* New York, NY: Oxford University Press, 2010.

Perche', Archbishop Napoleon Joseph. "Receipt dated November 1, 1873 signed by George Soulier." *Collection, VI-2-o, Archives of the University of Notre Dame.*

Pere' Regis-Marie de la Teyssonniere, Chaplain of Lourdes. *Le blog du Pere Regis-Marie.* August 1, 2011. http://pereregismarie.blogspot.com/ (accessed September 1, 2011).

Plauche, Brian. *Brian Plauche Photography and Photographs.* 2012. http://bpnola-photographs.smugmug.com/keyword/olgc%20stained%20glass/1/938198798_sqRhH#!i=938143310&k=KsWRw (accessed May 16, 2012).

Raphael, Mark S. *History of Notre Dame Seminary.* New Orleans, LA: Notre Dame Seminary, 1997.

Reeves, Sally Kittredge. *Legacy of a Century Academy of the Sacred Heart in New Orleans.* New Orleans: Walsworth Press Co., Inc., 1987.

Rice, Anne O'Brien. *Called Out of Darkness - a spiritual confession.* New York, Toronto: Alfred A. Knopf, 2008.

Simeoni, Fr. John. "Fr. John Simeoni to Archbishop Napoleon Joseph Perche, 25 January 1874. ." *Archdiocese of New Orleans Collection, VI-2-o, Archives of the University of Notre Dame.*

Sister Therese de Jesus, (D.C.). "Sister Therese' de Jesus (D.C.) to Archbishop Napoleon Joseph Perche', 1 August 1879." *Archdiocese of New Orleans Collection, VI-3-a, Archives of the University of Notre Dame.*

St. Charles Borromeo Church. *St. Charles Borromeo Church.* May 5, 2012. http://www.st-charles-borromeo.org/ (accessed May 5, 2012).

St. Joseph Catholic Church - A Brief History. *St. Joseph Catholic Church.* http://www.stjosephchurch-no.org/history.htm (accessed May 13, 2012).

St. Scholastica Academy. *St. Scholastica Academy.* 2012. http://www.ssacad.com/PageDisplay.asp?p1=1639 (accessed April 6, 2012).

Sunday Advocate Magazine. "St. Martin de Tours - The Mother Church is Restored." *Sunday Advocate Magazine*, July 29, 1973.

Teyssonniere, Pere' Regis-Marie de la. *Le blog du Pere Regis-Marie de la Teyssonniere.* August 31, 2011. http://pereregismarie.blogspot.com/2011_08_01_archive.html (accessed September 7, 2011).

The Advocate. "St. Martin de Tours reflects area's French heritage." *The Advocate*, February 18, 2002.

The Bayou Catholic. "Sacred Heart History since 1800's." *The Bayou Catholic*, August 21, 1985: 18 - 34.

The Dominican Sisters. *Rosaryville - God's Kaleidescope - 50th Anniversary Souvenir Booklet.* Ponchatoula: The Dominican Sisters, 1989.

The Medical Standard, Volume 26. Vol. 29, in *The Medical Standard, Volume 26*, 314. Chicago: G. P. Englehard and Company, 1903.

The Morning Star and Catholic Messenger. "A Great Collection of Holy Relics." *The Morning Star and Catholic Messenger*, February 1, 1874: 3.

—. "A Miniature Grotto of Lourdes." *The Morning Star and Catholic Messenger*, February 15, 1874: 4.

—. "Achbishopric of New Orleans." *The Morning Star and Catholic Messenger*, March 22, 1874: 4.

—. "Address of the Ancient Order of Hibernians at the Most Rev. Archbishop." *The Morning Star and Catholic Messenger*, December 31, 1876: 1.

—. "Address of the Archbishop of New Orleans at the Congress at Poitiers." *The Morning Star and Catholic Messenger*, September 19, 1875: 4.

—. "Another Miraculous Cure at Lourdes." *The Morning Star and Catholic Messenger*, September 28, 1873: 3.

—. "Archbishopric of New Orleans." *The Morning Star and Catholic Messenger*, March 22, 1874: 4.

—. "Arch-Confraternity of Our Lady of Lourdes." *The Morning Star and Catholic Messenger*, May 11, 1873: 8.

—. "Confraternity of Our Lady of Lourdes." *The Morning Star and Catholic Messenger*, Mary 17, 1874: 4.

—. "Cures Apparently Miraculous at the Holy Grotto of our Blessed Lady of Lourdes, May 1, 1873." *The Morning Star and Catholic Messenger*, June 15, 1873: 1.

—. "Cures by the Water of Lourdes." *The Morning Star and Catholic Messenger*, April 6, 1873: 3.

—. "Father Hermann." *The Morning Star and Catholic Messenger*, December 27, 1868: 7.

—. "Letter from "Our" Pilgrim - Arrival at Lourdes and Devotions at the Shrine of Our Lady." *The Morning Star and Catholic Messenger*, July 5, 1874: 4.

—. "Miracle at Liege." *The Morning Star and Catholic Messenger*, March 27, 1870: 6.

—. "Ordinations." *The Morning Star and Catholic Messenger*, May 2, 1875: 4.

—. "Our Blessed Lady of Lourdes." *The Morning Star and Catholic Messenger*, February 19, 1871: 2.

—. "Our Lady of Lourdes - Pilgrimage of St. Henry's Congregation to Her Shrine in Carrollton." *The Morning Star and Catholic Messenger*, December 13, 1874: 4.

—. "Our Lady of Lourdes." *The Morning Star and Catholic Messenger*, October 17, 1869: 1.

—. "Our Lady of Lourdes." *The Morning Star and Catholic Messenger*, November 30, 1873: 4.

—. "Our Lady of Lourdes." *The Morning Star and Catholic Messenger*, February 1, 1874: 4.

—. "Our Lady of Lourdes." *The Morning Star and Catholic Messenger*, December 7, 1873: 4.

—. "Pastoral Letter of His Grace The Archbishop of New Orleans, Announcing the Inauguration of the Monument Erected in Honor of Our Lady of Lourdes, in the Metropolitan Church of New Orleans." *The Morning Star and Catholic Messenger*, November 2, 1873: 5.

—. "Promises Made by Jesus Christ to Blessed Margaret Mary; Religious of the Visitation in Favor of Those Devoted to His Sacred Heart." *The Morning Star and Catholic Messenger*, March 29, 1874: 3.

—. "The American Pilgrimage - Contributions Received." *The Morning Star and Catholic Messenger*, March 29, 1874: 3.

—. "The Archbishop's Departure." *The Morning Star and Catholic Messenger*, April 25, 1875: 4.

—. "The Ceremonies at the Cathedral ." *The Morning Star and Catholic Messenger*, December 14, 1873: 4.

—. "The Holy Father." *The Morning Star and Catholic Messenger*, October 5, 1873: 1.

—. "The Most Reverend Archbishop of New Orleans." *The Morning Star and Catholic Messenger*, May 19, 1872: 4.

—. "The Pilgrimage to Lourdes." *The Morning Star and Catholic Messenger*, November 3, 1872: 8.

—. "The Water from the Grotto of Lourdes." *The Morning Star and Catholic Messenger*, February 4, 1872: 2.

—. "Triduum at the Cathedral." *The Morning Star and Catholic Messenger*, November 30, 1873: 4.

The National Shrine of Our Lady of Lourdes. *The National Shrine of Our Lady of Lourdes.* 2012. http://www.emmitsburg.net/grotto/history.htm (accessed January 28, 2012).

The Picayune. *The Picayune's Guide to New Orleans - Sixth Edition.* New Orleans: The Picayune, 1904.

The Times Picayune. *175 Years - Our Times New Orleans through the pages of The Times Picayune.* New Orleans: The Times Picayune, 2011.

—. "A Lecture on Lourdes. Father McGarry Pictures the Place and Tells Its Story." *The Times Picayune*, November 22, 1909.

—. "Angola Grotto Blessing Held." *The Times Picayune*, February 12, 1958.

—. "Archbishop Rummel Visits France's Grotto of Lourdes." *The Times Picayune*, August 27, 1949: 5.

—. "Archbishop Shaw Will Bless Grotto." *The Times Picayune*, February 4, 1934: 10.

—. "Archbishop Will Dedicate Grotto." *The Times Picayune*, February 1, 1958: 12.

—. "Archbishop Will Dedicate New Holy Cross Building." *The Times Picayune*, September 10, 1955: 8.

—. "Cardinal and Archbishop Honor the Celebration of the Semicentennial of the Miracle of Our Lady of Lourdes." *The Times Picayune*, February 10, 1908.

—. "Cardinal Gibbons." *The Times Picayune*, February 10, 1908.

—. "Centennial Chapel for the Ursulines." *The Times Picayune*, 1914.

—. "Church to Present Benefit Film Show." *The Times Picayune*, June 7, 1924: 9.

—. "Close of the Novena of Pilgrimages." *The Times Picayune*, June 1874.

—. "Close of the Novena Pilgrimages. Solemn Consecration of the Diocese and Province to the Sacred Heart of Jesus." *The Times Picayune*, June 16, 1874.

—. "Consecration of a Bishop." *The Times Picayune*, April 10, 1899: 1 & 7.

—. "December 8 at the Ursuline Convent." *The Times Picayune*, December 12, 1904.

—. "Dedication of Grotto Set Today on Orphanage Lawn." *The Times Picayune*, June 23, 1951: 8.

—. "Famous Lourdes Grotto, Reproduced Here at the Church on Napoleon Ave." *The Times Picayune*, July 19, 1908.

—. "Fr. Berthault Rites Monday." *The Times Picayune*, April 13, 1975: 18.

—. "Fr. Coburn Will Conduct Novena." *The Times Picayune*, February 15, 1958: 11.

—. "His Eminence, Cardinal Gibbons, on his Annual Visit. Welcomed at Depot by Crowd of Admiring Friends. Will Participate in Our Lady of Lourdes Jubilee." *The Times Picayune*, February 1908.

—. "In Memoriam. Yesterday's Celebration Commemorative of the Death of Pio Nono." *The Times Picayune*, February 21, 1878.

—. "Lady of Lourdes Program PLanned. New Orleans to Observe 75th Anniversary of Apparition." *The Times Picayune*, January 29, 1933: 2.

—. "Lourdes Grotto Replica Erected. Shrine at Notre Dame Seminary Erected." *The Times Picayune*, May 14, 1943: 21.

—. "Lourdes Lecture. James L. Small to Illustrate Talk on Famous Shrine." *The Times Picayune*, March 7, 1925: 21.

—. "Maison Blanche - Stone Figures." *The Times Picayune*, April 29, 1959: 29.

—. "March Slated to Cathedral - Rally to be Dedicated to Our Lady of Lourdes." *The Times Picayune*, June 21, 1958: 16.

—. "Nooks and Corners of St. Louis Cathedral." *The Times Picayune*, September 22, 1907.

—. "Our Lady of Lourdes Celebration Ends." *The Times Picayune*, February 12, 1908.

—. "Our Lady of Lourdes. Semicentennial Triduum Continues at Church Here." *The Times Picayune*, February 11, 1908.

—. "Our Lady of Lourdes. Semi-centennial Triduum Continues at Church Here, Father O'Shaunahan Preaching the Sermon at Last Night's Inspiring Service." *The Times Picayune*, February 1908.

—. "Present for Mgr. Guidi." *The Times Picayune*, September 3, 1902: 2.

—. "School Building Dedication Held." *The Times Picayune*, September 12, 1955: 12.

—. "Silver Jubilee of the Association of Our Lady of Lourdes." *The Times Picayune*, August 13, 1900.

—. "Statues in St. Patrick's as Memorials of Love." *The Times Picayune*, April 11, 1904.

—. "The Fountain of Lourdes. A Beautiful Shrine Fitted Up in the Cathedral." *The Times Picayune*, December 10, 1883.

—. "The Grotto of Lourdes, Recently Erected in the Church of Our Lady of Lourdes, Napoleon Avenue." *The Times Picayune*, March 14, 1909.

The Tri-Weekly Capitolian. "Archbishop Perche'." *The Tri-Weekly Capitolian*, November Unknown, 1881: Unknown.

Thompson, T. P. *The St. Louis Cathedral of New Orleans, A Sketch. Restoration Souvenir.* 1918.

Uter, Frank M. *Stones Beside the River - A History of the Church on the East Banker of St. James Parish 1809 - 2009.* 2009.

Vatican City State. *Vatican City State.* 2012. http://www.vaticanstate.va/EN/Monuments/The_Vatican_Gardens/ (accessed May 6, 2012).

Wapler, C. "Invoice dated September 9, 1873 from C. Wapler to Archbishop Napoleon Joseph Perche', Archdiocese of New Orleans." *Collection, VI-2-o, Archives of the University of Notre Dame.*

Wikipedia. *Wikipedia.* 2012. http://fr.wikipedia.org/wiki/Dominique_Peyramale (accessed May 16, 2012).

—. *Wikipedia.* 2012. http://en.wikipedia.org/wiki/Pope_Pius_IX (accessed January 16, 2012).

Wilson, Sam. *St. Patrick's Church of New Orleans.* New Orleans, 1992.

Wiseman, Vincent, O.P. *The Immaculate Conception.* 17 2003, October. http://campus.udayton.edu/mary/resources/kimmac.html (accessed May May 11, 2012, 2012).

Zacherie, J. S. *Outlines of the History of New Orleans.* New Orleans: F. F. Hansell and Brother Publishers, 1893.

References:

http://www.merriam-webster.com/dictionary/grotto Retrieved March 31, 2012

http://www.thefreedictionary.com/indult Retrieved April 5, 2012

http://dictionary.reference.com/browse/voiture?s=t Retrieved April 27, 2012

http://www.merriam-webster.com/dictionary/triduum Retrieved April 27, 2012

http://www.thefreedictionary.com/Pallium Retrieved April 27, 2012

http://www.thefreedictionary.com/Ex+voto Retrieved April 27, 2012

http://dictionary.reference.com/browse/rochet?s=t Retrieved April 27, 2012

http://dictionary.reference.com/browse/crozier?s=t Retrieved April 27, 2012

http://dictionary.reference.com/browse/mitre?s=t Retrieved April 27, 2012

https://sites.google.com/site/finicoincequoique/themes/langues/latin (prayer pro Retrieved April 27, 2012

http://education.yahoo.com/reference/dictionary/entry/catafalque Retrieved 4/22/2012

http://www.merriam-webster.com/dictionary/patois Retrieved 6/24/2012

Index

A

B

C

D

L

M

N

O

P

R

Residential Grottos

Over the years, many people have expressed their devotion to the Blessed Virgin under her many titles by erecting grottos in their yards, gardens or even inside their homes. The garden grotto or personal replica is always unique to the person who has elected to build it and visit it as a means to pray to, meditate upon and express their love for the Blessed Mother.

In my case, I made a simple garden grotto in my backyard adjacent to my gazebo. This picture shows how easy it is on the one hand but also how lovely a simple garden grotto can be on the other.

We have hopes of attracting photos of many more garden grottos with an eye toward publishing a second edition of this book to include all those that currently exist, but also, all of those which we ardently hope will spring up in many homes and gardens as the word of this devotion is re-ignited in our communities. Here are photos of my simple grotto:

Backyard garden grotto located at Mary Engler's house in Destrehan, LA

www.ingramcontent.com/pod-product-compliance
Lightning Source LLC
Chambersburg PA
CBHW041427290326
41932CB00054B/3489
* 9 7 8 1 5 9 8 0 4 6 6 7 0 *